Politics and Power

THE UNITED STATES SENATE

1869–1901

A PUBLICATION OF
THE CENTER FOR THE STUDY OF
THE HISTORY OF LIBERTY IN AMERICA
HARVARD UNIVERSITY

Politics and Power

THE UNITED STATES SENATE
1869–1901

David J. Rothman

☆ ☆ ☆ ☆ ☆

HARVARD UNIVERSITY PRESS

CAMBRIDGE · MASSACHUSETTS

1966

141012

Library of Congress Catalog Card Number 66–13185

Printed in the United States of America

The work of the Center for the Study of the History of Liberty
in America has been supported by grants from the Carnegie Corporation
of New York and the Lilly Endowment, Inc.

TO MY MOTHER
AND IN MEMORY OF MY FATHER
MURRAY ROTHMAN

Foreword

In the last three decades of the nineteenth century the federal government grew in power and complexity. Civil War, reconstruction, and industrialization raised issues that focused unprecedented attention on decisions reached in Washington. A political system which had theretofore emphasized decentralized controls had to develop the means of enlisting and coordinating the support of the diverse interests, regions, and groups in the nation.

In a period of relatively weak Presidents, the burden fell largely upon the Congress, and within that body, upon the house which had the greatest continuity of membership—the United States Senate. In these years the Senate became the pivotal political institution of the republic. In the process, it acquired and retained an unenviable reputation. The charges that David Graham Phillips would popularize in *The Treason of the Senate* would often be uncritically repeated by historians. They would also animate the movement for direct elections that culminated in the Seventeenth Amendment.

Emphasis upon failings of the Senate has obscured its function in the development of the modern American polity. The institution by 1900 had acquired the character and form it was to retain through the twentieth century. The decisive influences upon its evolution are the subjects of Professor Rothman's careful analysis. His striking reinterpretation clarifies a significant phase of the history of free institutions in the United States. The committee system, seniority, party controls, and the personal and social traits of the members fall into a suggestive pattern that provides a basis for understanding the role of the Senate in contemporary politics.

Oscar Handlin

Acknowledgments

In the course of preparing this volume, I have received generous assistance from many sources. I began my research under a fellowship from the Graduate School of Arts and Sciences of Harvard University, and the subsequent award of a Sheldon Traveling Fellowship enabled my wife and me to spend a pleasant year investigating manuscript collections scattered throughout the country. Under a grant from the Social Science Research Council, I completed my research and put the study in order.

During a stay in Washington, interviews with Senator Paul Douglas, then Congressman William Scranton, and columnists Doris Fleeson and William S. White clarified many current Senate practices. In Cambridge, P.M.G. Harris introduced me to the quantitative study of social mobility; his willingness to answer my frequent questions and to share his own findings with me were of great help. My colleague at Columbia, James P. Shenton, improved the manuscript with some useful suggestions. William E. Leuchtenburg gave the work a searching criticism; and although his dissent probably still stands, he did lead me to reconsider and reargue several key contentions. My friend Charles Halpern read the entire manuscript with a lawyer's eye for clarity and logic, saving me from many infelicities and errors. My debt to librarians—too numerous to mention—is great. The staffs at the Library of Congress, the Henry Huntington Library, the libraries at Duke University and Stanford University, and especially the Harvard University Library were particularly generous with their time.

My two greatest debts rest elsewhere. This project was conceived in discussion with Oscar Handlin, and his encouragement, his readiness to discuss methodology and substance, and his close reading of two drafts of the manuscript have benefited me in every way. Even more important, the opportunity to study history under a teacher whose perceptions illuminate the potentialities that exist within the discipline has been, and will continue to be, an inspiration. Finally, my wife, Sheila M. Rothman, shared fully in this work. Her editing skills were welcome, but, as many librarians could testify, her research talents were indispensable.

David Rothman

New York
September 1965

CONTENTS

TABLES

Charts

Illustrations

Politics and Power

THE UNITED STATES SENATE

1869–1901

I am as glad to see Brutus in Plutarch as in a book of his own. I would rather choose to know truly the conversation he held in his tent with some one of his intimate friends on the eve of the battle than the speech he made the next day to his army; and what he was doing in his study and his chamber than what he was doing in the public square and in the Senate . . . Spend more time on plans than on events, more on what comes from within than on what happens without.

Montaigne, "Of Books"

Introduction

Americans in the nineteenth century persistently asked visiting foreigners to evaluate their institutions. Newcomers learned that the inquiry was logical, for political, social, and religious organizations reflected the quality of life in the United States. A uniquely American relationship linked representatives to constituents, bishops to priests, fathers to sons. Moreover, in a nation spread over three thousand miles and populated by every European stock, institutions provided a starting point for discussion, offering a semblance of stability to those seeking evidence for their generalizations.

Scholars also favored this sort of inquiry. By the start of the twentieth century, studies of the Congress, the Family, and the Church crammed library shelves. All too often, however, these investigations isolated their materials. An author's preface noted that vital connections tied his subject to some fundamental characteristic of democratic society; still, the text invariably lost sight of larger issues. In these volumes government structures took on an independent existence, immune to any nonpolitical influence. Social histories confined families to the four walls of the home, while church studies rarely deviated from doctrinal exegesis. The narrowness of this approach weakened these efforts. To separate institutions by category was, to be sure, a useful device. Unfortunately, students neglected to tie together what they had arbitrarily torn apart.

Not surprisingly, institutional histories soon suffered a decline in reputation, and contemporaries have avoided what appears to be a sterile form of inquiry. But in one discipline at least, American political history, the attitude is unwarranted. In attempting to understand the exercise of power, institutions offer unparalleled methodological advantages. The Constitution, wedded to concepts of federalism, checks and balances, and separation of powers, divided authority once and then again. As government decisions became more vital and more varied, the researcher was frequently forced to wander like a tourist in search of respectable conclusions. The maze was nearly as complex in the decades that followed General Grant's inauguration in 1869 as it is today. And therefore, when I tried to penetrate the labyrinth and describe the process of politics in post-Civil War America, I looked first to an institution for help.

Recent studies of politics between the administrations of Grant and Theodore Roosevelt (1869–1901) offered few insights into the structure of party and power in the nation. Numerous biographies recounted the histories of outstanding personalities, but valid generalizations only infrequently emerged from their restricted frameworks. Accounts of the major parties analyzed presidential conventions and elections to the neglect of all other processes. Political scientists' descriptions of government bodies did not bother to relate the information to broader questions of American life. Chapters, paying scant attention to chronology, dissected an organization into its component parts but never connected one to the other. The only narrative account of these years, Matthew Josephson's *The Politicos* (1938), was so full of factual errors and dubious interpretations as to stand best as a spur to further research. In this context, it seemed that an institutional account might prove especially rewarding.

The most important decision—which institution to select—was surprisingly simple. To generalize about party and power from an intensive analysis of only one of many structures was not without its drawbacks. Our constitutional legacy includes town councils, county boards, state legislatures, the Congress, the Court, and the presidency. Still, in the years that followed Reconstruction, one particular body, the United States Senate, was of such importance that it was able to sustain the effort.

Contemporaries were convinced that the Senate dominated the government and, in point of fact, most major pieces of legislation took final form within that chamber. Senators themselves enjoyed political preeminence, exercising significant authority over events in the state legislature, the House of Representatives, and national conventions. Then too, during these years a seat in the chamber was the goal of most ambitious politicians. True, the White House remained the higher honor, but the President was usually less than equal to a match with the Upper House. To understand how the Senate performed its share of the tasks of ruling the nation would help to define the accessibility, distribution, and uses of power in the last decades of the nineteenth century.

The Senate had not always enjoyed such prominence. Its lawful powers were, of course, set down by the Constitution, but that formal allocation by no means pointed to the Senate's political supremacy. Members, two from each state elected by the legislatures for six-year terms, were to share legislative duties with the House of Representatives. Senators could not initiate financial bills, although their concurrence was necessary before sending any act to the President for his signature. They did enjoy several exclusive prerogatives: to advise and consent to executive appointments and to ratify treaties. Nevertheless, in the first years of the Republic, the Senate, meeting behind closed doors, did not attain the stature of the House. It took an integral part in the government, in no way resembling its British counterpart, the House of Lords. But as yet it offered few hints of its eventual authority.

However, the institution soon increased its power. Its sessions were opened to the public and its membership, when compared to that of the bulky House, appeared more selective. As competition for office increased, the six-year term gave it new attractions and when House discussion became conscious of the clock, the Senate tradition of unlimited debate heightened its distinction.

The Websters, the Calhouns, and the Clays made it their home
and the chamber's influence swelled. By 1860 it surely matched
and probably surpassed its Capitol rival. In the decades that followed, there was no question of its preeminence.

My choice of the Senate as the most appropriate institution for
the study of post-Civil War politics was based on another, even
more vital, consideration. During these years the Upper House
assumed its modern form. Party leadership and party machinery
took on the significance in its proceedings that they hold today.
The Senate of 1869 was very much like its predecessors; by 1901
it had come to resemble its successors. *This alteration, its causes
and implications, supplies the theme of this book.* To understand
why new practices transformed the institution is, in many ways,
to explain the political history of this era.

Senators in the 1870's usually performed their tasks without
party superintendence. No one had the authority to keep his colleagues in line, and positions of influence were distributed without
regard for personal loyalties. Democratic and Republican organizations rarely attempted to schedule legislation or enforce
unity in voting. In brief, senators were free to go about their
business more or less as they pleased. By 1900 all this had
changed. The party caucus and its chieftains determined who
would sit on which committees and looked after the business calendar in detail. Members were forced to seek their favors or
remain without influence in the chamber. At the same time, both
organizations imposed unprecedented discipline on roll calls.
The Senate never achieved the standard set in the House of Commons; yet by 1900 the parties exercised key powers over the
chamber's proceedings. The caucus and its leaders had assumed
their modern importance in Senate affairs.

Most histories of these years have ignored these innovations
and their implications. Republican senators of the 1870's, such as
Roscoe Conkling or Oliver Morton, are typically labeled the
bosses of a radical Republican cabal, busily determining vital

Senate decisions. In fact, there is little evidence to support this assertion. The 1872 bolt by Liberal Republicans is often presented as a reaction to and a casualty of party rule. But as yet no effective discipline bound the members. On the other side of the aisle, Democratic "Bourbons," in league with business, ostensibly ruled their colleagues with equal ferocity. But here again the assumption cannot stand. No one in either party controlled the chamber's proceedings at this time.

Moreover, the altered position of party in the 1890's is rarely appreciated. Now that the caucus dictated voting decisions and senators disregarded personal and sectional interests to respect its decisions, the organizations won a new prominence. Although never the sole determinant of legislative behavior, party's weight on the scale frequently tipped the balance. The results of this shift were widespread. Party, more than equal to external pressures, became the forum to which competing interests appealed, and no one could be confident that his request would be granted. Then too, the welfare of the organization became important in its own right and the tactics of compromise ruled in Washington. The history of these years gives ample testimony to the consequences of this change.

Why was the structure of the Senate so fundamentally altered in the decades that followed the Civil War? The second part of this study seeks to answer the question by taking the story beyond the boundaries of Capitol Hill. The skills of the chamber's leaders, men like William Allison, Nelson Aldrich, and Arthur Gorman, were obviously important; but their talents alone could not have revolutionized traditional practices. This institution did not operate in a vacuum, subject only to internal pressures. Events in the Senate reflected vital changes in the place of party and politics in the life of the nation.

By 1900 senators shared fundamental attitudes that differed markedly from those of their predecessors. They entered the chamber prepared to accommodate and promote party organization and leadership. Their political careers, in very personal and immediate ways, trained them to value discipline and order. They came to the caucus willing to compromise for the sake of party. This new breed of senator helped change the character of the institution.

No simple explanation can account for this phenomenon. Rather, a series of events, one reinforcing the other, extended the power of party in post-Civil War America. By the turn of the century, most senators had devoted their adult years to politics. The chamber was a gathering place for professionals, not a millionaire's club. There were few novices among them; members, regardless of social origins, were political veterans, accustomed to the demands of official life. Coming to Washington with a deeply ingrained respect for the machinery of organization, they appreciated the connections between ambition and party loyalty. They had no intentions of adopting the role of maverick.

As the nation increased in size and the tasks of legislating grew increasingly complex, political life became more demanding. Government service turned into a full-time occupation. The occasional amateur, when faced with the rigors of Washington service, quickly lost any inclination to stay at the task. Party committees began to order the chamber's proceedings when dedicated politicians monopolized the committee places.

The impact of these changes was evident in and reinforced by the structure of state politics. Paying complete attention to their tasks, leaders effectively mastered their organizations. State power and the Senate seat became inexorably linked as legislatures calmly sent the party chief to the Capitol. Arriving there after this sort of apprenticeship, senators knew firsthand the virtues of discipline and unity. Moreover, the various economic interests in newly industrialized America also encouraged and were affected by these alterations. Political organizations, buttressed by campaign contributions, became less vulnerable to outside pressures. Corporations, unintentionally, helped weaken their own influence in politics.

Finally, during these years a fresh appreciation of the relationship between party and democratic government justified the new practices. Although English thinkers had long appreciated the virtues of party loyalty, Americans had paid little heed to their arguments. Only when Democratic and Republican organizations dominated the affairs of government did this nation discover for itself what others had long professed: two-party politics was indispensable to the maintenance of freedom. Devotion to its interests was proper and efforts on its behalf were patriotic. These ideas sanctioned the growth of party, helping to alter its place in the nation and in the Senate.

The people did not witness these events in silence. They grasped many of the implications of the change, and their distortions and misunderstandings were also significant. The Senate was not a popular institution in post-Civil War America, and by 1900 the success of the movement for direct election was clearly only a matter of time. The upper house of Congress did not satisfy the nation's expectations; party rule appeared to be a dangerous innovation. Dissatisfactions provoked a dialogue between citizen and government that directly affected the political history of these years, and its implications carried well into the twentieth century.

Before undertaking this research, I was warned of the Whig bias that dominates the studies of this period. Nevertheless, I was astonished at the extent to which Mugwump-Populist-Progressive attitudes have been entrenched in the texts. Several generations of historians have echoed the unfounded accusations voiced at the time; Josephson cited a Mugwump to substantiate a charge and his conclusions in turn are used to document later opinions. The self-perpetuating quality of these assertions, one repeating and supporting the other, has allowed diatribe to masquerade as fact.

To confound matters, by the 1890's the cry "in the pay of the corporation," had become part of the campaign rhetoric, a convenient flag to wave once the bloody shirt was tossed away. This phenomenon was encouraged by the simplistic and facile side of

the Populist-Progressive mentality—an outlook that was far too
eager to posit direct relationships between two events without
any documentable connections. Charles Beard argued that portfolios determined voting behavior in a constitutional convention,
and his contemporaries agreed that any senator who had once
served as a corporation attorney would necessarily remain a slave
to its interests when responding to roll calls.

Despite a new sensitivity to the complex determinants that
make up political behavior, the senators of the Gilded Age are
still understood in simplistic terms. These notions have enjoyed
their monopoly long enough; it seems time to review the evidence.
Judgments need not be absent. But surely they should be vin-
dicated by the events of the period.

Part One

The Origins of the Modern Senate

☆ ☆ ☆ ☆ ☆

☆ **I** ☆

THE LIMITS OF PARTY

No one is *the* Senator. No one may speak for his party as well as for himself; no one exercises the special trust of acknowledged leadership. The Senate is merely a body of individual critics . . . The weight of every criticism uttered in its chamber depends upon the weight of the critic . . . deriving little . . . gravity from connection with the designs of a purposeful party organization.

Woodrow Wilson, *Congressional Government,* 1885

Americans in 1869, concluding a tumultuous decade of rebellion and reconstruction, looked to a future of stability and amity. Grant's simple statement, "Let us have peace," stood in welcome contrast to Lincoln's eloquent pleas for increased devotion, and the General, personifying order, was elected to exercise his talents. However, the intensity of the expectations, the overwhelming faith in Grant's abilities, revealed the pervasive doubt that the nation could simply resume its ways. "I looked for the 4th of March to bring Grant and Peace and Rest," Wisconsin's Timothy Howe confessed after the inauguration. "But Peace and Rest," he sadly concluded, "seem as far off as ever."[1]

Uncertainty was widespread in politics for the very survival of the parties appeared doubtful. Two decades earlier no one had anticipated a Republican organization. Would it soon share the oblivion of the Whigs? This prospect did not frighten people accustomed to the disintegration of alignments; most Americans had already paid allegiance to two or three successive parties. Though eager to settle into comfortable routines, the country sensed that politics promised confusion not coherence, vacillation not permanence.[2]

Political veterans anticipated the dissolution of the party that had fought the war for ostensibly its purpose was fulfilled. "There is no doubt that a feeling more or less deep seated prevails," the partisan *New York Times* admitted, "that the work of the Republican party, properly so called, ends with the adoption of the Fifteenth Amendment." Joseph Medill, editor of the *Chicago Tribune,* unhappily shared the outlook. "The great party issues are about settled," he warned Vermont's senator Justin Morrill. "Since the election of Grant party lines are melting away with extreme rapidity."[3] The passage of Negro suffrage legislation seemed to close the Reconstruction questions, and it was now appropriate to turn attention elsewhere. The catchword "new departure" gained wide vogue in both North and South. To the consternation of leading Republicans, however, its spirit appeared to lead away from their party.[4]

The future was even less promising for the Democrats. Many Americans, convinced that the minority in obstructing the war effort had all too regularly crossed the thin line into treason, judged the party's disappearance in the national interest. For their part Democratic spokesmen continued to debate the well-worn issues of the war, wondering whether they would ever settle factional disputes, much less convince the country of their ability to govern. There was without question a place for an anti-Republican movement, but its supporters often preferred to join together under a conservative or neutral banner. In all probability, some new organization would capture power.[5]

Despite the many doubts that plagued Washington when Grant cautiously intoned his inaugural address, the parties did not disintegrate. When the tensions of the war years relaxed, the anticipated reactions against the two organizations never achieved critical proportions. Nevertheless, after the threat to the Union ended, the ties that bound one colleague to another loosened and members resumed independent habits free from the sense of emergency. Senators were still easily identified as Republicans or Democrats, but, for all its obvious presence, party could not maintain significant control over the legislative process. As the chamber exerted its prerogatives, filling the vacuum left by Lincoln's assassination, party returned to a weak and limited place. Those familiar with its history there were not surprised.

Party influence was comparatively new in the Senate structure. For example, the committee system, so vital to the chamber's proceedings, had not been dominated by this consideration until well into the nineteenth century. Members originally met in small and specialized groups to evaluate and frame legislation, and to provide the full body, the committee of the whole, with a text for debate and amendment. By the start of Andrew Jackson's administration, the majority usually controlled the working committees but the opposition still held several important chairmanships. Committee positions were determined by an open vote in the chamber with personal preferences often outweighing other loyalties. Lines were casually crossed and minority senators captured key places.[6]

Not until the mid-1840's did procedures change. Then the majority composed, discussed, and approved the committee slate in caucus and submitted it to the Senate for the formality of a vote. Ranks held firm and chairmanships became the exclusive privilege of the dominant party. Moreover, the majority also determined the minority proportion on the committees allowing the rival caucus to fill the quota. When the first Senate Republicans protested that the allotments were far too unequal, James Bayard, the patrician Delaware Democrat, unequivocally declared: "The political party having the majority will necessarily control all the committees of the body, because they are responsible, as a party, for the business of the body . . . The majority always must, as a party, protect themselves against the chance of the control of the business of the body going into the hands of their opponents."[7] Had this doctrine been firmly established in 1789, the Senate might have emulated the British model with its working committees staffed exclusively by the majority. The delayed entrance of party responsibility into the chamber, however, started a tradition that was never broken.

Although the party considered itself responsible for the chamber's business in pre-Civil War America, its powers were confined to organizational questions, the election of committees and officers. Senators' votes on these matters defined their affiliation. Democrats cast their ballots for Democratic majorities on the committees and a Democratic President *pro tempore;* representatives of regional factions revealed their national sympathies by voting for a particular slate while mavericks exhibited their independence by abstaining. To remain in good standing, that is, to receive committee assignments from the caucus, members had only to demonstrate their loyalty at the start of each session. The demands were light for party was of little significance in the vital labors of the Senate. Colleagues at times consulted and voted together but did not create permanent institutional party structures. No caucus or informal committee determined general political policies, or designed specific measures, or enforced discipline, or looked after desired legislation. Senators performed their tasks as individuals rather than as Democrats or Whigs. If at times they gave weight to the recommendations of a platform or the suggestions of a President, that was testimony to a coincidence of aims, not to the power of party.[8]

During the crises of slavery, secession, and war, the Senate organizations assumed an authority unprecedented in intensity and effectiveness. A senator was required not only to support a committee slate but to accept substantive policies. When Stephen Douglas balked at following the Democratic stand on the expansion of slavery in 1858, he was summarily removed from the chairmanship of the Committee on Territories. The exigencies of the time brought a similar discipline to the Republicans, and even issues peripheral to the Union effort were frequently decided by calls to solidarity. The party strength that could be mustered in support of a tariff proposal or the conviction of an impeached President was great enough to obscure its novelty and its impermanence.[9]

With the end of hostilities and the passage of the last Reconstruction measures, members threw off discipline with a startling urgency. Only a few retained the new habits; most regarded them as temporary, if necessary, deviations. "The Republican party has no longer the uniting element of the war," former Illinois governor Richard Yates cautioned his Senate colleagues. "We have no longer the uniting element of opposition to human slavery and aspirations for freedom." Lyman Trumbull, the state's senior senator, agreed. "The party is very much demoralized. The war pressure is pretty much taken off."[10] Legislators, like battle-weary infantrymen, anxiously returned to the liberties of former days.

The weakness of party discipline reflected the lack of Senate leadership. During the war no special coterie formulated or supervised the enactment of legislation. The Democrats, few and powerless, had no incentive to organize their forces. But the story might have been different for the Republicans. Party chieftains could have profited from the unity and regularity instilled by the crisis. Perhaps the responsible performance of the members obviated the need for authority, and the skills and influence of Lincoln at one end of Pennsylvania Avenue left little room for its development at the other. In any event, control did not become entrenched in a few hands and no one proved able to direct the actions of colleagues and the course of legislation. After the vital issues had been resolved, personal authority could not sustain party discipline.[11]

The quality of legislative leadership always depended upon individual skills and genius. To invest a post with power in the hope that its occupant would exercise determinative influence was as optimistic as to expect a patronized artist to deliver a master-piece. Nevertheless, subsidies did have their place and would-be leaders attempted to win strategic offices. Their decisions were then sanctioned and legitimized, so that they did not need appro-bation for every maneuver. The prospects for party unity in 1869 were therefore all the more bleak because the Upper House pos-sessed no viable tradition of leadership. Existing positions seemed to carry little or no potentiality for power. The war years had inaugurated no permanent changes, and in this sense the Senate continued to resemble its predecessors, not its successors.

Hamilton Fish, Grant's astute Secretary of State, recognized the predicament facing the Republican-dominated chamber. "The Republican party," he wrote historian George Bancroft in January 1870, "is suffering from a want of a Leader in each House."[12] Henry Anthony, chairman of the party caucus, was personally popular with his colleagues—unfailingly sending each of them a turkey for Thanksgiving—but he enjoyed little au-thority. As a Providence, Rhode Island, newspaper man, Anthony had assisted the conservatives during Dorr's Rebellion, was re-warded with a Senate seat in 1859, and was then elected caucus chairman ten years later. Still he served only on minor working committees, exerting negligible influence over legislation.[13] As head of the caucus, Anthony selected the Committee on Commit-tees for each session; this group arranged the Republican com-mittee positions, and their slates were rubber-stamped by the party after minor revisions. Anthony himself never served on the committee and did not regularly reappoint the same senators for the task. Most important, he exercised no favoritism in his selections, and during Grant's first term no one group or would-be leader exercised any undue influence over committee arrange-ments. There seemed little chance that the Rhode Island Senator would alter Hamilton Fish's judgments.[14]

The caucus also elected the President *pro tempore,* but the office carried no power. Anthony held it twice while serving as chairman but refused the place in 1875, no doubt pleased to be rid of its formal duties. Any consequential functions had long since passed to the caucus, and the right to recognize speakers on the floor was never of significance in a body obsessed with unlimited debate. The honor was more likely to impress a constituent than a colleague.[15]

The tasks of the Committee on Committees were not mechanical. It exercised a wide range of discretion, for the guidelines of seniority were not yet firmly established. Senators, noteworthy only for their sectional diversity, determined the vital decisions. This was a random group; the five to seven committeemen represented nothing more than the various geographic regions of the nation. Senators of long tenure served as chairmen, but anyone could be appointed after a few years of service. Its members did not themselves hold notable assignments, and the heads of outstanding working committees exerted no unusual influence. Moreover, no one party faction dominated the group; neither the supporters nor the critics of Grant, for example, secured any advantage. At the end of the nineteenth century, Senate leaders would use the leverage of committee assignments to control the chamber's business, and the ability to reward friends and punish enemies would entrench their power. In 1869 this possibility seemed remote.[16]

The caucus was the oldest form of Senate association and its practices and prerogatives had only slightly altered in the decades that separated Washington from Grant. From the start colleagues discussed pressing political questions, airing particular views, and no one objected to the practice. When party identity came to determine committee places, the slates were settled there, and members, regardless of any personal grievance, voted appropriately in the chamber.[17]

But less harmony prevailed when in 1867 the Republican caucus attempted to designate the subject and order of Senate business. Antagonisms quickly mounted and debate soon broke out in open session. Massachusetts' fractious senator, Charles Sumner, refused to concede that a party gathering could limit the topics for consideration; under the Constitution, senators "must attend to the public business of the country. They cannot tie their hands in advance." When Joseph Fowler, the Unionist from east Tennessee objected ("I am perfectly willing . . . to agree that no other subject shall come before the Senate except that which the majority of this body regard as the important subject"), Ohio's long-time senator, Ben Wade, sprang to Sumner's defense. The chamber had always opposed any closing of debate, yet now it "would limit the very subject of debate," a doctrine surely more pernicious. "I ask my friends here who were in this body a year ago," Wade continued with disarming logic, "when we were in a lean minority, how they would have felt if the ingenuity of our enemies had conjured up such a rule as this, and they had been told 'You shall not debate the subject of slavery.' "[18]

Despite this common experience, William Fessenden, Maine's first Republican senator and Lincoln's Secretary of the Treasury, summed up the predilection of the party: "It is undoubtedly the right of the majority of the body," he judiciously announced, "whatever may be the consequences, to decide what shall be the order of business . . . It may outrage the rights of the minority; but for all that it is responsible to the people." The Fessenden view prevailed, and in the following Congress, the Forty-first, the Republican caucus selected the subjects for discussion. It created no advisory committee to schedule a weekly program but did draw up a broad outline for the session's business.[19]

The most perplexing inquiry a freshman senator could make of his colleagues in 1869 was also the most obvious: after attending the caucus and discussing pending legislation was he bound to abide by its decision? His duty to stand in rank on organizational questions and to accept the general order of business was clear; but all else was subject to disagreement. The newcomer would have been spared some concern upon learning that formal votes in the caucus were rare. Most issues were resolved through discussion to the satisfaction of all present or simply left undecided. But when differences remained and the sense of the meeting was determined by counting numbers, what was the minority to do on the floor? Senators with limited memories, not recalling the days before slavery agitation, believed the answer was patent. Richard Yates declared:

Those of us who are familiar with the consultations of party caucuses understand distinctly that when we go into caucus upon any question to ascertain what the will of the majority of that body is, we meet for the purpose of acting together in favor of the will of that majority . . . After we have deliberated together as a party, and a majority have decided, then to say that we are not bound by that decision is introducing a new rule into the well-known history of American politics.[20]

To many others, however, the matter was not so obvious. Some believed that only those who cast their votes in the caucus had to stay by the party in the Senate; abstainers could do as they pleased. Others contended that party loyalty was demanded only on "grave" issues or argued that participants should feel "bound by the decision of a caucus . . . so far as it is only a matter of judgment." And invariably a colleague would defend the view that no one was ever obliged to alter his opinions or votes: "I am a Senator of the United States," proclaimed Charles Sumner. "My obligations as a Senator were above any vote in a caucus."[21] This multiplicity of opinion may have assisted the astute initiate to grasp one vital truth: any senator who acted as he pleased on an issue, in spite of a caucus decision, would not be disciplined by the party. No one possessed the power for reprisals. Senators knew full well that while party whips ordered the House of Commons, they themselves had devised no such posts; nor had they the leadership to enforce such discipline. "I think the Senators are quite competent to express their own judgment without any whip," Maine's Lot Morrill reminded his peers. "We have never had what is called a whip in the American Senate."[22] Members were free to perform their duty as they saw fit. There were certain limits to the freedom from party dictates, but on any specific political question they could act with impunity.

The Appropriations Committee assignments in the 1870's revealed both the frequent absence of party considerations and the outer limits of acceptable behavior. When the Forty-first Congress convened, William Fessenden headed this most important group; but he soon died, and the vacancy had to be filled. The next in line presumably, although not inevitably, moved up the ladder; but the Committee on Committees passed over the ranking Henry Wilson, Sumner's colleague, naming instead Lot Morrill, just appointed by Maine's governor to complete Fessenden's unexpired term. The choice of a freshman senator for an outstanding chairmanship was not intended as a slap to Wilson, who was then serving on the caucus committee and probably approved the move. Rather, everyone agreed that Maine deserved the post. It would have held the chairmanship had Fessenden not suddenly died and it ought not to be punished for an act of God. The proprietary rights of states to committee places did not always dictate caucus action. But in 1870 it could still outweigh all other considerations.[23]

Morrill continued to serve as Appropriations chairman, even after election to his own term, until severe illness excused him. The ranking member, California's Cornelius Cole, wanted the place, but so did former Vice-President Hannibal Hamlin, who was not on the committee, and also George Edmunds, a recent and talented appointee. Cole found it imperative to become active in his own cause; and yet the lines of influence were so weakly established that he believed the President of the Senate, the nation's Vice-President, held a vote on committee assignments. Schuyler Colfax corrected him: "You had forgotten that the Vice-President also is never invited into the Republican caucus and hence I have never thrust myself or attempted to do so." Colfax, who was fond of Cole, warned him that since he knew of "another Senator or two who would like your place, it is best to guard every point," and promised to "allude to the subject to some members of the Committee arranging them friendly to you, but with the delicacy which propriety renders necessary."[24] Custom was followed only after such assistance, and the California Senator gained the chairmanship.

Cole failed to be re-elected in January 1873, and when the Forty-third Congress assembled two months later, the post was once more vacant. Next in succession stood William Sprague, the quixotic Rhode Island senator. Heir to a leading textile manufacturing concern, the adventuresome Sprague won his election during the Civil War, captured the Capitol's imagination, and soon married Justice Salmon Chase's ambitious daughter, Kate. In an attempt to keep his mills running, the Senator seems to have engaged in illegal cotton trading with the enemy, and if this was still hidden from the public in 1873, his wife's growing attachment for New York's pretentious senator, Roscoe Conkling, was not. Moreover, the panic of that year sent Sprague's faltering mills into bankruptcy. As his private world disintegrated, the Senator began to deliver long harangues in which he attacked the corrupting powers of the new wealth. A future full of evil and misery was inevitable unless the country liberated itself from bondage to the corporation, he argued.[25] Some colleagues took him seriously, more dismissed him as a crank. Venturing far beyond opposition to his party on a specific issue, repeatedly and intensely attacking what he took to be its wicked course, Sprague excited not only disagreement but distrust. The party, believing itself betrayed, would not permit him to head Appropriations and quietly passed over the one-time wonder of Washington. Impunity did have its limits.[26]

Charles Sumner even more dramatically and obstinately violated the tolerable limits of anti-party behavior. Yet the penalty, his removal from the chairmanship of the Foreign Relations Committee in March 1871, for all the accompanying uproar, entailed no unusual exercise of discipline. In fact Sumner's behavior illuminated the inherent difficulties any potential leaders faced, for, as Hamilton Fish observed, after "long continuance in Senatorial position . . . jealousies and disappointments develop in old Senators."[27] Any party chief would first have to overcome cantankerous independence.

An active opponent of Grant's foreign policy, especially in Santo Domingo, and more than sensitive to any slight, Sumner saw in the President's dismissal of John Motley as Ambassador to England a wrong second only to the crime of slavery. Despite appeals that there was no comparison between the political removal of an intimate friend and the reduction of four million men to chattels, that plans to dismiss Motley were well underway before Sumner voted against Grant's Santo Domingo treaty, and that the Ambassador had failed to represent the administration's viewpoint in London, Sumner would not be placated. Exaggerating the injury, he would neither let the incident pass nor reach an accord with the administration.[28] Normally tolerant men like Fish and Senator Justin Morrill lost patience as the Massachusetts Senator greeted their conciliatory efforts with enmity. When Sumner refused to meet or talk socially with the Secretary of State after having long since halted all conversation with the Chief Executive, he overstepped the bounds of party tolerance. The Committee on Committees asked the Republican caucus of the Forty-second Congress to remove Sumner from his Foreign Relations chairmanship.[29]

The move provoked a debate that spread from the privacy of the caucus to the gallery-filled chamber. Motley's removal was a blow aimed at Sumner, his partisans contended; the Committee on Committees had jumped to the lash of a vindictive President. Timothy Howe, heading the caucus committee, repeatedly and earnestly denied the slur. In frustration he instructed Elisha Keyes, his ally in Wisconsin, to make certain that at least the state's Republicans did not "believe that anybody has struck

Sumner. Don't let them believe that anybody has been struck for opposing Santo Domingo." When Sumner snubbed Grant and Fish, the committee thought it wise to select a chairman "who would afford to speak to one or the other." His outrageous behavior could not be ignored.[30]

Nevertheless, Sumner's friends persisted in their accusations, exaggerating the significance of the maneuver. Henry Wilson, for example, argued that the removal was an attempt to restrict the Republicans. "We hear something about disciplining men. We have a class of politicians who have an idea that if they can show the scalps of their political friends they are mighty war chiefs." Indignantly he charged: "This disciplining process is to begin here in the Senate. My colleague is to be disciplined . . . I warn our friends here today that they may pay too dearly for this kind of discipline . . . You have just as much as you can do to bear the banners of your party to victory, without putting discipline on your old and trusted leaders."[31]

To most Republicans the issue was not so portentous, and despite the hyperbolic rhetoric, they did not lose sight of realities. Convinced that Sumner had selfishly and irresponsibly nursed his wounded pride, the caucus majority supported his removal twenty-six to twenty-one. As usual, party discipline on organizational questions remained intact; nearly all the minority sustained the verdict in the chamber. John Sherman, destined to play a vital part in the politics of the next three decades, concluded that this sort of decision should be yielded to at once. New Hampshire's Aaron Cragin, after voicing his objections, bowed to the will of the majority, and William Buckingham, a fellow New Englander, confessed: "If I vote for it, it will be because I went into the caucus."[32] Indiana's aggressive senator, Oliver Morton, was less than sympathetic to Sumner's plight and announced without any ambiguity: "I hold the Republican party superior in importance to any man who is a member of it. I intend to stand honestly and in good faith by its organization."[33] A senator's freedom of action was circumscribed, if very broadly. William Sprague could not with impunity continuously brand his party corrupt, and Charles Sumner was not at liberty to stop all intercourse with the President and the Secretary of State. But only the most bizarre and flagrant behavior was ever called into question.

When Grant's administration opened, the Senate party compelled unity on organizational questions but its authority did not encompass substantive issues. "Many people," claimed a prominent veteran of the Wisconsin GAR, "ignore the fact that the Republican party is made of material that cannot be controlled by leaders." Confidently he declared: "This party will not be controlled by a man or set of men called leaders."[34]

The events of 1872 confirmed his contentions. Convinced that both parties were ignoring pressing questions and disgusted with Grant's administration, some dissident Republicans joined forces to establish the Liberal Republican party. Their central credo, that a new departure was long overdue, need not have provoked a revolt; many sympathizers tried to combat lethargy within the older organization. Of course, the strong expectation that novel political alignments would soon emerge simplified the break; and any nostalgia could be offset by pointing to the name Republican in the new label. Nevertheless, something more than dissatisfaction with current policies and presidential actions prompted the decision to bolt.[35]

Disaffected members were convinced that the Republican party no longer permitted the minority to express or uphold its convictions. As Senator Lyman Trumbull, an influential spokesman, explained: a cause of "the present agitation in the country and the disruption of parties is to be found in the attempts which from time to time have had their origin in the Senate to establish despotic rule and party intolerance." Efforts have been made "to put those who did not agree with the dictation of some caucus, under the control of the majority of the dominant party, but of really a minority of the Senate. A few members of the Senate making use of party organization seek to control first a majority of the members belonging to that organization and then of the Senate." Continuing his attack, Trumbull asserted that senators, "instead of voting their own convictions, are to be coerced by party discipline and party machinery to vote as they shall be dictated to"; Liberal Republicans were successful if they only freed the representatives of the people to "vote their own convictions, instead of voting as party requirements dictate."[36] Allies everywhere repeated the argument. Some denounced the "tyranny of a despotic organization," others, the "prison bars of party rule."[37]

The sentiment was sincere but misguided. In no instance had party discipline coerced Trumbull's colleagues to vote against their wishes; most of them agreed that Sumner's removal was warranted, and those who refused to support the caucus did not face later reprisals. No Senate office carried the power to discipline recalcitrants. John Sherman, ever accommodating, headed the 1871 group that arranged the committees, and Trumbull himself held the eminent chairmanship of Judiciary.[38]

Nor was control effectively imposed through the authority of a hostile President. Federal patronage, it was true, had not been available to future Liberal Republicans, and knowledgeable observers could have accurately predicted which senators would quit the party in 1872 by listing those not distributing offices. But Presidents always rewarded their favorites, and Grant was no more efficient or ruthless than Jackson or Lincoln. Furthermore, patronage considerations rarely determined political contests. They did affect events in New York and the South; the Collector of the Port, who disposed of innumerable jobs, conceivably could alter the balance, and in Reconstructed states many Republicans served only for the sake of the spoils. But these peculiar situations were not typical of state politics. Finally, not all Republicans cut off from patronage abandoned the party, and others, like Lyman Trumbull, would not have switched allegiances for the dubious possibility of distributing offices.[39]

The cry of coercion was misleading and inaccurate. It did, however, express the resentment of those excluded from patronage and, more important, it revealed the novelty of party government. When Trumbull and his admirers estimated that a Republican majority was still only a Senate minority, they demonstrated how alien party rule was to the chamber. Without the rationalization of a national crisis, even a discipline limited to approving committee slates could seem oppressive and dangerous.

The defection of the Liberal Republicans strengthened the authority they so abhorred. Sympathizers who remained loyal Republicans were discredited, losing power and prestige in the caucus. In December 1872 the Committee on Committees, the first to assemble after the revolt, was almost exclusively staffed by senators intolerant of the bolters; their report recommended the removal of defectors from committee places, leaving it to the Democrats to make the assignments. "Any other course would be a mere absurdity," the Republican press chanted, and Senate party consciousness, provoked by blatant and destructive hostility, was strong enough to punish opponents of the state and national nominees. Members once again followed the commands of discipline on questions of organization.[40]

After the Liberal Republican revolt, a faction dominated by the arrogant and brilliant Roscoe Conkling began to exercise authority that was sensitive to other, more subtle, considerations. The New York Senator, skillfully gathering power, enjoyed a unique and privileged status in the chamber. Nevertheless, his leadership never ordered its proceedings.

No public figure of his day excited as much devotion or disdain. Admirers considered Conkling more able than any senator they had known, including Clay and Webster, and judged him a loyal ally. Admitting that he could be impatient and domineering, they excused these failings as prerogatives of his genius. Critics, on the other hand, considered the New Yorker haughty and unprincipled, his ornate dress and imperious tones reflecting an incredibly narcissistic personality. Contending that his influence had been attained through corruption, that his prominence exemplified all that was rotten in politics, they could in no other way fathom Conkling's Senate strength.[41]

The game of politics was familiar to Conkling. His father and older brother had served in Congress, and the family home in Albany was a stopping place for such notables as Van Buren, Weed, and Seward. With the help of these friends, Conkling's own initiation to office was early and when only twenty-nine years old, he became one of his city's first Republican congressmen. After four undistinguished terms in the House, and despite the opposition of Reuben Fenton, a leader of the state Republicans, Conkling's party connections were strong enough to win him the 1867 Senate election. Two years later Fenton joined him in the chamber where they continued their struggle for state control. Conkling at first appeared the more vulnerable but gained the advantage after bringing Grant to his side. By 1873 Fenton was allied with the Liberal Republicans and Conkling commanded the New York Regulars.[42]

Conkling excelled in the Senate. Many colleagues were soon accepting his guidance and the New York Senator commanded a loyal following. In 1877, soon after entering the chamber, Wisconsin's Angus Cameron accurately noted: "Conkling is the leader of the Republican party."[43] Some of his admirers were attracted by the talents that brought success at the bar, clear headed logic and a booming voice. Conkling had also grown more intimate with Grant, and those who stood with the President at conventions were usually allied with the New Yorker in the Senate. Conkling was younger and more vigorous than the General's other supporters, and oldtimers like Zach Chandler and Simon Cameron seemed content to have the burdens of leadership fall to him.[44] As it became evident that Conkling could bestow tangible benefits on his friends, the ranks of his faction swelled. As he captured control over the Senate, he cleverly turned it to advantage. Power fed upon itself, and the Senator enlarged his authority.

Intimacy with Conkling now brought notable committee assignments. In 1875 J. P. Jones, the Nevada mine owner and perhaps Conkling's closest friend, received a much coveted place on Finance after having barely settled in Washington.[45] For Timothy Howe, another favorite, the benefits of the association were even greater. The Wisconsin lawyer had entered the chamber in 1862, and for the succeeding nine years served only on minor committees, making little imprint on the proceedings. In December 1871 he chaired the caucus committee that reported Sumner's deposition and filled the vacancy on Foreign Relations. "In a quiet way," he confided to his niece, "I am influencing affairs. I take but little part in debates but . . . I am more consulted than I ever was . . . Conkling can express my own ideas so much better than I can that I much prefer to have him do it. And he has much confidence in my opinions."[46] Two years later Howe began to serve on the important Railroad Committee and soon assumed places on both Judiciary and Finance. His suddenly acquired power reflected Conkling's new stature.

The faction, after 1873, usually dominated the Committee on Committees and thus could selectively staff the working committees. Henry Anthony continued as caucus head and as his allegiance to Conkling deepened, he used his privileges well; the chairman of the group arranging the slate might not always be an ally, but a majority could be counted upon to fill Conkling's requests.[47] Control of the Commerce Committee was a case in point. Any presidential appointment to a port or harbor post was first referred there for advice on the nominee's fitness; appreciating the connection between Commerce and his stake in the Collectorship of the Port, the New York Senator in 1875 asked for and out of turn received its chairmanship. The unexpected defeat of Zach Chandler had created the vacancy, and the next in line, Alabama's George Spencer, was a firm Conkling supporter.

Serving on the Committee on Committees at the time, Spencer undoubtedly respected the Senator's wish and may have looked after its implementation. Then in October 1877, anticipating the difficulties with President Hayes, Conkling desired the personal loyalty of a majority of Commerce. Again the caucus committee obliged, removing the inimical Rhode Island senator, Ambrose Burnside, and substituting the trustworthy J. P. Jones. Conkling was well protected when he set out to battle a hostile executive.[48]

Yet, for all this, the New York Senator's power was still more potential than actual. His leadership was not uncontested for Oliver Morton, one-time Indiana war governor, was nearly as much a rival as an ally. "The combination against me here is very strong," Morton complained to his wife. Conkling, Howe, and their friends "are pulling every string."[49] Conkling's personality, his short temper and overbearing habits, were not suited to political management, and even close supporters wondered whether Morton was not his superior in this art. Furthermore, the New York Senator's control was severely limited; able to reward friends, he could not prevent the progress of enemies. In 1877 Stanley Matthews, a known Hayes admirer, entered the Senate and received an assignment on Foreign Affairs. At the same session Massachusetts senator Henry Dawes, no ally of Conkling, filled the vacancy on Finance.[50]

Nor was the faction's influence over legislation noteworthy. Its members were slowly gaining valuable committee positions, but they could not exert significant control over substantive political matters. During these years party cohesion in Senate roll calls was not great (see Chart I, Chapter III), and Conkling usually stood with the minority on such vital issues as currency and railroad regulation.[51] The caucus, a potential lever of influence, obviously had not increased in power. In December 1874 William Sprague, denouncing the caucus, resigned from the party; those ignoring its dictates, he charged, would no longer be considered in good standing. Anthony immediately denied the allegation. Whenever a senator inquired if he must vote with a caucus majority, he was invariably told no. Participants gathered to facilitate the interchange of opinion, and no one was expected to surrender his convictions. The validity of Anthony's reply was affirmed a few months later when Senator Isaac Christiancy, after defeating Zach Chandler in the Michigan legislature with Democratic support, announced that he would enter the Republican fold. The newcomer indicated his willingness to follow the party's dictates in selecting committees and officials and agreed to consult with it on public questions. Under no circumstances, however, would he abandon private judgment in the face of a majority. Placed on the Judiciary Committee, Christiancy suffered no penalties for his stand.[52]

A curious innovation in the Republican caucus also revealed the narrow scope of Conkling's authority. The lack of Senate leadership was well known, and the *New York Times* accurately concluded: "Congress with nearly unlimited right to legislate, within the Constitution, is without distinctly recognized leaders. Business is left to the initiative of individuals or of numerous unconnected committees. A great deal is proposed and little carried through."[53] Not surprisingly, when Republicans gathered in December 1874 and heatedly debated the session's order of business, they were unable to agree upon a program. After long and fruitless argument, they decided to appoint a committee to prepare a schedule for the consideration of a future caucus. Some proposed to give it more detailed and exact guidance, but after further altercations, the committee left uninstructed. The experiment worked well, and in December 1878 the caucus reappointed a similar body. Significantly, a majority of the five members were not tied to the Conkling wing. Within a decade, this innovation would become established party practice, familiar as the Republican Steering Committee. But Conkling neither founded nor controlled it. The legislative proceedings of the Senate felt his power only obliquely.[54]

The faction might possibly have extended its power over the Senate, but its leader prematurely tested his strength against two successive Presidents. Conkling's authority was too new and limited to withstand both encounters; he survived the feud with Hayes and Sherman only to succumb to the onslaught of Garfield and Blaine.

When Hayes calculatingly appointed Conkling's opponents to the key offices of the Port of New York, the Senator was prepared. The Commerce Committee tagged along as he first delayed action and then fought the nominations. The President eventually obtained Senate consent for his choices, but the victory hinged on Democratic support; Republicans stood loyally by the Senator. Some certainly favored the institution in a conflict with the executive, while others, like White House aspirant and Senator James Blaine, did not admire Conkling but liked Hayes less.[55] But of the New Yorker's personal strength there could be no question. Hayes himself lucidly assessed the situation: "Senatorial courtesy, the Senatorial prerogative, and fear of Conkling's vengeance . . . control them;" "vengeance" was the President's peculiar expression for Conkling's ability to affect his colleagues' future.[56] John Sherman, who had quit the Senate for the cabinet, managed to lure away some supporters with the bait of present rewards, but Republican ranks remained remarkably united behind the chamber's leader. A few dissidents joined the Democrats to give Hayes a majority, but Conkling's stature was undiminished.[57]

The Hayes imbroglio was not simply the first in a series of battles between Stalwarts—the popular designation for Conkling's camp—and Half-breeds—the group reputedly following James Blaine. The incident was isolated. No permanently organized factions dominated all aspects of Senate proceedings during these years. On substantive issues, the division was entirely irrelevant. Conkling's friends stood together on organizational, not legislative, issues and their alliance by no means ruled the chamber. To label all opponents Half-breeds was even more misleading for it implied a cohesiveness which did not exist; there were vital differences among the men who disliked Conkling. Sherman, supposedly a Half-breed, thought the New York Senator was greatly "overrated," but he also believed that Blaine was an annoying "meddler." Blaine, presumably the Half-breed chief, consistently voted to uphold Conkling against Hayes.[58] Moreover, newcomers were not forced to join one or the other of the camps; no set lines split the chamber. Half-breeds and Stalwarts did not structure the business of the Senate and certainly did not necessitate conflicts with the White House.[59]

The New York Regulars did not support Garfield in the 1880 convention, and their rivals, the old Fenton wing of the party now led by William Robertson, were crucial to the Ohio nominee's success; nevertheless, Conkling's relations with the party's choice began well. Garfield carefully placated the New York leader, and Chester Arthur, vice-presidential candidate and a long-time Conkling lieutenant, helped sustain the harmony. A month before inauguration, Garfield conferred with the Senator and found him "frank and friendly." He saw no reason why they could not join together in "independent and mutual respect."[60]

The need for unity was imperative for the Senate parties in 1881 were so evenly divided that control of the chamber depended upon the vote of General William Mahone, the newly elected Readjuster from Virginia. The Readjusters, determined to scale down the state debt contracted before the war, had offered a separate state ticket while supporting the national Democratic nominees. Having led them to success, Mahone was rewarded with Senate election; he unexpectedly announced that he would stand independent of both national organizations. Wasting no time, George Gorham, Conkling's close friend and secretary of the Senate, set out to capture him for the Republicans.[61] The Conkling men were willing to accept Mahone's vote without ado, but Garfield, Blaine, and Sherman hesitated to ally with a debt repudiator. No one, however, proved difficult to convince. Promises of control over the state patronage, fine committee assignments, a liberal share of the Senate offices, and the withdrawal of the Republican ticket from future Virginia elections secured Mahone's vote. Assurances that Virginia's debt would be honestly settled and a reminder of the satisfactions inherent in controlling the Senate won over Garfield and his friends.[62]

Conkling now believed that Garfield would also support his wing of the state party. However, when they met again toward the end of February 1881, only a few days before inauguration, the President announced his intention to reward the New York insurgents who had helped him capture the nomination. When Conkling suggested that they be allotted foreign missions, Garfield hastily replied: "They did not deserve exile, but a place in the affairs of their own state." Prepared to "keep the peace," but determined not to abandon his supporters, the President sent to the Senate the nomination of William Robertson, leader of the anti-Conkling party, for Collector of the Port of New York.[63]

Garfield's efforts to secure a place for Conkling's opponents eventually might have proved acceptable to the Regulars, but they would not tolerate the loss of the state's most strategic political position. The conflict spread from New York to Washington as for the second time in as many administrations, Conkling attempted to block a presidential appointment. The Chief Executive was well supported. Sherman, back in the Senate, was experienced in marshaling anti-Conkling forces, and Blaine, now in the cabinet, was prepared to pull wires that Garfield would hesitate to touch.[64] Nevertheless, to topple Conkling from his Senate ascendancy would not be easy and in the course of the effort, onlookers finally discovered the extent of his power. John Hay, the young author and future diplomat, informed *New York Tribune* editor Whitelaw Reid: "You see the caucus today was completely under Conkling's thumb . . . It would amaze you to see the pusillanimity of some of our great men. Conkling seems to have a magic influence over them. They talk as bold as lions to me . . . and then they go into caucus, or the Senate, and if he looks at them they are like Little Billee of the ballad . . . Senators who owe him nothing, now or prospectively, are eager to lick his boots."[65] There was nothing magical about the ability to repay your supporters.

Nevertheless, Garfield did subdue Conkling. Two months after the affair began, J. P. Jones testily informed his wife that the Robertson appointment had been agreed to in the caucus without asking for the ayes and noes. At first Jones thought to have the roll called so as to see who was who—to see which Senators in his estimation were willing to bow in submission to the President in return for favors of patronage. But he quickly thought better of the notion, fearing it would only identify those decent enough to defend the right.[66] Jones' explanation for the defeat carried some validity, for Garfield, vowing it would be "no rosewater war," had without pretense "let several Senators know, that the vote on R[obertson]'s confirmation was a test of friendship or hostility to the administration."[67] Hayes had issued similar threats without gaining significant Republican support, whereas Garfield managed to defeat Conkling in the caucus. The Democrats, convinced that Conkling was "the most dangerous and most vindictive man in the Republican party," would gladly have aided Garfield; but in this instance their intervention was superfluous.[68]

Much more determinative was Garfield's popularity; he was able to attract and win over all those not firmly bound to Conkling. Then too, the New Yorker had difficulty in mustering strength for his second successive struggle. But most interesting was the President's record of the struggle. "I find," he noted in his diary, "a good deal of strong and hearty support among Senators who have long been restless under the arrogant domination of the N. Y. Senator."[69] Conkling's power was still new to the chamber. When those outside the magic circle joined with outright opponents, he could not master the alliance.

The aftermath of the defeat was puzzling. Conkling and his co-senator, Tom Platt, immediately resigned, asking the New

York legislature for re-election. Friends were bewildered by this gesture, foes viewed it as a "freak of insanity," and Hamilton Fish concluded that after all his service in Washington, he still could not fathom the game of politics. To win re-election would impress no one; defeat compelled permanent retirement.[70] In the absence of any satisfactory explanation, J. P. Jones wondered whether the latter alternative attracted Conkling, and Whitelaw Reid also speculated on this possibility. When the New York legislature, responsive to the intervention of Blaine, failed to send the Senator back to Washington, it may well be that Conkling received his wish.[71]

Resignations, retirements, defeats, and death soon ended whatever power remained with the Conkling wing, and the 1883 failure of George Gorham, a steadfast ally, to win re-election in the caucus as secretary of the Senate signaled the close of their day. Members instead selected Anson McCook, one-time Ohio congressman. While in the House, McCook customarily took his meals at the Arlington Hotel and there he came to know Senators William Allison, Nelson Aldrich, and Orville Platt. With their prodding assistance, he accepted the nomination and secured the election. Some members of the press speculated that a new group of men might soon assume power in the Senate.[72]

In the decade that followed Reconstruction, Republicans remained leaderless and undisciplined. Conkling could not command his colleagues, and no one succeeded where he had failed. Members paid little heed to the caucus, infrequently utilizing its machinery. The vacancy left by the New Yorker's departure would not long remain open, but fifteen years after Grant's inauguration Republican senators were still free from party control.

Democratic party machinery also played a minimal role in the Senate during these years. When the Forty-first Congress assembled, the minority numbered only eleven, and four years later it could point to but eight additions. Thereafter, its ranks swelled, but Democrats controlled the institution just twice between 1869 and 1901. The history of the Senate in this period, then, was unavoidably the story of the Republicans; still, the minority fit into an almost identical pattern. In the 1870's the absence of discipline was as evident on one side of the aisle as the other.

The paucity of members at first obviated any need for organization. As the minority, they had no important tasks; the order of business and the committee chairmanships were out of their control. Personal relationships were very intimate—Southerners often knew one another before coming to the chamber—and regardless of outlook, Democrats held together by the ties of friendship, not of party.[73] The results were often startling. The Westerner, Allen Thurman, noted for loudly and rudely blowing his nose into an abnormally large red bandana, was a close companion of the aristocratic, impeccably dressed Thomas Bayard, the fourth generation of his family to serve in the Senate. It did not seem to matter that the two men also disagreed on most political questions.[74] The few decisions requiring party discussion, the allotment of minority committee places, for example, were disposed of informally. Thomas Randolph, senator from New Jersey, described the Democratic structure in the 1875 chamber as very weak; more accurately, it was nonexistent.[75]

Democrats gained majority Senate control for the first time since the war in 1879 and they immediately elected, as they had two years before, Pennsylvania's William Wallace chairman of the caucus. Wallace had entered the chamber in 1875, and his rapid rise revealed the fluid quality of the newly established organization. He served at the same time as head of the Committee on Committees but held no important chairmanships himself. The Democrats, perhaps profiting from the Republican example, appointed a group to report on the order of business and put it under the charge of Allen Thurman, the President *pro tempore*.

(The Republicans, incidentally, ridiculed the duplication of their *ad hoc* committee, referring to it as the Democratic Thinking Committee. Innovations were slow to take root.) But although Wallace and Thurman occupied the outstanding offices, the organization did not enjoy firm and united leadership.[76]

The party contained neither one dominant group nor several cohesive and competing factions. Personality did not divide it, and no one to the left of the aisle even approximated Conkling's power. No neat division existed between senators favoring the corporations, the so-called Bourbons, and those representing the people, the anti-Bourbons. To be sure, it was by no means obvious which political decisions deserved to be labeled Bourbon and which anti-Bourbon. Railroad regulatory legislation was favored by some businessmen, such as the coal owners of West Virginia, and opposed by others, such as the entrepreneurs of the Texas & Pacific. Many manufacturers preferred high tariffs, while certain merchants, producers, and farmers preferred low rates; some capitalists urged inflationary measures and still others advocated currency contraction. But in any event, few senators fitted into either category. Among the Bourbons, some regularly voted for higher tariffs, railroad regulation, and currency contraction; their colleagues habitually defended transportation interests and labored to expand the currency. Variation was the rule, not the exception.[77]

An absence of factionalism on organizational questions duplicated the lack of legislative unity. Party posts were not filled by a careful selection of Bourbon or anti-Bourbon candidates. There may have been some vague differentiation between members more sympathetic to the demands of industrialism and those concerned with its effects upon the entire population; but these considerations did not influence the party structure. In 1879 the same majority that had imposed a sinking fund on the Pacific railroads and inflated the currency, also elected William Wallace to head its caucus. Wallace had begun his career as a lawyer in a small Pennsylvania town. His talents and inclinations, however, brought him into the legal service of the Pennsylvania Railroad, and he soon became a valuable and wealthy vice-president for the Texas & Pacific.

An excellent political manager, Wallace attempted to control the Pennsylvania Democrats as tightly as his friends the Camerons dominated the state's Republicans; although he could not equal their authority, he was able to gain Senate election. Sam Randall, Speaker of the House of Representatives, led the state Democratic opposition, denouncing the railroad vice-president as a friend to all monopoly schemes. Wallace's reputation preceded him to Washington; yet two years after his arrival, the Democratic party, about to regulate railroad finances, elected him their caucus chief. Moreover, Wallace, after a typical Bourbon career, proceeded to vote with the party majority in its attempts to regulate the western roads and expand the currency.[78]

Other offices were bestowed with a similar lack of attention to Bourbon or anti-Bourbon proclivities. Allen Thurman, who labored untiringly to curb railroad abuses and increase the money supply, chaired the committee to order the Senate business; Thomas Bayard, in disagreement with both of these positions, headed Finance.[79] The Democratic as well as the Republican organization functioned in an open, haphazard manner, and its members recognized the absence of unity or leadership. Eli Saulsbury, whose family's rule in Delaware commenced where the Bayards' ended, confided to a colleague in 1879: "We ought to maintain, as far as possible, harmony in our ranks . . . [But] we have more *talent* than *wisdom* in the Senate and unless the latter can be increased the former will be of comparatively little service either to the party or the country."[80] John Tyler Morgan, the popular senator from Alabama's black belt, wondered whether Cleveland's inauguration would encourage Democratic harmony.

Although pleased with the election of the new President, he soberly conceded: "We return [to power] as the Jews did from Babylon, speaking many tongues and draped in the garb of a foreign people. We have much to do yet to raise the old standards over a united army."[81]

In 1885 the Senate parties were still without coherence, exercising only limited influence. Yet all efforts to compensate for their authority by investing greater precision in chamber rules inevitably failed. Attempts to tighten proceedings by revising parliamentary codes were never successful; if the parties did not regulate in detail the order of business, it was useless to alter the procedures for taking bills from the Calendar. By the time Grover Cleveland entered the White House, it should have been evident that formal practices could not discipline or control the Senate business. Only extrainstitutional organizations, that is, the parties, could perform the task.

Senate rules before 1869 specified that after the opening Morning Hour, devoted to reading the Journal, the petitions and executive communications, the General Orders Calendar, listing all committee reports, should be called. Measures entered first were considered first, but any bill could be raised out of turn by a majority vote. Vital business, such as appropriation bills, was assured of prior attention if a two-thirds vote put it on the separate and privileged Special Orders Calendar. The General Orders Calendar, however, did not differentiate between the increasing number of public and private bills, inconsequential or of some importance, that demanded action.[82]

In 1872 Henry Anthony suggested an improvement. From the close of the Morning Hour, usually at 12:30, until 1:30, bills should be taken from the General Calendar under a proviso limiting each speech to five minutes or less; if a single senator objected, the measure would be put aside for later consideration without any limitation on debate. Anthony expected non-controversial measures to be quickly passed or defeated and the chamber adopted his proposal.[83]

In February 1882 Senator George Edmunds sought to supersede the Anthony Rule with more stringent procedures. Immediately after the Morning Hour, in the absence of special business, the General Calendar would be called in strict chronological order; any attempt to alter the rankings would not be debatable and would now require a two-thirds, not a majority vote. The entire legislative day was to be tightly regulated. With no discussion permitted and a two-thirds vote needed to alter the legislative order, the Senate would save time and increase its efficiency.[84]

Most senators objected to the change. John Sherman doubted that the chamber was "prepared to vote for a rule which prevents a majority from taking up a bill at its discretion." Moreover, a colleague declared, the body had enough rules; the difficulty was that they were not observed. "We cannot establish a rigid, inflexible, castiron system," John Ingalls informed his peers, "because there is prevalent here a great abiding, penetrating sense of courtesy and good will, a disposition to oblige on the part of the majority, that always results in the temporary abrogation of rules."[85] The fate of Edmunds' suggestion was typical of all restrictive measures. It was amended so that a majority, and not two thirds, could bring up business out of order and was used along with, not instead of, the Anthony Rule. Edmunds' recommendations were accepted only after the key provisos were omitted; so long as a majority could disregard the Calendar order, legislation would not be handled efficiently. Senate practices could not enforce the necessary regularity.

Similar hostility greeted other attempts to tighten procedures. Pride in unlimited debate was immense. Massachusetts senator George Hoar instructed his colleagues in all seriousness: "One of the great historians of Rome has declared that the liberties of Rome perished when the freedom of debate was terminated."[86] A majority also objected to the mild suggestion that the rule be amended so that no other business should be considered before the conclusion of the Morning Hour, standard Senate practice in any event. Even the attempt to enumerate the chamber's officers was defeated.[87] The sentiments were constant: no institutional barriers should block freedom of action. The Senate should not limit its prerogatives.

In 1885 Woodrow Wilson, then a graduate student at Johns Hopkins, published *Congressional Government,* his study of American party politics. Arguing that Congress sorely lacked leaders, he asserted: "The public now and again picks out here and there a Senator who seems to act with the instinct of statesmanship and who unmistakenly merits the confidence of colleagues and of people. But such a man, however eminent, is never more than *a* Senator. No one is *the* Senator . . . No one exercises the special trust of acknowledged leadership. The Senate is merely a body of critics."[88] Incessantly, Wilson returned to this theme: power was not concentrated, but doled out among petty chieftains. Within Congress there was "no visible and therefore no controllable party organization," and party action could not produce consistent legislation. Unable and unwilling to follow the haphazard proceedings, the public first ignored Congress and then abandoned its role in the democratic process.[89]

Wilson's insights and oversights resulted from his willingness to compare Britain and America. In the House of Commons, parties were controlled by ministers responsible for the measures they introduced and passed; party structure there inspired the public discussion so vital to the success of democratic government. By contrast, the American system was ineffective and disorderly.[90]

But if the future President recognized the chaos of congressional government, he could not incorporate the congressional party organizations into his observations. Misunderstanding the role of the Senate party machinery, he did not realize that the confusions were less complete than he imagined and might soon undergo a significant ordering. Grasping the importance of committees and their chairmen, he forgot that parties determined which members gained key positions. Only in his very last pages did he discuss the caucus; but then he failed to assess its relationship to his main argument.

Wilson concluded that the caucus supplied "the cohesive principle" in the Senate, that it was "the drilling ground of party." With British examples always in mind, he even exaggerated its power when asserting: "Its whip seldom fails to reduce individual malcontents and mutineers into submission . . . The man who disobeys his party caucus is understood to disavow his party allegiance altogether."[91] Wilson could not and did not, however, integrate this statement with his earlier view that Congress had no controllable organization. To reply that the privacy of the caucus, its "invisibility," inhibited its powers was unsound; the British never opened their caucuses to the public either. The point at issue, after all, was whether the caucus enforced legislative responsibility; and since Wilson overestimated its authority, his answer should have been yes. Only by ignoring his misconceived exaggerations did he reach the valid conclusion that Congress was disorganized.

In 1885 party could neither discipline its members nor drive malcontents from the ranks. With no leader to enforce regularity and no caucus to compel obedience, it still was unable to control the business of the Senate.

☆ II ☆

THE DYNAMICS OF LEADERSHIP

Both in the [Senate] committees and in the offices, we should use the machinery for our own benefit and not let other men have it.

Advice to William Allison,
Republican Senate Caucus Chairman, 1895

The Senate establishment is almost the antithesis of democracy. It is not selected by any democratic process. It appears to be unresponsive to the caucuses of the two parties. It is what might be called a self-perpetuating oligarchy.

Senator Joseph Clark,
Congressional Record, 1963

"The Senate of the United States," declared Moisei Ostrogorski in 1902, "no longer has any resemblance to that august assembly which provoked the admiration of the Tocquevilles." To the Russian-born, French-educated political scientist, the reason for the decline was obvious: less than two decades after Woodrow Wilson lamented the lack of party discipline, Ostrogorski decried its dominance. "The caucus," he concluded, "was one of the principal, if not the principal agent of the fall." Its "iron discipline," and unlimited authority strangled all independent judgment.[1] Ostrogorski, unlike Wilson, distrusted party rule, but for all his heightened sensitivity to its abuses, his conclusions were as valid in 1902 as Wilson's had been in 1885. Within these years, party organization transformed the Senate until it no longer resembled its predecessors, the bodies that Tocqueville had praised. The Senate of the 1890's was similar to the institution that Eisenhower confronted, not to that of Jackson or Grant.

On the Republican side of the aisle, the skills of such leaders as William Allison, Nelson Aldrich, and their hand-picked allies helped alter Senate practices. The dimensions of the changes and their role in bringing them about were most vividly illustrated in the Fifty-fifth Congress, convened in March 1897.

The first duty facing the party that year was to elect a caucus chairman to succeed John Sherman, who had just resigned to enter the McKinley cabinet. The choice presented no difficulties; William Allison, having served longer than any other Republican, succeeded to the place. Calculations of seniority rather than of party strength determined the decision, for the authority of the chairman, even at the end of the nineteenth century, was still not fully appreciated. George Edmunds had occupied the post from 1885 until 1891, exhibiting little talent for leadership, and during the following six years, John Sherman was far too feeble to exercise vital influence.[2] Party connections, rather than length of service, would come to dictate selections only after the caucus became crucial to the control of Senate business. The efforts of Allison and his friends contributed to the change.

When Allison chaired the Republican caucus, the faction that he and Aldrich dominated acceded to power. In the course of their rule, they established and clarified the authority that Senate party officers could wield. Realizing the potentialities for control in the chamber, they entrenched and tightened personal leadership and party discipline. Their example would not always be emulated; a severe shrinkage in members, a lack of capable senators, or excessive factionalism, could in future years return the party to its former condition. Nevertheless, they institutionalized, once and for all, the prerogatives of power. Would-be successors or Senate rivals would now be forced to capture and effectively utilize the party posts. Allison understood clearly that "both in the committees and in the offices, we should use the machinery for our own benefit and not let other men have it."[3] His heirs had no choice but to follow his dictum.

The privileges of leadership could never be simply invested in specific positions. But personal magnetism was more easily translated into political influence once the route to power was well marked. After the persistent maneuvering of Allison and Aldrich, the opportunity for control was always present in the Senate Republican party; only the aptitude for leadership had to be periodically reintroduced.

The members of the ruling circle were well known to the public and their importance was justly appreciated. They were a surprisingly diverse and interesting group. Perhaps the most convenient place to meet them together was at the home of Senator James McMillan some weekday night. In his imposing residence on new but fashionable Vermont Avenue, McMillan had handsomely equipped a spacious den. A billiard table on one side and a sizable card table on the other, several carpets, easy chairs, and leather-covered straight backs composed the furnishings of the bronze-colored room. Here the School of Philosophy Club gathered for its steady post-dinner game of poker.[4] The game had begun sometime around 1890, antedating the group's political supremacy, and some of the original participants, such as William Washburn of Minnesota and Charles Manderson of Nebraska, left after suffering defeat for re-election. The sessions took on a new significance, however, when Allison assumed the party post.

Politics, to be sure, was only infrequently discussed for although the stakes were not especially high, the play was intense.[5] Yet a strong personal comradeship united the men gathering there. At times the friendships induced a participant to vote against his better judgment but most often the fellowship simply insured that good feeling prevailed among the gentlemen who dominated the Senate.[6] No doubt it served them well as they settled public questions and adjusted private ambitions.

McMillan, elected Michigan's senator in 1889, was the perennial host; he gave little thought to the cost of entertaining, having amassed a fortune in shipping and manufacturing.[7] Allison, his closest friend, was always present at these evenings and Aldrich also attended regularly, his skills at the table proving as outstanding as his talents in the Senate. As many would have guessed, he was "hell on jackpots" and the most frequent winner.[8] Maine's Eugene Hale and both Connecticut senators, Joseph Hawley and Orville Platt, were members, and Mark Hanna took a place soon after entering the Senate. George Wetmore, Aldrich's co-senator and staunch supporter in Rhode Island, also joined. Before coming to the chamber, Wetmore used his fantastic inheritance to travel and collect art; everyone was quite certain he would prove "very acceptable" in the Club.[9] John Spooner, the hand-picked successor to Wisconsin's millionaire lumberman, Philetus Sawyer, looked forward to these sessions and missed them greatly whenever he was away from Washington. "I look back upon those little gatherings," he told William Washburn, "and their freedom and frankness and friendliness, with the utmost delight . . . If I were President I think I should want them to be in the Cabinet, and if either of that crowd were President I think I should want to be in the Cabinet."[10]

The harmony that united McMillan's guests also prevailed among the Senate leaders and their party colleagues. William Allison, short, stocky, and full-bearded, was the most popular member of the group, known to veterans and newcomers alike as a "conciliator and adjustor." A native of Ohio, Allison worked his way through school to enter the law and soon became active in Republican affairs. Dissatisfied with his professional and political progress, he settled in Iowa just before the outbreak of the Civil War and devoted his attention to the new Union party. His rise to prominence was rapid and from 1863 until 1871 he served in Congress. In the following year, with the decisive help of Grenville Dodge, chief engineer of the Union Pacific and head of the Iowa Republicans, he was elected to the Senate. In the course of thirty-five years of service there, Allison mastered the politics of the possible, willing to compromise whenever necessary so that he might ultimately win his point. He possessed the tact to follow a course without antagonizing its staunchest opponents; rather than hunt with a brass band, like Conkling, he conducted his business quietly. Without pretense but with extraordinary regularity, he achieved his goals.[11]

Aldrich was the most brilliant of the group. Distinguished in appearance despite the weight of 210 pounds on a five-foot, eleven-inch frame, he was at ease in committee rooms, but not on the Senate floor. Born into a poor Rhode Island family, the future senator entered the grocery business and as his mercantile and stock holdings increased, he became involved in local and state politics. His allegiance to state leader Henry Anthony fluctuated; supported for Congress in 1879 by the organization, he won Senate election two years later without its aid. Immediately after Anthony's death, the now wealthy and experienced politician consolidated his power. Aldrich joined Charles Brayton, a professional political manager, conceded control over the state party in return for the security of re-elections, and for the next thirty years was free to pay full attention to Washington affairs. In debate his comments and questions were invariably laconic and penetrating, if not endearing. With some cause he prided himself, albeit inordinately, on an ability to master the most confusing and detailed piece of legislation.[12]

In 1899 New York's Tom Platt, now back in the Senate, took the opportunity of a temporary absence to pay obeisance to the rule of Allison and Aldrich. "If I were a Chandleric Senator [coined after New Hampshire's irritating William Chandler] or a recalcitrant member," he wrote the caucus chairman, "you might consider my presence necessary on some important questions; but as I have told you, I am with and for the Government, and I consider the interests of the Government as embodied in you and Senator Aldrich. What you say goes. Kindly keep me posted as to what you do, so that I may not go astray."[13] Undoubtedly he was kept well instructed.

Allison and Aldrich attracted talented allies. John Spooner, after an outstanding career in the law, utilized his legal abilities to maneuver many bills through the chamber. Orville Platt, elected as a dark horse by the Connecticut legislature, proved an imaginative senator, and unlike most compromise candidates, continued to win re-elections. Maine's Eugene Hale was among the most hard-working members; never able to inspire enthusiasm from a stump gathering, he nevertheless worked so effectively at his tasks that he enjoyed one of the longest tenures of any United States senator.[14] James McMillan rounded out the group. Usually content to listen rather than to give counsel, his conviviality and hospitality made him a welcome addition. When Anthony Higgins, a backbench Republican senator, learned that Aldrich would take up a piece of business, he rightfully concluded: "This means the action of what I call the 'Junta' of the Senate: Aldrich, Allison, Hale and McMillan and a few others." Their rule was far from invisible.[15]

Utilizing and extending the privileges of the caucus chairman, Allison secured tight control over the Senate proceedings. His faction's power was recognized but neither critics nor supporters understood the base of its influence. Muckrakers denounced the corrupting influence of campaign contributions while sympathizers exaggerated the charms of personality. Few, however, looked for a clue where it actually was, in the workings of the Senate party.[16]

One of the first duties Allison faced in 1897 was to select the chairman and members of the Republican Steering Committee. By the mid-1880's the *ad hoc* groups that helped settle the legislative schedule had been transformed into the biennially appointed Committee on the Order of Business, less formally known as the Steering Committee. Previous caucus leaders had usually appointed other senators to head it; Allison, however, invariably chaired the committee himself.[17] Moreover, when choosing the remaining members, he again regularized practices that predecessors had followed erratically. Repeated service on the eleven-man committee was not exceptional before 1897, but most often a majority of the group was replaced at the start of each Congress. Allison, concentrating authority, habitually named the same senators to fill the places.[18]

His freedom of choice was almost unlimited. Some geographical diversity was necessary, but no section held such strong claims to a particular place that Allison was compelled to alter a proposed selection. When Michigan's James McMillan died, his post went to a western senator without debate; and it coincided with the chairman's plans to put Lodge of Massachusetts on the committee when fellow New Englander, Orville Platt, left the chamber.[19] The leading working committees traditionally advised on the order of business but their prerogatives prompted few restrictions. Allison headed Appropriations, Aldrich chaired Finance, and their associates were equally well established. Any member, not necessarily the chairman, could represent a working committee on Steering, and Allison had no difficulty in placing his favorites in strategic posts. When Mark Hanna in 1900 wanted to join the caucus committee, William Frye, chairman of Commerce, wrote Allison: "Please put Senator Hanna on your Committee on the Order of Business. The Committee of Commerce is entitled to one." That Commerce was already represented by Oregon's George McBride did not prevent Allison from granting the request.[20]

After filling the Steering Committee, Allison turned to the Committee on Committees. Caucus chairmen normally enjoyed great leeway here, confined only slightly by broad considerations of regional representation. In December 1895, however, dissident Republicans compelled John Sherman to report his choices to the full caucus; for the first time, the party reviewed and approved a chairman's slate. During the 1870's, members sporadically examined the opinions of Finance Committee nominees, at times to insure a majority in harmony with their views on currency. But never before had they scrutinized a Committee on Committees listing to guarantee geographical diversity and political sympathies. In this instance western senators from newly admitted states instigated the demand, in search of favorable assignments and loyal majorities. Their numbers were sufficient to win Sherman's unhappy consent, and five of his nine choices met their requirements.[21] Two years later, however, Allison faced no such difficulties. The dissenters were too few and too weak to impose any conditions upon the party. The chairman was free to name the Committee on Committees as he pleased.[22]

Various members of the Allison-Aldrich circle intermittently occupied key Senate positions before 1897, but after Allison assumed power they monopolized party offices. When Ostrogorski published his comments on caucus rule, Allison headed and Aldrich, Hale, McMillan, Orville Platt, Spooner, and Hanna served on the Republican Steering Committee. A majority of the Committee on Committees was responsive to Allison's requests, and its chairman unfailingly belonged to the ruling clique. McMillan held the post in 1897 and was succeeded by Aldrich in 1899; two years later Orville Platt performed the duties and Eugene Hale next assumed them. Moreover, Allison unofficially sat with the group and together with the chairman, exercised skillful oversight. The Steering Committee and the Committee on Committees were firmly controlled by the men who gathered at McMillan's.[23]

The faction's dominance over the party offices helped entrench its power over business. Most Senate legislation was shaped by the working committees, and the increasing complexity and widening scope of Senate action after the Civil War increased their prominence.[24] Not surprisingly, the Allison-selected Committee on Committees was fully cognizant of the implications of its decisions. "If we do not meet until we meet in Washington," Allison wrote John Spooner in 1899, "I hope you will be there at least some days before the opening of the session as it is of utmost importance that we should make no mistake in re-organizing the committees of the Senate."[25] With appropriate cal-culations, they determined the assignments, always attempting and usually managing to further their own ambitions.

Now, before the first session of each new Congress, the Com-mittee on Committees gathered in the chairman's office, immedi-ately directing the secretary to dispatch a note to all Senate party members. "In behalf of the Republican Caucus Committee on Committees," dictated Eugene Hale when chairman, "I would be glad to learn from you what your preferences are in the matter of Committee assignments . . . An early answer will facilitate our work." Replies were soon returned as rumors and speculations engaged reporters and senators alike. The group then set about its business in private meetings, without keeping minutes.[26]

The obligation to respect the Senate's traditions somewhat simplified its tasks. Vacant chairmanships were assigned to the ranking members, and no one who objected was removed from his place. The rule of seniority in selecting committee heads was common knowledge; the frequent practice of the 1870's had become an iron-clad formula two decades later. Nevertheless, the job of the caucus representatives was not simply mathe-matical, adding and correlating years of service with assignments. Rather, they exercised the critical authority to fill committee vacancies; a senator could not ascend the ladder to a chairman-ship until he had occupied one of the rungs. Here the Committee on Committees used its discretion for the claims of seniority did not dictate its choices for the openings.[27]

Francis Warren, Wyoming's leading stockgrower, went on Ap-propriations soon after beginning his Senate service. "There are Senators elected to four or five terms," he boasted to an admirer, "who have regularly every two years asked for a place on Ap-propriations and never received it."[28] Orville Platt could have filled a Judiciary Committee vacancy despite the ambitions of Massachusetts senator George Hoar, his senior in service. "It does not make a bit of difference," George Edmunds informed Platt. "We want you on this committee, we do not want Hoar."[29]

The great number of committees, forty-nine in all, with comparatively few members, an average of thirteen, made every vacancy the focus for contentions and rivalry. Still the turnover was rapid. Between 1895 and 1900 fourteen openings occurred on Finance and Appropriations alone, and places were even more frequently available on lesser committees. Moreover, newly elected senators had to be assigned to posts and again preferences were exerted. The Committee on Committees had ample room to wield its authority.

When seniority first grew current, committee assignments were still distributed unsystematically, and before personal allegiances and factional ambitions were carefully calculated, the practice appeared as equitable as any other. The custom became more firmly established after the Civil War, simplifying an almost impossible task; a random gathering of senators would have been forced to reach decision after decision faced only with colleagues' qualifications and desires. Thus, by the time the Allison-Aldrich circle came into power, the procedure could have been disregarded only by creating great opposition and dissatisfaction. But no one considered the change for little would be gained. Republican chieftains, veterans to the chamber, stood to win most contests determined by years of service. More important, seniority helped stabilize the authority of leadership; the committee assignments of one year would affect chairmanships ten years later. As long as the Committee on Committees enjoyed more than adequate power, Allison and Aldrich were content. Welcoming the tradition of seniority, they made its place in the Senate's proceedings secure.[30]

The Committee on Committees was able to satisfy many requests, because a diversity of taste and interest as well as differing estimates of utility characterized the chamber's members. Finance, in charge of monetary and tariff policies, and Appropria-

tions, responsible for the federal budget, were by common agreement the two most important committees. But among Commerce,
Foreign Relations, Interstate Commerce, and Judiciary, for example, personal considerations determined any rankings.[31] Offered the vacancy on Commerce in 1895, McMillan prudently
evaluated the alternatives. Aware that "there are a number of the
most important of the Lake improvements within the jurisdiction
of Michigan," and that until recently "there had been a Michigan
senator on that Committee," he finally concluded to take the
place and "look after the general interests of the Lakes."[32] When
he was offered the committee's chairmanship six years later, the
choice proved more difficult. Commerce, McMillan reasoned,
"would help me in the state," carried a fine committee room and
"the amount of work that would be done would rest entirely on
me." Still, each senator was entitled to only one chairmanship
and McMillan already headed the District of Columbia Committee. The local duties of running the capital had proved exceptionally pleasant and he was not anxious to quit them. In the end,
taste took precedence over strategy; McMillan kept his old place
and ceded the Commerce chairmanship to the second in line.[33]

John Spooner, on the other hand, was discouraged by the
minor duties of the Claims Committee. When accepting the post
in 1885, he had expected to meet with the Senate's most prominent men. Overwhelmed with investigating pleas for government funds from irate citizens, he soon tired of its laborious
tasks. "Your advice," he confided to a knowledgeable acquaintance in 1888, "not to let semi-private committee duties keep me
out of the general business of Congress, is sound, and thoroughly
appreciated. I am not on a single committee the duties of which
either give me an opportunity, or compel me, to become thoroughly familiar with any question of broad public policy, and if I
knew everything that ever will come before the committee . . . it
would be of little use to my constituents."[34] Burdened with "over
a thousand things that nobody ever hears of, that few people care

anything about," Spooner incessantly bemoaned his fate.[35] William Stewart, his colleague on Claims, surveyed the prospects quite differently. "I have been forced," the Nevada senator confessed, "to do more drudgery in the way of Committee work than was reasonable." Placed on Claims "because I will work, they load me down with cases to investigate." Nevertheless, "I find it a great advantage to do the work because it places so many Senators and members under obligations to me."[36] For some, the worst predicaments offered consolations.

Senators realized that if left to chance, their committee assignments would not satisfy their ambitions. To inform the caucus committee, as did Indiana's Charles Fairbanks in 1897, that Appropriations was his first choice, followed by Foreign Relations, Finance, and Judiciary, only publicized an ignorance of realities. It was, of course, Fairbanks' freshman year and none of his requests was granted.[37] Wiser senators, however, learned to concentrate on one preferred place, marshaling all conceivable arguments to bolster their appeal.

Petitions most frequently emphasized the need for geographic diversity on the working committees. The Committee on Committees calculated the sectional origins of the membership especially when filling openings on Finance, Appropriations or Commerce, and to a lesser but still significant extent, on other, non-pocketbook, committees. In 1899 two members from New England, the Mid-West, and the West, and one senator from the Mid-Atlantic and Far West made up Appropriations. Noting the arrangement, William Chandler unhappily concluded: "Of course I cannot go on Appropriations for New England now has two members."[38] Geography proved more of an asset to William Stewart in 1891. "I would be much gratified," he informed the chairman of the caucus committee, "to be placed on the Committee on Appropriations. I make this request because it seems proper that the Far West should be represented on that committee." The contention was accepted and he received the place.[39]

Regional interests often facilitated unexpected accommodations by prompting senators to seek the chairmanships of committees with specialized concerns. Through such circumstances, Orville Platt finally won a seat on Finance. Platt was the Allison-Aldrich choice for the vacancy in 1895, but the strength of the western silver senators that year made his anti-inflation record a seemingly insurmountable hurdle. A curious chain of circumstances began, however, when Idaho's senator, Fred Dubois, grew tired of standing second on Public Lands to South Dakota's Richard Pettigrew. "I beg to say," Dubois impatiently told the Committee on Committees, "that my first and real desire is, the chairmanship of the Public Lands Committee."[40] Pettigrew, cognizant of his state's large Indian population, was just as anxious for the Indian Affairs chairmanship, but he ranked second to Platt, who in 1895 was in line to receive it. Dubois attempted to convince Platt to move off Indian Affairs; Pettigrew would then take its chairmanship and Dubois could head Public Lands. Platt agreed, provided that Dubois and Pettigrew secured him western support for the Finance Committee. The circle was completed and the bargain struck. "Pettigrew and I," Dubois later noted, "got busy and induced the Committee on Committees to increase the Finance Committee by two, one Democrat and one Republican." The silver strength was not diminished—the one Democrat was an inflationist—the two western Senators secured their chairmanships and Platt went on Finance.[41]

It was evident by 1897 that although local diversity and peculiarity could help some senators gain positions, success ultimately depended upon winning the favor and support of the leaders. Not every Republican expected an invitation to dine at McMillan's, but all understood that the men who gathered there controlled their colleagues' future in the chamber. Albert Beveridge paid homage to this lesson; and if his successes were at first only modest, that was testimony to the grandeur of his schemes rather than to any error in plotting the lines of power.

In January 1899 Beveridge, the youthful and popular Republican orator, received Indiana's second Senate seat, despite opposition from Charles Fairbanks, the senior senator and state party head. For attacking Fairbanks, who was now in alliance with Aldrich and Allison, the word went out, supporters informed Beveridge, "that you belong to the genus mugwump."[42] Frantic that unless the description were corrected he would waste considerable energy in combatting wrong impressions and still not receive favorable committee assignments, Beveridge urged his Washington friends to contradict the rumors. "You may be sure," Charles Dawes, a prominent Republican functionary, comforted him, "that in every way possible I am endeavoring to create a proper impression of your personality and your abilities."[43] But despite warnings that he might be "endeavoring to do too much," the Senator-elect presumptuously informed Allison: "While I earnestly desire the Foreign Relations, Finance, Judiciary, and Relations with Canada, I am willing to sacrifice everything for a place on the Foreign Relations Committee, though I hope this will not be necessary."[44] Beveridge also let it be privately known that if Allison and his friends "do not put me on the Foreign Relations Committee, it will be a shame, a plain unvarnished shame . . . I expect this statement seems a little 'nervy' but it is so nevertheless."[45]

Shrewd as well as ambitious, Beveridge concentrated on influencing the caucus chairman. With no attempt at modesty, he first outlined his qualifications: the study of international affairs and a recent trip to the Philippines fitted him for Foreign Relations. He had learned constitutional law in the office of a specialist (Judiciary) and satisfied Indianapolis bankers and laborers alike (Finance). Not content to let his abilities stand alone, Beveridge assured Allison of his personal loyalty and subservience, declaring: "I leave my fate in your hands." He concluded his appeal with a certain candor. "I feel that the greatest single point is gained in the possession of your friendship," the young Senator told the caucus chairman. "I will labor very hard, strive very earnestly to deserve your consideration."[46] Beveridge could give himself no better advice.

Lest Allison have any remaining doubts, the indefatigable newcomer courted other key Senate figures. Aldrich received letters commending the Indiana Senator to his attention, Foreign Relations chairman Cushman Davis was advised of Beveridge's talents, and Teddy Roosevelt mentioned to Henry Cabot Lodge how appropriate the appointment to Foreign Relations would be. Yet for all these efforts, Beveridge did not immediately gain the committee of his choice; Allison probably remained dubious of the new Senator's fidelity, and others found him a young man too much in a hurry.[47]

The setback in 1899, however, was only temporary. Beveridge had played the game correctly and in disappointment did not alter his tactics. "As I have said to you before," he continued to remind Allison, "I value your intimate acquaintance and friendship most highly. If I can have that, I feel that my opportunities for usefulness in the Senate will be increased and the probability of my mistakes lessened."[48] Soon Beveridge was honored with membership on the Steering Committee and within a few years he was fully content with his assignments. Perseverance was finally rewarded.

The faction's influence was sharply delineated in the careers of more favored if less tenacious senators. Aldrich's co-senator, George Wetmore, whose inheritance obviated any familiarity with the drudgeries of a budget, received the vacancy on Appropriations soon after joining McMillan's table. He had proved quite acceptable to the Club. Mark Hanna, another regular, was granted his request for a place on Commerce, and John Spooner, now on Judiciary and Finance, no longer complained about the meaningless bother of committee work. When Clarence Clark of Wyoming entered the Senate in 1895, he was immediately assigned to Judiciary—an honor in a chamber rich with legal talent

—and was soon also serving on the much-coveted Foreign Relations Committee. Hoping to benefit his state, especially in swelling its share of appropriations, the Wyoming lawyer had resolved to win Allison's confidence and regard; in presidential conventions and Senate proceedings, he was always "unchangeably for Allison." The tactics brought even greater success than he anticipated.[49]

By the end of the nineteenth century, access to positions of influence depended upon the right connections. In 1899 Tom Platt filled a vacancy on Finance, not a surprising reward for a senator who believed that Allison and Aldrich embodied the interests of the government. Two years earlier, however, his desire for the seat had been thwarted when McMillan, in the Committee on Committees, nominated his junior senator and staunch supporter, Julius Burrows. No one argued Platt's qualifications as earnestly as McMillan praised Burrows; and the caucus acceded to the Michigan Senator's proposal. Others were closer to men in power, and Platt had to bide his time.[50]

Through such exacting oversight, Allison and his supporters dominated the Senate working committees as effectively as the party organization. Allison himself chaired Appropriations and was second on Finance; Aldrich headed Finance and also sat on Rules, Interstate Commerce, and Relations with Cuba. Orville Platt and John Spooner both served on Finance and Judiciary, and the Wisconsin Senator also chaired the Rules Committee. Hale was a member of Appropriations and headed Naval Affairs while McMillan occupied places on Commerce and Cuba, and chaired the District of Columbia Committee. Never before in the history of the Senate were the outstanding committees so monopolized by the party leaders.

Control of the Steering Committee also confirmed the power of the Allison-Aldrich faction over the Senate business. Arranging the legislative schedule in detail week by week, the committee extended the party leaders' authority unimpaired from the caucus to the chamber.[51] Senators knew that they had to consult the committee before attempting to raise even minor matters. For the first time one of its members managed the legislative proceedings, offering the required resolutions and directing the course of debate.[52]

The efficiency that marked the distribution of committee assignments was equally evident in ordering the program of business. The Steering Committee requested the chairmen of working committees to list bills warranting immediate consideration and it carefully studied the replies. Subsequently, it informed the caucus which measures were to be taken up and the order of discussion, frequently including some recommendations on substantive policy decisions.[53] Beveridge was understandably eager to join this group, only slightly exaggerating its significance when he informed J. C. Shaffer, president of the *Chicago Evening Post:* "This is the highest expression of confidence possible to be given to one Senator by the Senate. This Committee absolutely determines what shall and shall not be done in national legislation."[54]

Caucus meetings usually proceeded harmoniously, pointing to the effectiveness of the new Senate leaders. Meeting frequently at the start of the session, party members approved the slate presented by the Committee on Committees, no matter how blatantly it favored the ruling circle, and sanctioned the order of business. The once traditional task of voting on the distribution of Senate patronage—the secretaries, doorkeepers, and other minor officials—was now unnecessary; rather than encourage intraparty competition, each senator simply received an equal share of the offices.[55] Similarly, Senate honors no longer prompted attention, much less conflict. The President *pro tempore* lost any remaining preeminence once the floor manager controlled the proceedings; Orville Platt, without hesitation, announced his preference for a place on Finance to the presiding officer's chair.[56] As the session wore on, the caucus convened less frequently and members were often notified of the order of business by mail. Still, vital decisions were always presented for its approval so that differences could be smoothed over in private session. By the time the party assembled in the Senate chamber to cast its votes, ranks were usually in order (see Chart II, Chapter III).

When freshman Republican senators speculated on their duty to the party caucus, they could still hear conflicting statements. Nevertheless, their alternatives were now recognizable and unambiguous. They might be told "that the decision of a Republican caucus is like the decree of an ecumenical council . . . The decree is infallible and everybody is bound to obey or be anathemized." However, a member in good standing could honestly reply: "I have been here nearly 24 years and have attended every conference when I have been in the city, and the Republican Party has never undertaken to bind its members to vote on any question whatever."[57] Newcomers quickly learned that the remarks were only seemingly contradictory. The Republican caucus was not binding, and yet its decisions commanded obedience for party leadership was capable of enforcing discipline. Senators could no longer act with impunity unless they were willing to forego favorable committee posts and control of the chamber proceedings.

Allison and Aldrich firmly maintained Republican unity; effectively dispensing rewards, they promoted their friends and isolated their enemies. Senators who joined the alliance soon occupied vital committee places while dissidents were excluded from influence. To be sure, anyone could use the chamber as a forum and address the nation. Senators willing to abandon the opportunity to increase their authority could act freely, following their own inclinations. If their numbers increased, they could encourage opposition and resistance. But barring a take-over of the party offices, they could hardly affect the exercise of power. The country might honor their names but the Senate barely felt their presence.

Soon after arriving in Washington, Albert Beveridge suggested to Allison that the Republicans alter their procedures. The party meeting, technically known as a "conference," should be officially designated a "caucus." The new title would inaugurate a fundamental change: unlike the conference, the caucus would demand and compel obedience to its every decision, organizational or substantive. Participants would be bound, in advance, to uphold the majority's viewpoint. Allison confessed to "great reluctance in making so radical a change in the Senate." "We can get on without [it]," he remarked, confident that his leadership was not dependent upon so formal a rule.[58] "There seemed to be no necessity," an astute Democrat later observed, "of imposing a rule upon a party which holds its party solidarity without a caucus."[59]

Republican ranks were not always to remain united after the rule of Allison and Aldrich. Unskilled and irresolute successors would often fail to harmonize fractious or discordant members. Nevertheless, the example set by the first two Senate leaders was not forgotten. The opportunity for party control and Senate dominance was now always present.[60]

"Men who have personal independence of character," complained Democratic senator John Daniel in 1890, "when they become allied in political organizations and under the influences which are brought to bear about the great Capitol . . . bow and bend and surrender." Certain that "in their organization and political movements, parties do not differ with each other," that practices "are likely sooner or later much to resemble each other," Daniel concluded that the Senate Democratic organization, like the Republican, improperly dominated its members.[61] Arthur Gorman, however, the only Democrat comparable in stature to Allison, took more pride in party government. In 1894 he concluded that without an effective caucus "we should have passed through the session with divisions as wide upon this side as it is possible to conceive of within a party."[62] If Senate Democrats in some ways matched their rivals, Gorman was pleased.

Gorman served in his youth as a Senate page, and his early introduction to politics later helped guide him through the intri-

cate alignments of Maryland's Democratic party. Prudently joining one faction and then moving over to its rival, Gorman chose
sides so well that by 1880 he commanded the state organization
and won election to the Senate. His political talents continued to
serve him well and nine years later he chaired the Democratic
caucus.[63]

Fascinated by the party leader's personality and activities,
Horace Chilton, an observant Texas Democrat, set down his impressions in a never-completed memoir. Gorman was "the most
influential man of the Democratic side," Chilton wrote in his
Recollections of a One Term Senator, 1895–1901. Resembling
"a dignitary of the Church," with a pale, smooth-shaven face, he
was extraordinarily discreet and wary. Gorman's policy decisions
were often "the reflex of Democratic opinion," for he always preferred to gain "sufficient approval among the other Senators."
"But," Chilton quickly added, "it must not be supposed that he
was not a powerful agent in finding the common ground and
leading his colleagues to enter upon it. He was indefatigable in
his attention to all Democratic Senators," invariably employing
"the ingratiating influence of hospitality, favoring Senators in
regard to Committees, helping them concerning pet measures."
Unable to "make a Senator cast a vote which risked his position
at home," he usually gained his point on other matters. "For if
a man recognized as a leader, shows interest in the personal con-
venience of a Colleague—if he interests himself to get you a good
seat, if he picks an opportunity of helping you to do something of
decided importance to you, if he bestirs himself to get you a
congenial Committee assignment, you are sure to want to recipro-
cate." And Gorman rarely forgot a debt. Chilton aptly concluded: "He has a well-organized mind."[64]

The senatorial practices of the two parties in the 1890's were
similar, and the Democratic structure, in fact, was probably the
more conducive of the two to the emergence of energetic and
effective leadership. Gorman's election to the caucus chairman-

ship reflected his influence among party colleagues for seniority did not govern the Democratic choice; ostensibly, by winning the contest, he had already proved his authority.[65] The Maryland Senator, like Allison, chaired the Steering Committee and selected its members at will, vaguely limited by geographic considerations. But Gorman's appointments were permanent, and Democratic senators served as long as they remained in the chamber. Moreover, the Democratic chief himself headed the Committee on Committees, preferring not to delegate responsibility. Increasingly, he named the same men to help arrange the slate and determine the order of business, and soon the two committees simply merged into one. Thus even fewer Democrats than Republicans monopolized the party offices.[66]

Gorman's Senate allies controlled the positions of influence. Francis Cockrell of Missouri, a leading Gorman supporter in the 1892 Democratic Convention, served on both the Steering and Appropriations Committees. His appearance, always in a white linen duster with a well-chewed corn cob pipe in his mouth, belied his stature as one of the state's outstanding attorneys; still, his sympathies for the rural populace were real, and the St. Louis press depicted him as an enemy to progress. The rise of Alliance and Populist strength only secured his power and Cockrell continued to win re-elections without difficulty.[67] Kentucky's Joseph Blackburn, another promoter of Gorman for president in 1892, also served on Steering and Appropriations. Son of a wealthy planter and successful politician, he practiced law and served a long and distinguished career in the House before moving up to the Senate.[68]

Equally comfortable in both committee rooms was Gorman's good friend, Calvin Brice of Ohio. Beginning his career as a first-rate railroad attorney, Brice went on to head his own international railroad syndicate. Like Mark Hanna, he served his party first as Democratic National Committee Chairman and then as senator. Edward Walthall, protégé of L. Q. C. Lamar and opposed to the popular if less distinguished Vardaman clique in Mississippi politics, came to the Senate after President Cleveland promoted his patron to the Supreme Court. A loyal Gorman follower in national and Senate proceedings, Walthall soon received a place on Steering as well as on Finance.[69] When the Democrats controlled the Fifty-third Congress (1893–1895), a majority of the party's Steering Committee, not surprisingly, had worked for Gorman's nomination at the 1892 Democratic Convention.

California Democrat Stephen White, hoping to achieve Senate influence, used the same tactics as Albert Beveridge. A successful lawyer and keen student of politics, White had culled support from southern California and northern rural communities to become, in 1893, the first senator elected from Los Angeles. Appreciating the importance of valuable committee assignments, he methodically set out to fulfill his ambitions. "If you have any choice of Committees," his shrewd friend Charles Richards wrote from Washington, "make it known to someone near the throne. If you will give me a hint, I will whisper it to Senator Gorman of Maryland (with whom I have been somewhat intimate for 30 years) and who will have more to do with the new organization than any other Senator probably."[70] White did not ignore his injunction that "a little foresight ought to be exercised." Emphasizing that he was "the only democratic senator from this part of the United States," that he "had about as much experience as most men of my age in litigation," and was "capable of doing a good deal of work," White expected to be "treated a little better than common." Positions on Commerce, Foreign Relations, and Judiciary would satisfy his designs.[71]

White frequently corresponded with Gorman, and Richards had not exaggerated his closeness to the throne. When White's first session of service commenced, the California Senator was seated on Finance and Commerce—a key assignment since Los Angeles was desperately attempting to gain a harbor appropriation. Within two years White secured the full approval of the Democratic leader; for being "friendly to Mr. Gorman," he was awarded a vacancy on the Steering Committee.[72] Knowing the rules of the game helped on both sides of the aisle.

In April 1893, a few weeks after the Democrats announced the majority committee assignments, Wilkinson Call of Florida testified to the changes in the Senate. The Democrat took the floor to criticize the system of party rule and the distribution of committee places. Both Senate parties, Call declared, confirmed the maxim that "the history of all legislative bodies has been a history of encroachment and usurpations of power." And nowhere were their machinations more evident than in the assignments of committees, where "the final exercise of sovereign legislative power" rested. "The committees, in the history of every legislative body," he continued, "have been at different times made, as they may be made now, the mere toys to gratify personal ambition . . . and to give advantages to a few in the control of the powers of government over the whole constituent body." The cure for this nefarious system was patent: to appoint senators to their places by drawing lots, with the proviso that every state be assured a seat on one of the vital committees. Such a rule would "secure equality of power and privilege . . . [and] avoid the indelicacy of personal exultation and the humiliation of exclusion from the great duties of the Senate."[73] Call's resolution, striking at the very heart of party leadership, made no progress for the men of influence would not be turned out of power so simply. He had grasped the connections between caucus decisions and Senate actions but he could do little to change them. A plea for sectional distribution could no longer displace the authority of party.

A more limited proposal presented by Idaho's Silver Republican senator, Fred Dubois, was more successful. Sharing Call's sentiments, Dubois moved in December 1895 to distribute the many duties of Appropriations to particular Senate committees.

The Agriculture Committee, for example, would frame the appropriations dealing with agriculture; Military Affairs would determine the army budget, the District of Columbia Committee would settle the capital's finances. Heretofore in charge of all these matters, the Appropriations Committee had excessively burdening responsibilities. But solicitude for the hard-working senators did not prompt Dubois' concern; rather, he wanted each member of the Senate to "perform as much of the work, share as much of the care, enjoy as much of the honor, and be as much of a leader as possible."[74]

The Silver Republican was supported from all sides of the chamber. Newton Blanchard, a Louisiana Democrat, looked forward to ending the "monopolistic dominance" of Appropriations, and Republican Knute Nelson believed the proposal would soon return the Senate to a body of equals. For his part, New Hampshire's senator, Jacob Gallinger, thought it best not to "place the responsibility for legislation in a few hands." Call, recognizing that he and Dubois were attempting to rectify the same condition, warmly supported the measure; it would increase the "equal connection" of all senators and terminate the control of the party "juntas."[75]

Allison and his friends, voicing their opposition, delayed the move by referring it to the Rules Committee, which they, of course, dominated. But the pressure for reform was unabating; in January 1899 Aldrich reported, and the chamber passed, a rule that sent future agricultural, military, naval, pension, and post office appropriations to the particular Senate committees. The leadership salvaged some items, reserving for Appropriations the large District budget and Foreign Relations finances; still, the victory belonged to Dubois and Call. No one intimate with Allison, Aldrich, or Gorman favored the bill, but those cut off from power were more numerous and not altogether subservient. Moreover, by raising the issue in the chamber rather than in caucus, the minorities of both parties combined with independent senators to effect their desires.[76] The defeat was not vital; party chairmen, still dispensing the committee assignments, were not required to stake their leadership on the question. However, they did not welcome any dispersal of their authority.

Call and Dubois leveled their protests against both parties, but Gorman never attained the power that Allison and Aldrich wielded. Although his allies were loyal, the harmony shared by Republican leaders was not duplicated within the Democratic organization. Cockrell was admired by Populists who could not bear Calvin Brice; Joseph Blackburn received support from men who considered Walthall far too removed from the people. Chilton's writings accurately portrayed the compromising quality of Gorman's leadership; the caucus chairman attempted to find a common ground among members because mediation was his most potent tool. On many substantive issues, Democratic rulers divided. Attempts to enforce a party course often met the vigorous and effective protests of those closest to power, and Gorman could do little to instill discipline when members of his own coterie disagreed. Democratic senators therefore acted with impunity, confident of support in the top echelons of the party.

Gorman was helpless to increase his strength. Such designations as Bourbon or anti-Bourbon did not become pertinent to the Senate during these decades, and persuasive talents, not legislative policies, earned the Maryland Senator the caucus chairmanship. Gorman was in the uncomfortable position of selecting his intimates as best he could. Democrats united on the need to proceed cautiously with tariff reform deserted him on financial questions; members agreed upon monetary issues often allied on political matters with Grover Cleveland, his opponent in the White House. The caucus chairman's goals were inevitably limited and never over-ambitious. Attempting to gain support here for a tariff and there for blocking a presidential nomination, his successes were evidence of his skills. Realizing the impossibility of altering the majority's views on the need for silver coinage, Gorman typically chose to keep the helm rather than abandon ship; voting against currency expansion, he did not utilize his caucus position to halt its progress.[77]

The centralized Senate Democratic organization could not effectively discipline its members. No matter that a highly select and constant group arranged the committee slates and the order of business; divergent viewpoints necessarily diluted any concentration of power. Perhaps if Gorman had served regularly as majority chairman, he might have strengthened his position. As minority leader, however, the Maryland Senator bestowed only limited rewards without especial significance. When the stakes were smaller, the dealer was less important.[78] Republicans, not Democrats, dominated the chamber and effected most of the changes of these years. Realizing more fully the powers and potentialities of party unity and leadership, they transformed the character of the institution.

Most Senate Democrats, despite sporadic protestations over the unequal distribution of authority, were dissatisfied with the lack of party harmony. Whatever ambivalence they felt toward more powerful colleagues, the great majority keenly desired to bring stability to the organization. Since the chairman could not accomplish the task alone, they ruled all caucus decisions binding; in December 1903, upon Blackburn's motion with only two dissenting votes, the Democrats resolved that the vote of two thirds of the party compelled the obedience of every member in the Senate. Allison had considered a similar scheme superfluous, but Gorman enthusiastically urged its adoption.[79] The rule was right and just, the usually quarrelsome Ben Tillman later declared. "Any man claiming to be a Democrat and refusing to bow to the will of a two-thirds majority should be drummed out of the party and allowed to go where he may. We can have no discipline in any other way that I can see."[80]

The caucus, Democrats decreed, could not compel a senator to oppose instructions from his state legislature or to violate his oath in support of the Constitution. If "prior to his election he has pledged himself to his people" on a particular issue, the caucus had no right to demand that he "break his faith with his constituents." In all other instances, however, members were expected to adhere to its decisions. Newcomers now inquiring after their obligations would promptly learn that obedience was presumed. Should a senator be convinced that a party proposal would bring disaster or dishonor to the nation, he should "be a patriot rather than a partisan." The caucus defined "the duty of a party man," and anyone was at liberty to act outside his organization. Participants determined to contravene the caucus must now remember, however, that they were subject to penalties; anxious to enforce its will, the party was prepared to punish recalcitrants.[81] To be sure, caucus resolutions did not discipline members as efficiently as did determined leaders, and the two-thirds ruling could not regularly enforce unity. Nevertheless, the intent was clear, and an independent senator might be excluded from positions of authority. Patriotism now demanded personal sacrifice.

The Populist experience revealed the gulf that separated the Senate parties of the 1890's from their predecessors. Democrats and Republicans composed permanently established alignments, not likely soon to disintegrate. What had been problematical in the 1870's was now evident; the only open question was whether their ascendancy left any room for another party. Moreover, the Populists demonstrated that the changes in the chamber were not related to a particular outlook on national affairs; for all its fresh opinions, the new group emulated its rivals' practices. Discipline guided the actions of every organization in the Senate.

Well aware of the many blocks on the road to power, the first Populists delighted in comparing the progress of the early Republicans with their own. The antislavery party had suffered countless defeats before winning control, and the Populists, each hastened to assure the other, were actually faring better in 1892 than had their forerunners in 1852. Anxious to clarify why they had severed old allegiances, the new members again returned to the Republican story. Just as the Democrats had attempted to ignore the problem of slavery, so the contemporary organizations were avoiding the major issues of the day. Republicans had responded by founding their own party, and Populists were now compelled to adopt the same strategy. "Both the old party organizations," announced one-time Republican J. P. Jones, "persist in treating this most imperious of all questions [silver], as a mere tail to the party kites." Democrats and Republicans alike were out of touch with the people; only the Populists now recognized their interests. "New parties must spring from the ground," Jones concluded. "It was the operation of this principle that produced the Republican party," and forty years later brought strength to Populism.[82]

The Populists echoed the new definition of Senate parties even as they declared their own uniqueness. By the last decade of the nineteenth century, effective organization was the desideratum and the Populists hastened to present their qualifications. "The Populist party in the Chamber," insisted Marion Butler, senator and Populist National Committee Chairman, "is as distinct an organization and political entity as is the republican or democratic party. We have our conferences and our party organization and what we do is done systematically and after due consultation and deliberation." Yet conferences implied discipline, and Populists frequently denounced their rivals for restricting freedom of action. Party tyranny has made the politicians of the old parties contemptible, argued Marion Butler. "Republicans and Democrats alike in this chamber will bow their necks in meek submission to the yoke of their parties."[83] Populists acted systematically; their enemies, however, suffered under the yoke of discipline. In political oratory, the stance of the speaker made all the difference.

In 1895 and again in 1897, Populists held the balance of power in the Senate. The Republicans controlled a plurality but not a majority of the seats, and they would sink to a minority should the Populists ally with the Democrats. The new organization, however, steadfastly resolving to maintain its integrity, abstained from supporting either organization. "We have simply stood by the principles," Butler reminded the chamber. "We have let the two old parties fight it out. The Republicans had the most votes and they got the organization."[84]

Although the Republicans arranged the committees, they were dissatisfied with their predicament. "We are running," Francis Warren complained, "with throttle open having no political power. The reorganization of committees was more or less a farce, because with the populists holding the balance of power in nearly every committee, we were indeed in a pitiable condition." It seemed wiser to placate the new party rather than tempt them to join the Democrats, and so the Republicans assumed the chairmanships but allotted the Populists vital committee places. "Of course," Warren concluded, "it was a choice of two evils; we could not be worse off with a Democratic majority on the committees."[85] The Populists were aptly rewarded for their independence, while Republicans persistently reminded colleagues and countrymen that chairmanships alone did not constitute Senate control. Lacking party power, they denied responsibility and even rivals did not debate their contention.[86]

By 1899 the Senate returned to a safe Republican majority and the Populists were slowly disbanding. The two-party system handily had survived the threat, and many observers were content to recognize the "leavening" effect of a third party's program. "No political party," announced one-time Populist William Stewart as he returned to the Republican fold, "can always be right, but *one party or the other* must be trusted with the reins of government."[87] The efficacy of third party was quickly dismissed.

The Senate experienced the most vital changes in its history during the three decades that followed the end of Reconstruction.

Both parties became firmly established, and a new concern for order and discipline accompanied their stability. The increased importance of party government sharply differentiated the institution at the opening of the twentieth century from its predecessors. The battlelines for control of the Senate parties were clearly delineated; the strategic posts were known, their strength predictable. Dissident factions in 1907 or 1963 would recognize the power of party organization, and Senators Bob La Follette and Joseph Clark would share a similar determination and frustration as they attempted to capture it. Party leadership for the first time dominated the chamber's business, and the tactics of Allison, Aldrich, and Gorman were faithfully emulated by Lyndon Johnson. Authority within the institution was not related to stature beyond its walls; the senator who dominated the politics of New York might well stand meekly before the senator from Iowa or from Rhode Island. By 1900 the United States Senate had become modern, enjoying a life of its own.

THE LEGISLATIVE PROCESS

As the Democratic margin is so exceedingly narrow, it became absolutely essential to follow the leadership of the Committee. This naturally results in the incorporation of many features which individual Senators, including myself, do not like; but we are compelled to take our medicine or sacrifice the whole thing.

Remarks of Senator Stephen White
on framing a Democratic tariff, 1894

In order to get a bill through at all we have to vote together, and in doing that I am voting for some duties I don't like, and may have to take some bitter medicine before we get through.

Remarks of Senator John Spooner
on framing a Republican tariff, 1897

The preeminence of the party caucus and its leaders fundamentally altered the conduct of Senate business. By the end of the nineteenth century, Republican and Democratic organizations, through their meetings, committees, and chairmen, first formulated and approved, then scheduled and enacted the session's key bills. Now the prospects of particular measures depended upon caucus decisions and the course of legislation could no longer be considered apart from party considerations.

Party directed Senate proceedings in several vital ways. First, and perhaps most important, the caucus decided who would serve on each working committee and the decision was significant. Committees held the hearings, framed the issues, and fixed the details. At the very least they formulated the first tentative solutions for caucus review; in other instances, their proposals were approved without the formality of a roll call. Chamber leaders allotted these places with extraordinary care.

Senate organizations shaped legislation by other means as well. A caucus committee determined the schedule of business, arranging in detail the program for a working day. As might be expected, a place on the calendar directly affected the history of a bill. Party councils also often resolved the most divisive legislative questions. The especially controversial sections of a tariff or currency act would frequently be compromised to the majority's satisfaction. These meetings were not uniformly successful, but by the 1890's members invariably utilized the caucus machinery to settle their differences.

The party also controlled the fate of Senate bills through the ability to enforce voting discipline. Uniting its ranks, the caucus regularly transformed private decisions into public laws. To be sure, congressional cohesion on roll calls never equaled European standards. Students, relying only upon practices in the House of Commons as indexes of cohesion, have accordingly tended to dismiss American parties out of hand for not voting their members as a bloc in every instance. And certain that organizations here never exercised significant authority, they have also not appreciated the changes that occurred at the end of the nineteenth century. Such judgments are faulty and misleading. Statistics can tell only part of the story for the parties carried out vital duties even before a bill came to a vote. Roll calls do not reflect the significance of the power to staff working committees or to order the chamber's business. Moreover, the interpretation of congressional voting patterns has been too colored by cross-national comparisons. These contrasts may often illuminate unique sorts of behavior, but American performances should ultimately be viewed within their own sphere. The fact that Republicans and Democrats never achieved European discipline did not prove that parties were unimportant in the affairs of government.

In 1901 a young student of politics, A. Lawrence Lowell, published his first investigations of the influence of English and American parties upon legislation. Noting that "recently some political theories have been based upon the assumption that political action in America is almost entirely determined by the party machines," he set out to demonstrate that "vehemence in the outcry against party . . . by no means always corresponds with the actual extent of its power." A pioneer in the quantitative study of political history, Lowell revealed that party voting— nine tenths of the members of each party standing together— was less regular in Congress than in Commons.[1] Yet at the same time, his data, if not his inferences, made very clear that extraordinary changes had occurred in America.

The shift in Senate voting patterns was striking. In the Twenty-ninth Congress (1845–1847) party lines stood firm in only 16 per cent of the votes, although by this time the majority party controlled the working committees. In the Thirty-eighth Congress (1863–1865) the figure dropped to 6 per cent. By the Fiftieth Congress (1887–1889), however, Democratic and Republican ranks were united in 47 per cent of the roll calls and they maintained almost the same degree of harmony in the 1890's, despite the divisive issues of that decade. Parliament, of course, evinced still greater cohesion, but Lowell's figures pointed to the unprecedented authority of the Senate organizations in legislative activity.[2]

Moreover, his methodology tended to underestimate the congressional party's influence on voting behavior. Its efforts were more selective than those of its British counterpart. Caucus authority did not extend to all measures; leaders usually exerted their influence on the most important items of business. Lowell, however, set his gauge to measure British not American power. He included *every* Senate roll call in his calculations, from adjournments to the most significant public bill. And by equating the vote that gave Justice Waite's widow a pension with the ballot that passed the 1897 tariff bill, he, in fact, minimized the changes in the Senate.

Then too, Lowell's definition of a party vote—nine tenths of each party on opposing sides—was, at the very least, a strict measurement. A less inclusive, if more selective, compilation might provide a more accurate guide (see Charts I and II below, for examples). Despite these difficulties, Lowell's findings still verified the new energy of party in American politics.

Finally, the Senate debates, as much as committee slates and roll-call data, pointed to the transformation of the institution in post–Civil War America. The intervention of party in the legislative process was so new and so momentous that members felt compelled to defend and rationalize the innovations. A discussion of the tariff turned into an apologia for caucus action; a federal elections bill prompted an analysis of the place of party in democratic government. The participants understood full well the changes that marked these years.

The primacy of party in the 1890's stood in striking contrast to the practices of earlier decades. During the presidencies of Grant, Hayes, and Arthur, bills were usually enacted without party superintendence. The calendar received scant attention in the caucus, and questions of party influence rarely intruded into substantive discussions. Prominent issues were settled in open session, not in Republican or Democratic conclaves, and key votes were most often cast with little regard for dividing aisles. When achieved, party cohesion was testimony to a coincidence of aims, not to the effectiveness of organizational machinery or discipline. To appreciate the altered style of politics at the end of the century, it is well to begin with a description of how the Senate in the 1870's went about its business.

The need to stabilize the nation's currency was perhaps the most important and complex issue in the post-Reconstruction

Senate. The solutions bore few marks of party intervention. When Congress had agreed to issue greenbacks without a specie basis during the war, there were few protests because the steps seemed necessary to the Union effort. Once hostilities ended, however, the status of paper money demanded definition. The war debt was to be repaid—the greenbacks were eventually to be redeemed in specie. On this score, there was no argument. But the speed and method for retiring the currency prompted disagreement. Senators heatedly debated whether to maintain, contract, or expand the available money supply and the significance of the decision only intensified the controversy. Inflationists hoped to increase, at least temporarily, the amount in circulation; contractionists were determined to retire as much paper as possible. The parties did not help settle the conflict. Members usually gave little heed to their affiliations when framing and enacting the various proposals.[3]

In the opening years of Grant's presidency, the contending forces were evenly matched and neither side gained clear-cut victories. A bill to establish the public credit, declaring honest intentions, received broad Republican agreement, but particular proposals divided party ranks. Efforts by the Forty-first Congress (1869–1871) to redistribute currency circulation and banking establishments, for example, split the overwhelming Republican majority; one third of the members stood out against even modestly inflationary proposals.[4] The Senate, by a strict party vote, enacted the Funding Act, recalling certain government war bonds and reissuing them at lower interest rates, but the passage was testimony to the quality of the bill and the hard-working chairman of the Finance Committee, John Sherman, not to organizational discipline. The measure, well designed to placate all shades of opinion, was discussed only on its merits, and no party caucus intervened to iron out differences of opinion. Inflationists from both sides of the aisle tried to amend it and failed; contractionists' efforts met a similar fate. Since the proposal was a compromise that would obviously save the government money, Republicans voted to promote the reputation of the Grant administration.[5]

The Panic of 1873 brought a new urgency to the currency question and in the opening session of Congress in March 1874, the program underwent full review. No steering committee anticipated or scheduled the discussion; but when John Sherman introduced some minor legislation to clarify an earlier measure, a full and lengthy debate erupted. After fruitless argument, the chamber instructed the Finance Committee to frame a comprehensive measure for redeeming the greenbacks but the report only sparked further contention. The stumbling block was the amount of paper to be left in circulation for the next several years. Contractionists contended that $360,000,000 worth of greenbacks was more than sufficient while inflationists declared that $400,-000,000 was the smallest sum possible to avoid another severe depression. Sherman assumed his familiar posture in the middle, urging a figure of $382,000,000.[6]

Party spirit was as insignificant in the controversy as it was in provoking the debate, and the key decisions were reached in the chamber, not in caucus. Culling support from both sides of the aisle, the inflationists won; 57 per cent of the Republicans joined 48 per cent of the Democrats to carry the measure. Indiana's onetime war governor, Oliver Morton, stood with former Confederate general, Francis Cockrell, to vote yes, and Roscoe Conkling and Thomas Bayard, disregarding party lines, both voted no. The bill thus passed a Republican-controlled Senate, but few were astonished when Grant vetoed it. The legislation was not the work of either party and a Republican President felt no compulsion to make it law.[7]

In November 1874 the Republicans performed so poorly at the polls that for the first time since secession, the House, although not the Senate, came under a Democratic majority. The lame duck Congress in December would be the last session under complete Republican control, but few observers expected any important legislation from the short, three-month meeting. Although the funding program was still unsettled and no date for resumption had been fixed, it appeared unlikely that Congress would reach any essential decisions. Opinions were too divided and the press predicted a lengthy wait before the issue was resolved.[8]

To everyone's surprise, Republican senators, stunned by the November defeat and all too aware that their long reign was nearing its close, acted with unusual alacrity. The exigencies of the situation spurred organized efforts and an eleven-man committee, headed by Sherman, reported a funding bill to the caucus. Contractionists held a slight majority on the *ad hoc* group, but seven of the participants signed the document and the others urged all members to support the proposals. On December 20 the party agreed, and on the very next day the measure was introduced to the Senate. Contrary to all recent experience, Republicans refrained from discussion, leaving the Democrats to do all the talking; in disgust and frustration, Allen Thurman admonished the caucus for sponsoring legislation and prohibiting debate. The maneuver, however, was effective. Within twenty-four hours the bill received the chamber's approval by a strict party vote.[9]

Eager to act on the most pressing contemporary political issue before losing control of the government, the Republicans made extraordinary efforts to settle their differences. Their intentions were political, and if the caucus could not formulate a meaningful compromise between contending factions, no matter. They achieved unity here not by an authentic adjustment of antagonistic opinions but by a sham compromise, successful only because the crucial question was left ambiguously unresolved. Paper money, according to the Resumption Bill, was to be redeemed; but whether the greenbacks were to be reissued or destroyed after they were returned to the Treasury was left intentionally unclear. The caucus measure begged the real question, that is, how many greenbacks would remain in circulation after the introduction of specie payments. The party passed its bill only by avoiding the issue at hand—a portent of how it might conduct legislation if left to its own devices.

Party machinery was not again quick to shape financial measures. In 1877 Senator Stanley Matthews asked Congress to declare its opinion that government war bonds were payable in silver as well as gold. Neither the Democratic nor Republican caucuses took any part in the proceedings and slight majorities of both parties (55 and 65 per cent, respectively) joined to pass it.[10] When the most important monetary legislation of the decade, the Bland-Allison Act, passed, Senate organizations once more remained in the background. Allison introduced the bill that he had framed, together with the Finance Committee and John Sherman, the new Secretary of the Treasury, but Republicans immediately objected. The speed with which the Resumption Bill became law was not duplicated here; debate, from both sides of the aisle, continued for some four weeks. Connecticut's Democratic senator, William Eaton, regarded the lack of party unity with favor, pleased that financial questions did not resemble "a football to be kicked about at the mercy of partisans"; Republican Justin Morrill, on the other hand, revealed none of his fellow New Englander's equanimity: "Unless they [the inflationists] are cured of the paper-money mania," he harshly predicted, "we are as likely to split as the Democracy."[11] Sixty-two per cent of the Republicans and 73 per cent of the Democrats stood with Allison; and the act to remonitize silver was finally passed. Differences with the Democratic House of Representatives were ironed out in conference and when Hayes objected to the measure, Congress overrode his veto.[12]

Over the decade, financial decisions were reached, revised, and then disregarded with little consistency or regularity. Individual accommodations, not party organizations, put these assorted measures through the chamber, and legislation was freely altered after slight changes in the composition of the membership. After ten years of effort, however, the nation's currency structure was

settled at least for the moment.
credit.

The tariff legislation of these
influence of Senate Democratic
William Eaton persistently attem
from party machinery, and his co
suggestion that a board of private
"The members of the Senate and
Bayard in the 1881 debate, "are the
of different local interests all of wh
the transactions of the government
mission, on the other hand, would reach "proper adjustments,"
and Congress would undoubtedly accept their advice. No one
suggested that the caucus, by assuming party responsibility, could
adjust the various claims and fulfill the role envisioned for the
extra-institutional committee. With support from majorities of
both parties, Eaton's motion passed in March 1882 and a commission was named to recommend rates to the Congress.[13]

Although the commission reported its findings, the 1883 tariff
bill bore little resemblance to its suggestions. The Finance Committee did in fact lower the rates in line with the board's advice,
but in the course of Senate roll calls the schedules were freely
raised. "There is likely to be a combination of Senators," West
Virginia's Henry Davis shrewdly anticipated in advance of the
debate, "who are interested in different subjects on the bill and
who will agree to aid each other in voting thereon." Davis worked
to insure his prediction and by gaining sufficient Republican and
Democratic support, was able to raise the coal duties well above
the level suggested by the commission.[14] Senators interested in
sugar reached some sort of accommodation with midwestern colleagues concerned with lumber, and these two rates were also appreciably heightened.[15]

Party organizations exerted little discipline over the proceedings. Republicans made a limited effort to harmonize their viewpoints: "We had a caucus this morning on tariff and revenue,"

in Mitchell informed industrialist Wharton
me to no conclusion. The lamentable fact is that
a solid Republican majority in favor of protecting our
ustries, iron, steel, wollens [sic], etc."[16] Democrats fared
etter. Former Supreme Court Justice David Davis, now
ly courting his second wife from the Senate chamber, inter-
spersed his declarations of love with angry words for the party.
"The Democrats quarrelling and criticizing each other's views
consistently," had marred all attempts at tariff-making. Benjamin
Harrison, then serving as Indiana's senator, echoed similar complaints. "The situation of both parties in the Senate," he concluded, "is quite unfavorable to the best work on this subject."[17]

Through individual accommodations, the tariff bill made its
way through the chamber. All the Republicans and eight Democrats favored the measure, many admittedly hoping that the Conference Committee would improve the bill, that is, raise the rates
still higher, as it settled the differences between the two houses of
Congress. The Conference indeed enhanced the protective quality
of the tariff, but only haphazardly, increasing some duties but
not others. Chance meetings and unexpected selections of sympathizers to the Committee determined the success or failure of
particular interests. Nevertheless, by one vote, the Republicans in
perfect order passed the bill over united Democratic opposition.[18]

The cohesion marking the roll call was not the work of the
caucus or the result of an irresistible appeal to party duty. Up to
the moment of balloting, no one was confident of the outcome.
Some, like John Mitchell, were disgusted with the bill and yet
voted for it anyway. "It is a dangerous way of legislating," he
conceded, "practically leaving the whole question to three men
on a side, representing the two Houses, and making the law."
Uneven quality must be expected for "we do not have a party
united upon the *principle* of protection so firmly as to have it
observed uniformly."[19] Other Republicans realized that the 1883
tariff, like the 1874 currency bill, was the product of a Republi-

can lame duck Congress that would soon give way to a Democratic majority in the House. Thus, Justin Morrill, not at all happy with the schedules, supported the measure; it was, after all, protective in nature and might well turn out to be the lesser of two evils. Democrats, neither consulted nor involved in the discussions or decisions of the conference committee, found the revisions too adulterated for their taste and were content to let their rivals assume full responsibility.[20]

Nobody had a good word to say for the bill. New England Senators George Hoar and Justin Morrill received angry notes from the American Iron and Steel Association, and the wool growers informed John Sherman in no uncertain terms of their displeasure. The first experiment with a tariff commission was a total failure; the attempt to bypass party politics proved impractical. Without some authoritative superintendence, the most scrupulously conceived schedules would be liberally amended to suit individual preferences. Some astute members were beginning to understand that party machinery might supply such control.[21]

Democratic and Republican organizations once again failed to structure the legislation regulating the country's railroads. No matter whether the issue revolved on the wisdom of the 1872 Texas & Pacific charter, the advisability of a general incorporation law for the territory's railroads, or the justice of a sinking fund bill, the caucus took no part in the decision. Party loyalties did not sidetrack the debates or dominate the roll calls.

When the Pacific railroads failed to repay their government loans as scheduled, the Senate Judiciary Committee in 1877 formulated a measure compelling them to establish sinking funds. Although Judiciary was under a Republican majority, Democrat Allen Thurman introduced and defended the proposals; and opposition came not from a rival caucus but from another Senate committee. Democrat John Gordon, on behalf of the Railroad Committee, presented a milder and more lenient proposition for safeguarding the government's investment. Senators took sides with no concern for party lines; John Sherman and George Edmunds joined Thurman while Roscoe Conkling and Henry Dawes supported Gordon.[22] The proposals, not settled in the Forty-fourth Congress, were reconsidered in March 1878. The two propositions once more occupied the chamber, and the constitutionality, wisdom, and justice of the bills were again debated. The Republican party split down the middle, and although a sizable number of Democrats urged strict action, a substantial minority (18 per cent) defended the lines. The Senate soon passed the Thurman bill—another piece of legislation untouched by party.[23]

The best-known piece of railroad legislation in this period, the Interstate Commerce Act, was also enacted without party superintendence. First introduced in December 1884 by Republican senator Shelby Cullom, the bill found friends and critics on both sides of the aisle. Some Democrats, such as Richard Coke, were among its most enthusiastic supporters while others, such as Thomas Bayard, questioned its constitutionality. Proposals to regulate the lines were debated for some two years, but the source of the difficulty lay in the differences between the two Houses, not in those between the two party organizations. When a compromise was finally reached (and, as usual, it was the House that did most of the compromising) and the measure came up for a vote, majorities from both parties (63 per cent of the Republicans and 84 per cent of the Democrats), combined to pass it. The Senate took this significant step without the assistance or interference of party machinery.[24]

Senators' legislative behavior did not follow predictable party patterns because measures affecting the currency, tariff, or railroads were considered without reference to any guiding program. Some, like John Sherman, Justin Morrill, George Edmunds, and George Hoar, favored the protective tariff and currency contraction while heartily endorsing government supervision of the Pacific railroads. Others, like Stanley Matthews, Timothy Howe, and Thomas Bayard, worked for higher duties and currency expansion and resisted attempts to regulate transportation. Republican Don Cameron stood side by side with John Gordon on financial questions; but the Georgia Senator labored on behalf of the roads, while Cameron, a good friend of the Pennsylvania lines, backed the disciplinary measures. To be sure, some Democrats consistently opposed legislation that Republicans steadfastly supported; James Beck and Roscoe Conkling rarely voiced ayes on the same roll call. But in most instances alliances fluctuated. Here a senator aided a private economic interest and there he voted to restrict it; here a member adopted the seemingly unpopular side, there he joined the more numerous ranks. Complex variations were the rule not the exception.

Party organizations assumed some importance on questions of Reconstruction, where most unity might have been anticipated; nevertheless, caucus activity and discipline remained unusual. Republicans manifested little harmony as reconstructed states submitted their constitutions for congressional approval and Southerners appeared in Washington seeking Senate admission. George Edmunds fiercely debated his colleague, Matt Carpenter, on the legality of prescribing test oaths and he also persuaded a majority to thwart Oliver Morton's scheme for capturing a contested Louisiana Senate seat.[25] When Charles Sumner introduced his civil rights bill in 1872, dissensions were again evident. Republicans immediately amended and moderated its provisions; even so, a bare majority (53 per cent) did not agree to its desirability and nothing was accomplished.[26]

Certain Democratic proposals were, of course, guaranteed to solidify the opponents' ranks. In 1870 Kentucky senator Thomas McCreery introduced a resolution favoring the return of land currently in use as a Union cemetery at Arlington, Virginia, to its former owner's widow, Mrs. Robert E. Lee. The only question dividing Republicans was whether the bill should be expunged from the Senate *Journal*. When Democrats attempted to repeal legislation permitting federal troops "to keep the peace" at election polls, they again came up against firm opposition.[27] And just before the autumn election of 1874 and immediately after the death of Charles Sumner, Republicans followed the unusual course of framing a civil rights measure in caucus. Despite differences on the justice of separate but equal facilities—many members like William Allison saw nothing to fear in the practice —they consistently supported the bill and passed it through the chamber.[28] At times the party could unite on anti-Southern legislation.

Still the proposals that resolved the major political crisis of these years, the Hayes-Tilden controversy, were framed in bipartisan Senate committee meetings, not in the party caucuses. The eventual compromise to appoint a commission to count the electoral votes was supported by the Democrats and about half the Republicans. "Our side is divided," Henry Dawes complained to his wife, and only 57 per cent of the Republicans were persuaded to enact the settlement. The party councils nominated the members of the commission, but the vital tasks were performed outside the caucus without the exercise of discipline.[29]

Nor did party considerations affect other major legislation in these years. When Congress ostensibly "grabbed" a salary hike in March 1873, 54 per cent of the Republicans and 64 per cent of the Democrats backed the move. Efforts to reform the civil service were largely nonpartisan; the final votes taken on the Pendleton bill paid little attention to chamber aisles. Finally, the abortive effort to increase federal appropriations to education, the Blair bill, did not separate the two organizations. In 1884, for example, three fourths of the Republicans and three fifths of the Democrats lined up behind the bill.[30]

The more standard business of the chamber—the annual internal improvements appropriation, for example—also remained far beyond the limited scope of party influence. Whenever the decisions of the Appropriations or Rivers and Harbors Com-

CHART I. 1869-1887

SENATE VOTES ON:

Scale (Per Cent): 50, 60, 70, 80, 90, 100 Per Cent

#	Vote	Category
1.	Tariff Commission Appointment – 1882.	TARIFF
2.	Iron Duty – 1883 Tariff.	TARIFF
3.	Coal Duty – 1883 Tariff.	TARIFF
4.	Senate Version – 1883 Tariff.	TARIFF
5.	Conference Report – 1883 Tariff.	TARIFF
6.	Currency Act – 1869.	CURRENCY
7.	Funding Act – 1870.	CURRENCY
8.	Redemption Bill – 1874.	CURRENCY
9.	Resumption Act – 1874.	CURRENCY
10.	Silver Resolution – 1878.	CURRENCY
11.	Bland–Allison Act – 1878.	CURRENCY
12.	Appropriation for Michigan – 1876 Bill.	APPROPRIATIONS
13.	Appropriations Bill – 1876.	APPROPRIATIONS
14.	Mississippi parts of Rivers and Harbors Bill – 1882.	APPROPRIATIONS
15.	Rivers and Harbors Bill – 1882.	APPROPRIATIONS
16.	Repassage of Rivers and Harbors Bill – 1882.	APPROPRIATIONS
17.	Pacific R.R. Charter – 1872.	TRANSPORTATION
18.	R.R. Incorporation Act – 1874.	TRANSPORTATION
19.	Blaine Amendment to Thurman Bill – 1878.	TRANSPORTATION
20.	Thurman (Sinking Fund) Bill – 1878.	TRANSPORTATION
21.	To Recommit Interstate Commerce Act – 1887.	TRANSPORTATION
22.	Interstate Commerce Act – 1887.	TRANSPORTATION
23.	Test Oath for Senators – 1871.	RECONSTRUCTION
24.	Civil Rights Act – 1872.	RECONSTRUCTION
25.	Civil Rights Act – 1874.	RECONSTRUCTION
26.	Admission of Louisiana's Senators – 1877.	RECONSTRUCTION
27.	Army Appropriations Act – 1877.	RECONSTRUCTION
28.	Appointment of Electoral Commission – 1877.	RECONSTRUCTION
29.	Modifying Tenure of Office Act – 1869.	OTHERS
30.	Modifying Tenure of Office Act – 1869.	OTHERS
31.	Salary (Grab) Increase – 1873.	OTHERS
32.	Blair Act – 1884.	OTHERS

DEMOCRAT ▬▬▬   REPUBLICAN ▨▨▨

mittee touched local or regional interests, members brushed aside any thought of national affiliation. Inevitably, a state's senators worked together for the appropriation, permitting no other loyalties to hinder their cooperation. Although Allen Thurman usually preferred to oppose large-scale federal grants, he forgot his predilection where Ohio was concerned.[31] If constituents' welfare was in no way at stake and if other guidance was absent, senators often followed the lead set by party colleagues on the working committees; but voting behavior here, as might be expected, was erratic. In the consideration of the 1882 Rivers and Harbors bill, framed by a Republican committee and exceptional for its generosity with government funds, the Democrats were even more anxious than their rivals to increase the funds earmarked for commercial improvements. When the final vote came, 76 per cent of the Democrats and 51 per cent of the Republicans helped pass the measure. President Arthur, believing the sums too large, exercised his veto; but once again majorities from both parties overcame his opposition.[32]

In the decade and a half after Grant's inauguration, neither Democratic nor Republican organizations ordered Senate proceedings. Chart I,[33] plotting the percentages of party majorities in thirty-two roll calls between 1869 and 1887, is obviously selective, and thus subject to question. But since caucus activity was itself particular and the table includes votes on almost every major issue during these years, the findings are significant. It is immediately apparent that on most legislation, party harmony was negligible. Forty-two per cent of the votes revealed majorities of less than 70 per cent on both sides of the aisle. In another 28 per cent of the votes, majorities ranged between 70 and 89 per cent. In only 30 per cent of all roll calls did 90 per cent or more of the members line up in solid rank. An extraordinary currency or tariff measure, or bills particularly relating to the Negro and the South, could unite them. But these instances were uncommon and, even more important, unity was not achieved through

CHART II. 1889-1900

PARTY MAJORITY

SENATE VOTES ON:

1. Senate Version – 1889 Tariff.
2. Reciprocity Clause – 1890 Tariff.
3. Senate Version – 1890 Tariff.
4. Conference Report – 1890 Tariff.
5. Sugar Duty – 1894 Tariff.
6. Lumber Duty – 1894 Tariff.
7. Senate Version – 1894 Tariff.
8. Sugar Duty – 1897 Tariff.
9. Wool Duty – 1897 Tariff.
10. Reciprocity Clause – 1897 Tariff.
11. Senate Version – 1897 Tariff.
12. Free Silver Amendment – Sherman Act – 1890.
13. Sherman Act – 1890.
14. Repeal of Sherman Act – 1893.
15. Seignorage Bill – 1894.
16. Gold Standard.
17. Appropriations Bill – 1891.
18. Rivers and Harbors Bill – 1899.
19. Reagan Amendment – Anti-Trust Act – 1890.
20. Anti-Trust Act – 1890.
21. Raising Elections (Lodge) Bill – 1890.
22. Postponing Elections Bill – 1891.
23. Passing Over Elections Bill – 1891.
24. Cuba Arbitration – 1897.
25. Conference Report – Cuban Relations – 1898.
26. War Revenue Act – 1898.
27. Annexation of Hawaii – 1898.
28. Annexation of Phillipines – 1899.
29. Treaty of Paris – 1899.

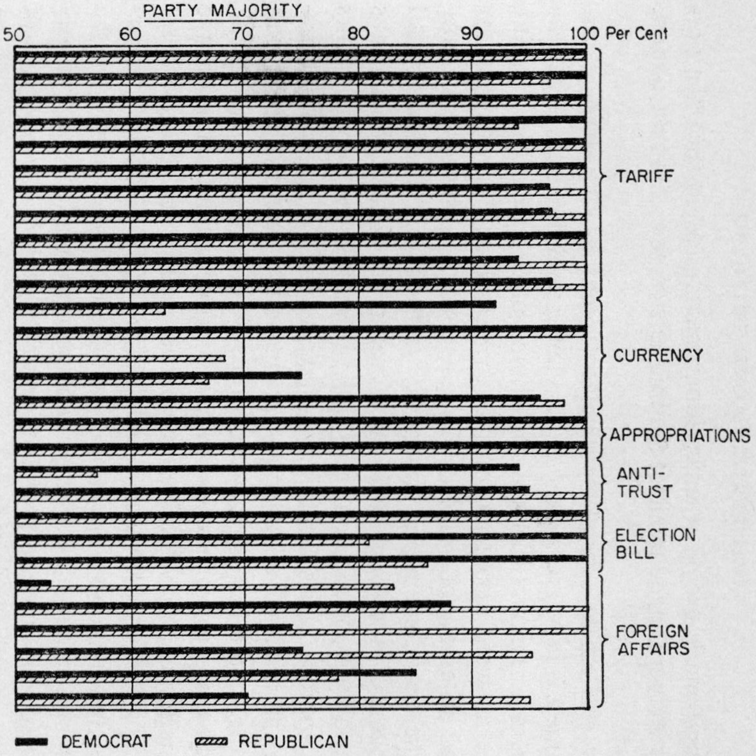

TARIFF

CURRENCY

APPROPRIATIONS

ANTI-TRUST

ELECTION BILL

FOREIGN AFFAIRS

50   60   70   80   90   100 Per Cent

■ DEMOCRAT   ▨ REPUBLICAN

the systematic use of organizational machinery. In sum, the parties rarely managed to affect the business of governing the nation.

By the last decades of the nineteenth century, the situation had changed. The prerogatives of the caucus and the authority of its leaders commonly dictated the course of Senate affairs. Voting patterns were also transformed. A. Lawrence Lowell's study, based on every roll call for selected sessions, revealed something of the new dimensions. Chart II,[34] setting out a more limited number of issues, highlights them even more clearly. Party ranks invariably stood firm on tariff bills; in matters of foreign affairs and appropriations, cohesion was expected. The free silver question often defied all attempts at harmony, but this result was unique. In the 1890's party unity on key roll calls became typical.

Nowhere were the new practices more evident than in the formation of the tariff. The two parties had begun to draw apart in their platforms on the benefits of free trade as against protection, but members need not have consolidated ranks in the chamber. Other subjects of campaign documents were regularly ignored and failed to promote legislative unity. The new role of Senate party organization, not national declarations, imposed the order. The chairman and the caucus were responsible for the change.

In 1886 there seemed little prospect for Republican agreement on the tariff. Admitting the need for an established party policy, Orville Platt unhappily conceded: "The difficulty is the old one, that Republicans are never ready to agree upon anything and will follow no leader."[35] Yet two years later, when the Democratic House of Representatives approved the Mills Tariff Bill, the Republican Senate majority was prepared to handle it. The act did not pass the House until July 21, 1888, but as early as March, Senate Republicans gathered in strategy sessions. Foremost in everyone's mind was the presidential election coming in the fall, and advice on treating the tariff poured into Washington in more than usual quantity. James Swank of American Iron and Steel told Justin Morrill that Senate Republicans should frame their own bill and bring it to the country. Others, like John Sherman, did not wish to argue schedules in the midst of the capital's summer heat while beleaguered with calls from home to come and campaign.[36]

On the night of July 25 Republicans met in caucus to determine their policy; should they appoint a committee "to report the first day of the next session, or to prepare a thorough revision of the tariff and to debate it until done?"[37] Allison took the lead in urging immediate work on the tariff and his arguments were effective. The party decision was clear. "With one exception," Allison's supporter, Frank Hiscock, informed editor Whitelaw Reid, "we last night were all in favor of the passage of a tariff bill by the Senate. The minority Senator favored it provided that each Senator would agree to stand by the bill on its consideration and every Senator pledged himself to do so."[38] William Chandler, for all his reputation for irritability, gleefully noted the "remarkable unanimity" of the party. And with some astonishment, John Spooner informed his old Wisconsin friend and ally, Horace Rublee:

Never since I came into the Senate have I seen anything like such a disposition among Republican Senators to stand together in the interests of the party and of the country. Every one seems willing to yield reasonably in order that a bill which shall meet the general approval may be passed.[39]

The details of arranging the rates put all the members' good intentions to the test. Morrill, chairman of Finance, was too ill to manage the bill, so Allison and Aldrich, next in line on the committee, exhibited their special talents for the first time. Duties on wool, lumber, and sugar proved the most difficult to adjust, but John Sherman, Don Cameron, and Matt Quay accepted compromises and on October 3, 1888, after weeks of labor in committee and in caucus, the Republicans raised the bill in the

Senate.[40] Democratic free trader Zebulon Vance greeted the measure with an ardent attack on the caucus machinery, and the ensuing debate centered around party practices and principles. Contending that Republican partisanship perverted all honest attempts to deal with the tariff, Vance labeled his rivals "the strongest party as a party organization known to the country." Gorman too denigrated party spirit, complaining, no doubt from envy rather than indignation, that Allison managed "to vote his party as a unit on every question."[41] The session drew to a close before Republicans could enact their measure, but they proved themselves willing and able to formulate a tariff and compromise their differences. Skilled leadership and organization were beginning to illustrate their effectiveness.

In the summer of 1890, attentive to the lessons of 1888, the Republican Senate passed the McKinley Bill. In accord with Allison's request, Aldrich assumed the tedious burden of tariff-making; together with a few colleagues from the Finance Committee, he adjusted the rates and presented the finished product to the full caucus. The members quickly approved the schedules and in order to expedite their enactment agreed to avoid lengthy debates in the chamber. The Rhode Island Senator adroitly managed the bill on the floor, giving it full priority. His decision "that he would not allow any business that would raise discussion to interfere with the Tariff" was strictly obeyed, and Republicans asked his permission before attempting to place an item on the order of business.[42]

The Democrats furiously attacked Republican tactics. "Vulgar tyranny," declaimed Alabama's black belt senator, John Morgan, "could no more indecently display its presumptuous arrogance than in the demand for silence while it taxes the people." But invectives hurled at the majority were immediately returned. "Party discipline," countered Justin Morrill, "appears to compel our free trade Democratic friends to assail the tariff bill."[43] Once the political maneuvers were completed, however, the individual schedules were raised and efficiently dispatched. Nearly every clause ponderously announced by Aldrich received unanimous Republican support; the party was faithful to its resolve. Occasionally, a break occurred. Senators allowed binding twine, a farmer's necessity, to enter the country duty-free although the committee had recommended a low rate, and they raised the sugar rates. Nevertheless, by approving the overwhelming number of provisions exactly as reported, they readily rubber-stamped the decisions of the caucus.[44]

The new efficiency prompted explanations. John Spooner informed his Wisconsin friends that now Republicans understood the necessity of standing together to accomplish anything great. With so many states presenting conflicting demands, senators were forced to adopt a broad spirit of tolerance; knowing that all interests could not be equally satisfied, members voted for specific rates that did not meet their approval. Local interests had to be compromised and, at times, even sacrificed to pass a party measure.[45]

When presented with the opportunity to frame their own tariff, Democrats emulated their opponents' tactics. Under the leadership of West Virginia's William Wilson, the House, in accord with President Cleveland's recommendations, substantially lowered protective duties in 1894. The bill then moved to the Senate where the Democratic-controlled Finance Committee reported a very similar measure to the party caucus. However, high tariff sentiment was much more current among the Senate members and the schedule immediately ran into determined opposition. "The Democrats," recalled one participant, "spent three full days in caucus on the Tariff . . . The whole subject was discussed fully— freely." But even after laborious debate, the caucus could not reach an agreement. Rather than adjourn and attempt to settle their differences on the chamber floor, they instructed the committee "to go back with our bill and readjust it so that it would be acceptable, if possible, to all Democratic members." The committee reworked the schedules and by raising particular duties finally managed to win party approval. The revised bill then went to the Senate.[46]

Debate now focused on party procedures, not on the tariff itself. Caucus adjudication demanded that members forego their own viewpoints for the sake of party legislation, and senators frequently found themselves supporting a bill containing many unacceptable clauses. The discomfort of the situation occasioned long rationalizations. "As the Democratic margin is so exceedingly narrow," asserted California's Stephen White, "it became absolutely essential to follow the leadership of the committee." Reiterating an argument that John Spooner had outlined four years earlier, White continued: "This naturally results in the incorporation of many features which individual Senators, including myself, do not like; but we are compelled to take our medicine or sacrifice the whole thing." For the sake of legislating, Louisiana's Newton Blanchard concluded, it was "necessary to make concessions to different interests, different sections, different States."[47] In quite similar tones, Democratic leader Arthur Gorman insisted that the "long hours of conference . . . [were] the only method known by which parties can be brought together."[48] Senators William Lindsay, Charles Faulkner, and Daniel Vorhees emphasized the duty to stand by the party, and the popular Roger Mills of Texas summed it all up by concluding: "Every act of legislation must necessarily be an act of compromise.[49]

"It is wise of the Democrats," observed Republican Henry Teller during the course of debate, "to try and compromise so that they can get the support of all their colleagues to pass the bill. We would do the same."[50] Most of Teller's party, however, would not publicly adopt his justly tolerant attitude. Convinced that damning party rule made good oratory, the Republicans launched long attacks on the sins of caucus control and discipline. No matter if the description fitted them as well; the chance to gain political capital could not be resisted. Images of Democrats trooping silently in a mournful procession under "the tyranny of the party lash" were evoked, and the evils of enslaving individual conscience to party dictation denounced. Any measure composed and enacted under such conditions would imperil the nation's fortunes.[51]

More justifiably, the opposition accentuated its lack of responsibility in framing the bill. A Democratic subcommittee of Finance fixed the rates, and the caucus reviewed them without any assistance from or consultation with the minority. The legislation was clearly "in every sense a party bill," noted Allison, "and any suggestion from a Republican as respects the subject receives no consideration."[52] Still, Republicans had learned something about the role of the minority. McMillan believed it absurd to filibuster in hope of preventing the passage of the measure, and Edmunds as well as Morrill shared his outlook. The Democrats, they conceded, were responsible for the business of the Senate; having set a tariff, they were responsible for its effects. The place to defeat the proposals, concluded the Michigan Senator, was at the polls in time of election.[53]

When senators in caucus were determined to compromise any differences for the sake of party, special economic interests could not anticipate satisfying particular demands. In 1894, for example, coal companies feared that the schedules would be set too low, but the consuming industries, such as Standard Oil, were anxious to keep costs as cheap as possible. Both groups pleaded their cause to Senate Democrats; the mine owners urged a fifty cent tariff and the consumers argued for less. Republican senator Stephen Elkins worked for coal while Cleveland's former Secretary of the Navy, William Whitney, represented Standard Oil. Neither could report substantial success. "I confess," Elkins informed Henry Davis, one-time West Virginia senator and now a leading coal producer, "I have always been a little afraid of Whitney's influence with Gorman, but we are doing the best we can."[54] The duty was finally levied at forty cents, falling between the two camps. Regardless of any personal sentiments, all Democrats voted to enact the rate.[55]

The various sugar interests contested each other's proposals even more frantically. The growers insisted upon full protection from foreign competition and badgered the Louisiana Senators with their demands; the refiners, on the other hand, wanted raw sugar to enter the country free, while processed sugar, in competition with their own product, was locked out by high tariff walls. The two sides made extraordinary efforts to carry their points, but after innumerable conferences and consultations the Democrats concluded a compromise. Neither interest was satisfied, but the united party passed the schedule.[56]

The Senate Democrats altered the 1894 tariff so thoroughly that President Cleveland and the House leaders voiced outright indignation. When the bill went to Conference, the representatives at first remained adamant in their stands; but in the end the joint committee agreed to the Senate schedules, and the House accepted the change. The closed ranks of the Upper House, concluded William Wilson, brought it the victory.[57] The caucus had performed its tasks well.

In 1897 party discipline and organization once again helped the Republicans, with a plurality but not a majority of Senate seats, to pass a tariff. The Dingley Bill made its way through the House in March of that year with a speed that testified to the Speaker's new powers and stature; in less than two weeks, after discussing only some 15 per cent of the provisions, the measure was dispatched to the Senate. There, the Republican majority on Finance took charge. As was now expected, it conducted meetings without the presence of Democrats; the minority was simply allowed to examine the finished product briefly before its introduction to the Senate. Some debate on the various schedules went on in the caucus, but Allison and Aldrich, firmly settled in positions of power, were less constrained by the party's members.

With only the help of the Finance Committee, Allison confidently framed the schedules; and all but three of the Republicans agreed in advance to stand by his decisions.[58]

The party kept to its pledge. McMillan appropriately praised the "Republican organization and caucus action," telling friends: "I think you will be inclined to give the Republicans credit for an amount of expedition unparalleled in years." Refrains already familiar to the gallery were again faithfully repeated. "The country has become so large . . . that there had to be mutual accommodations," the host to the School of Philosophy Club declared.[59] The Republicans, answered Ben Tillman, "under the stress of party orders, I suppose, given by the caucus, sit by quietly and vote. They say nothing . . . and every schedule prepared by the party caucus [he should have said Finance Committee] is voted for by them unanimously."[60] Only Stephen White, the California Democrat, departed from the traditional orations. "I do not," he began facetiously, "desire to criticize and I do not for a moment criticize, the majority because they have kept together . . . in such a wonderfully cohesive manner that we have not been able to break through in any case . . . except in one instance." Nevertheless, White reminded his opponents that they had chided the Democrats in 1894 for following the same practices. "We have some very distinguished imitators," the Westerner concluded.[61]

"The party has stood unitedly by the Committee of Finance," McMillan observed as the roll calls were underway, "and without an exception worthy of the name has voted down every amendment proposed by the other side."[62] The twelve Independents in the chamber, holding the balance of power, at times forced a change in the committee's rates, but on most duties they either abstained from voting or split their ranks. "If the silver Senators had stood in the way of such legislation," William Stewart explained, "the administration would have laid the blame at their doors, and the tariff as an issue would not have been cast

aside, as it is now."[63] In July 1897 united Republican support
passed the measure over solid Democratic opposition; in joint
conference, the Senate as usual gained its points, and the Dingley
Bill became law.[64] Senate party practices had revolutionized the
making of the tariff.

Critics of tariff legislation often complained that high schedules
encouraged the formation of trusts. Whatever the justice of the
argument, Senate parties did not treat the two issues similarly.
Members energetically deliberated tariff rates and the frequent
caucuses helped win united support. The trust question, however,
prompted no such action. Neither Senate Democrats nor Republicans considered it a party matter. In this sense the issue was
not vital to them.

Popular agitation for limiting the trusts was slow to develop
in post-Civil War America; by 1890 the sentiment, although
present, was not very strong. Both national platforms in 1888
supported the action in principle, but it provoked little excitement. When a bill declaring combinations in restraint of trade
illegal came before the chamber in December 1889, few found
cause to disagree with a restatement of common law principles.
By the 1890's, however, the absense of caucus involvement on an
item of business pointed to its uncontroversial character and suggested that few members were excited or offended by its provisions. After its reception in the Senate, it should not have been
surprising that the Anti-Trust Act proved a rather innocuous
piece of legislation.[65]

Caucus leaders also helped determine which of the many
measures introduced into the Senate would eventually be considered. The powers inherent in this responsibility became apparent when a federal elections bill awaited action. "Efficient
legislation to secure the integrity and purity of elections" was
optimistically promised in the Republican platform of 1888, and
two years later Massachusetts' new congressman, Henry Cabot
Lodge, introduced an appropriate bill into the House. While still

under consideration there, Senate Republicans expectantly debated in caucus whether to press the issue actively; despite their preparedness, however, they finally elected to postpone any decision until the House action was clear.[66]

Republicans met again in caucus once the Lodge measure passed. For three hours members debated various possible calendar arrangements but reached no decision on priorities, for the tariff and currency also required action. A lengthy caucus session discussed the suggestion that the Senate break all precedents and pass a cloture rule; by curbing debate all the necessary legislation could probably be enacted. The party even went so far as to charge a special committee to report back an anti-filibuster rule. But it seemed unlikely that they could alter Senate procedures so fundamentally.[67] "We could not get a sufficient number of Senators," revealed Connecticut Republican Joseph Hawley, "to support a proposition to change the rule to provide for a previous question. We have had many private caucuses, or conferences as we call them, in which we struggled to preserve unanimity and good feeling among ourselves."[68] Without an effective method for limiting discussion, the movement to consider Lodge's measure suffered a key setback. "I was one that did not believe in taking up any Election Bill under the present system," McMillan informed his son; the Democrats could have thwarted not only its passage but the enactment of any other legislation as well.[69]

By mid-August 1890 the bill's most energetic friends were in despair. "It looks now," John Spooner divulged to one interested supporter, "as if enough Republicans had gone . . . over to the Democrats to postpone until next session, which means to kill it, the Federal Elections bill, in order to secure an earlier passage of the tariff bill."[70] But the Wisconsin leader was overly pessimistic. Four days later, "after a good deal of row," noted McMillan, the Republicans "decided to hold a private conference at my house this evening, where it is to be hoped some satisfactory solution of the question may be found.[71] The meeting was on the whole successful. "We have," recorded Senator Hawley, "come to an agreement among ourselves by which the elections bill will be taken up on the first Monday in December and pressed to a consideration, even if it becomes necessary to adopt a modified previous question. We have made no bargain with the Democrats to make this postponement . . . Our party was united in sufficient strength."[72] Spooner was also pleased by the party's cooperative efforts. "The bill," he affirmed, "goes over to the next session on terms satisfactory to those in favor of the elections bill."[73] The caucus had ostensibly accomplished its duty.

January 1891, however, brought unexpected disappointment. Although Republicans more intent on tariff schedules were responsible for the postponement in 1890, silver senators dealt the measure its death blow in 1891. William Stewart, representing the inflationary forces, depicted the election legislation as a threat to American liberties and a party ruse to avoid silver coinage.[74] Thus, the hopes aroused by the earlier caucus agreement were shattered. "Enough abandon us on the election bill," Spooner unhappily confessed, "to constitute, with the Democrats a majority of the Senate, and the trouble, therefore, is not with the great body of Republican Senators, but the few who for reasons of their own desert us."[75] Seven Republicans, all inflationists, voted in the chamber against taking up the measure; determined to place silver above all considerations, they voted as they pleased.[76]

Perhaps the federal elections bill would have succeeded if the Republicans had established some sort of control over Senate discussions; with much justification Maine's senator, William Frye, contended that opponents of the rules change were responsible for the measure's defeat. The caucus leadership could not suppress a small but determined bloc of senators, and even the heightened awareness of party power and responsibility could not alter the custom of unlimited debate. Members favoring effective curbs argued that the majority was accountable for the business of the

Senate and so should be permitted to enact its program without obstructions. "If we have no power to legislate upon any subject except by your consent and according to your domination," Aldrich told Senate Democrats, "then the responsibility does not properly belong to this side of the chamber."[77] But those opposed to any cloture rule countered with statements on the necessity of two party politics; accentuating the essential role of a loyal opposition in a democracy, they warned against limiting its privileges. "If there was not a minority party in this country," asserted Henry Teller, "there would be little prospect for the maintenance of American liberty."[78] One side was as determined as the other, and the tradition of unlimited debate continued unchanged.

Party leaders made serious and repeated efforts in caucus to instill harmony on the most sensitive and pressing political questions. Few issues were as divisive as the currency, and yet the organizations performed quite creditably, utilizing every prerogative to unite party ranks. The attempts, however, were not uniformly successful; there were limits to their capabilities.

Although currency legislation played no part in the 1888 presidential campaign and was not discussed at any length in Harrison's inaugural, the subject came before Congress in 1890. William Windom, Secretary of the Treasury and a former Minnesota senator, unexpectedly outlined a program for expanding the use of silver. The House improved upon his rather fanciful suggestions and soon proposed that the government purchase $4,000,000 of silver monthly and then issue treasury notes valid for public, but not private, transactions.[79]

The bill went next to the Senate, where a majority favored even more inflationary legislation. Republican caucus leaders attempted to find agreement somewhere short of free silver coinage but their efforts failed. After a sharp fight, reported Richard Pettigrew to his South Dakota friends, the inflationists won out. "It took the eastern chaps a long time to find out they were in the minority, but they accepted defeat with good grace."[80] Fully aware that a free silver amendment would be tacked on to the House measure, the Steering Committee scheduled the bill and took steps to ensure the presence of a quorum. The Senate roll was called and party ranks dissolved. "So great are the interests involved," announced Colorado's young senator, Edward Wolcott, "that in view of them party lines are obliterated and forgotten." The issue, John Mitchell of Oregon righteously declared, cannot be compromised by any means, by the caucus, the conference, or the party leadership. "It is not a party question," and "mere partisan politics" were of little use.[81]

The Senate passed the free silver clause and sent the measure into Joint Conference with the House. There, under the experienced hand of John Sherman, Republicans formulated a substantially new piece of legislation. The Secretary of the Treasury was instructed to buy 4,500,000 ounces of silver each month and release legal tender notes, redeemable in gold or silver at the government's discretion. Silver Republicans now agreed to stand by the party; realizing the impossibility of passing free silver through the Lower House and over an anticipated presidential veto, they were content to return to the ranks. The truisms about the necessity for compromise replaced the slurs at "mere partisan politics," and rivals did not neglect to chastise those who "bow and bend and surrender" to party organization. The Republicans joined to enact the measure over united Democratic opposition.[82] The Sherman Silver Purchase Act seemed to promise that acceptable currency measures would be worked out through the mediation of the caucus.

Nevertheless, the next significant piece of financial legislation followed an atypical course from the start. Grover Cleveland, even before his second inauguration, was determined to repeal the Sherman Act and he, not Congress, instigated and superintended the move. Soon after taking office, he consulted with William Vilas, a close friend, on the best possible strategy; the Senator advised him to convene a special session in October 1894, expressly for the purpose of revoking the law. The President agreed and on June 13, 1894 issued the call. Five weeks later the members assembled.[83]

Without much fuss, the House speedily passed a measure embodying the executive's demands, and Daniel Vorhees, on behalf of the Finance Committee, soon reported it to the Democratic-controlled Senate. There was no question of the President's resoluteness. "If there are some nominations," he had instructed his private secretary, Henry Thurber, in August, "that the Senators who are inclined to be mean, as well as opposed to what we want, especially desire, it might be well to postpone sending in such nominations [to the Senate] until my return." And although Cleveland probably did not win any votes that he would not otherwise have received, at least everyone understood the stakes of the game.[84]

Despite the President's determination, strong Democratic opposition was immediately apparent. Since Republican support for the measure was questionable at best, most members of the majority, certainly Gorman if not Vorhees, anticipated some sort of compromise. Cleveland, however, remained adamant, refusing to consider any legislation short of unconditional repeal. The leaders of the Democratic Steering Committee considered sending a delegation to the White House, but they canceled their plans after being distinctly forewarned of an icy reception. Furious at this rigidity, the bill's opponents began to filibuster, halting all progress in the chamber. "This kind of session," confessed a weary Senator McMillan, "does not help me to like this kind of business."[85]

In a deadlocked Senate, cries for caucus intervention and compromise solutions were now heard over and over again. For all the previous attacks on Senate party government, members from both sides of the aisle turned to the party machinery as soon as the proceedings reached a standstill. "The Senate Democrats," grumbled John Morgan, "have not held a single conference on the bill to explore party sentiment; dissidents have not once been consulted." "Seven-tenths of all legislation in this chamber results from compromise," Marion Butler reminded his colleagues; why was it not turned to here?[86] John Sherman, who at first generously hoped that "in dealing with such a question we surely ought to dismiss from our minds all party affinities or prejudices," soon changed his tone. "Whenever Republicans were in control" and faced a divisive issue, "we met in conclave, compromised and came to an agreement." Party action ought to close the debate; if the Democrats were unable to rule, they should resign their majority.[87]

Toward the end of October, Senators Cockrell and Morgan and other champions of the filibuster ended their dilatory tactics. Vorhees had invoked day and night sessions to wear down the opposition, and then too, "some sense of party exigency . . . led to an acquiescence by the other side in the inevitable result."[88] Moreover, the Republicans had determined to vote with Cleveland's supporters, thereby guaranteeing the bill's passage. They were not at all happy to join with the opposition, but toward the middle of October the members in caucus decided to let Sherman speak for the party in favor of repeal. Everyone agreed to stay on hand, preventing early adjournments, and to refrain from debate, shortening the proceedings. Even when the filibuster continued unabated, Republicans again in caucus reaffirmed their decision to sit back and wait upon the majority.[89]

In retrospect, Sherman and his colleagues judged the 1890 act a dismal failure, and opposition for its own sake seemed foolhardy. Still, McMillan was delighted when the majority almost compromised the issue among themselves and formulated a measure which Republicans could not support; had the legislation won Democratic approval, the minority would have been spared the embarrassment of the alliance.[90] The Democrats, for their part, were equally dissatisfied. Critics denounced Cleveland for compelling the Senate to accept Republican assistance; his foolish obstinance cost the party the esteem of the public. "If we who are charged with the responsibility," countered the President, "inaugurate a measure of relief, our countrymen will give us full credit for it and will not inquire whether Republican votes helped us or not." He smugly concluded that the nation would not be content with any sort of compromise, "even though it was passed by Democratic votes alone."[91]

Content that his obligations to party responsibility were discharged, Cleveland proceeded to fulfill his design. Willing to risk enmity and dissension, he dealt strictly and harshly with all antagonists. "Those of us who represented the sentiments of our people in the extra session of Congress on the silver question," Texas senator Richard Coke informed Governor James Hogg, "are as completely cut off from any participation in the counsels of the administration or in the giving out of patronage as if we belonged to the Republican party."[92] Left to its own devices, the Democratic caucus might have effected a workable compromise; significantly, senators now turned to it in hope of settling their differences. But a hostile President together with a divided membership were too formidable, and party unity collapsed before the combination.

The strength of the Populist party in the last years of the nineteenth century prevented the enactment of any important currency measures between 1894 and 1900. Convinced that the nation had been "brought to the verge of ruin," that the two political organizations struggled only for "power and plunder" and made "no serious effort" to correct the many "grievous wrongs inflicted on our people," the Populists set out to right these evils. Their dissatisfactions far outweighing any sense of party loyalty, they offered the electorate a new ticket. Success was uneven; nevertheless, by 1895 enough independents were elected to deadlock Washington proceedings. As J. P. Jones noted, the silver men had enough strength in the chamber to prevent at the least the passage of any gold bill. However, no unlimited coinage bill could be enacted either, and in December of that year the Nevada mine owner conceded that this session of Congress would be dull and insignificant. The parties were so divided that aggressive legislation would be impossible.[93] In January 1896 McMillan informed Republican supporters not to expect any action, and in February, Stephen White wrote his followers that "the Senate is in a condition where non-performance is a necessity and doing anything effective an impossibility."[94]

Populists prided themselves on their organization and like their older rivals met in frequent caucus to set policies. In 1896, for example, they resolved that no tariff bill would pass through the chamber without including a free silver clause and they kept to the decision.[95] Democrats and Republicans also continued their conferences, now, however, devoted more to strategy than to substantive legislative programs.[96]

By the opening year of the new century, the strength of the silver forces was depleted, and the Republican majority was able to enact the Gold Standard Bill. Allison and Aldrich conferred frequently and party colleagues bowed to their leadership. "In this as in all matters, I rely upon your judgment and wisdom," one typical member told the caucus chairman,[97] and soon the gold dollar became the sole monetary unit of the nation. Henry Teller immediately criticized the measure when it came up in the Senate as a caucus bill; but then he reminded himself and others that legislation could not be condemned merely because it was framed in caucus. When Aldrich declared "that he knew of no one else on his side of the Chamber who intended to discuss the measure," Teller felt justified "in speaking of this as a caucus measure." Nevertheless, he quickly conceded that only the bill's merits warranted attention.[98]

Teller's label was, of course, correct. Republicans first submitted their rough plans to a professional board of monetary experts and then met to debate and approve their recommendations. In fact, the legislation was never even considered by a Senate working committee for the caucus usurped its duties. Discipline was again evident as every Republican member, with one exception, balloted for monetary reform and the Democrats joined together against the measure.[99] Party chieftains once more dominated the chamber's proceedings.

Other substantive issues also revealed the new powers of party. The Senate organizations, for example, assumed a vital role in America's imperial adventures at the end of the nineteenth century. The votes on the various treaties negotiated during these years pointed to a significant degree of party cohesion (see Chart II). Moreover, caucus machinery helped instill the discipline. With good cause Democrat Stephen White noted that the proposal to annex Hawaii, "were it not that the Republican party is making an issue upon this subject . . . would be beaten out of sight."[100] Relations with Puerto Rico did not let Republican Charles Fairbanks forget that "the unity of the party on all questions is of paramount importance. Free trade or a tariff for Puerto Rico is of insignificant consequence compared with the solidarity of the Republican party." The treaty with the Philippines was no exception. "I know too how many men in the Senate," observed George Hoar, "feel constrained by mere party fidelity . . . to vote for the treaty."[101] By 1900 a legislative history of the Senate demanded a keen sense of party politics.

Finally, Senate leaders superintended the important routines of the chamber. Although a few select working committees and not the caucus determined what funds would go to government administration and internal improvements, party chairmen, carefully allotting committee places, still extended their authority. An opening on Appropriations, for example, whetted many senators' ambitions, and Allison, Aldrich, and Gorman exercised every privilege of their positions to dictate the assignments. Ambitious functionaries as well as enterprising villagers felt the impact of their verdicts; "You understand," wrote Francis Warren with forgivable oversimplification, "Mr. Allison is chairman of the

Appropriations Committee and therefore in many ways the most influential man perhaps in the Senate."[102]

The detailed legislation was rarely discussed or contested in the Senate. Party members tended to uphold their committees' decisions, and even the formalities of a vote were often unnecessary. Local interests could at times induce a senator to break ranks or sponsor new amendments, and independent action here rarely prompted reprisals. Still, dissension was uncommon. Between March and July 1897 the Senate passed a Rivers and Harbors and an Appropriations bill, and in almost every instance the committees' proposals became law without even the bother of a roll call. Caucus leaders were not surprised at the display of harmony; by then they had every right to expect it.[103]

The transformation of the Senate was not the exclusive work of Democratic or Republican leaders, for talented caucus chairmen alone could not have secured these changes. Personalities, of course, were significant; Allison was more skilled than Conkling and Gorman more tactful than Wallace. But events beyond the walls of the chamber vitally affected the proceedings within it. Not that a mere increase in membership or the quantity of business would necessarily have stimulated discipline. The rise in numbers, from seventy-five senators in 1869 to ninety in 1899, and a bursting calendar might just as easily have promoted chaos as order. Rather, the history of the institution during these years cannot be understood if it is left isolated and stranded atop Capitol Hill.

The career lines that carried men to a seat in the chamber and the sorts of lives they led there affected the exercise of power. The structure of state politics and the pressures exerted by private interests reinforced some tendencies and stifled others. New ideas on the proper role of party in democratic government also were important to these events. The story of the Senate requires the tableau of America as well as the vignette of Washington.

Part Two

Politics and Society
The Elements of Change

☆ ☆ ☆ ☆ ☆

☆ IV ☆

THE ASCENT TO POWER

We must not forget that governing the United States is an art . . . and it cannot be learned in a week or two by smart lawyers, merchants, ministers, and authors, who have had no experience in the management of men and parties . . . The management of parties requires a certain tact, adroitness, and worldly wisdom which are only gained by long experience.

Whitelaw Reid, editor, *New York Tribune*, on post–Civil War political careers

Senators at the end of the nineteenth century came to Washington after a long and systematic apprenticeship. First holding minor posts and then moving into more responsible positions, they finally won seats in the chamber. Significantly, political organizations promoted and at the same time profited from this lengthy training. Ambitious politicians, facing the hurdle of successive elections, welcomed assistance; and party chieftains preferred to support and promote those prepared to link private ambitions to the organization's welfare. By 1900 professionals filled the Capitol's offices. It was no coincidence that at this point in the Senate's history, the caucus and its leaders assumed critical importance.

Men from all social origins climbed the political ladder. Party organizations, far more concerned with what a man did than with what he was, rewarded performance not inherited position. The well born enjoyed some advantage in being able to devote attention to politics more easily than less wealthy colleagues. Nevertheless, to a remarkable degree, every circumstance of birth was represented among the membership. Similarly, full-time politicians, not bored millionaires, dominated the chamber's halls. Lawyers typically entered the Senate after maintaining quite ordinary practices; their political efforts, not income or status, carried them to power. Businessmen, on the other hand, commonly enjoyed greater financial success; but they too began public careers at the bottom and methodically worked their way to the top. There was a very practical sort of democracy in professional politics.

Seated in the firm leather and mahogany chairs, almost half (40 per cent) of the Senate could look back on lives begun in considerably less comfortable surroundings. Whether elected in the 1870's and thus well along in their careers before the Civil War, or in the 1890's, their professional pursuits postponed until after the close of hostilities,[1] members gave neither a hint nor a promise of future fame in their early years. Born into families that could not offer any significant assistance, they were in every sense responsible for their achievements. Fathers struggling to subsist were, at most, able to offer food and clothing. There were no surplus funds to provide for education, no personal friends to offer crucial aid, no reputable family name to open opportunities. These future senators characteristically made their own way (see Table 1).

Of the members born into subsistence households, three quarters spent their childhoods on humble farms in small and remote settlements. Nelson Aldrich inherited a barren and hilly homestead in depressed Rhode Island, and future colleagues surveyed similar patrimonies in western New York and on the Georgia frontier. Kentucky's John Carlisle began a career that brought him first to the Senate and then into Cleveland's cabinet on a farm far more notable for rocks and boulders than fertility, and Alabama's John Tyler Morgan shared the same experience. A few colleagues knew urban rather than rural hardships. Some 9 per

Table 1. Senators' social origins, 1869–1901, by father's occupation
(per cent)

Occupation	Per cent in occupation	Origin		
		Subsistence	Substantial	Elite
Farmer	50	76	40	20
Businessman	17	13	21	18
Professional	27	2	34	59
Laborer	3	9	—	—
Other	3	—	5	3
Total for Senate		40	42	18
Status known (number)		(88)	(100)	(44)
Father's occupation unknown (number)		(13)	(4)	

Source: See Appendix A.

cent were sons of luckless shopkeepers or itinerant peddlers. For most senators the unyielding soil rather than the frugal boss or the haggling customer was the family villain.

An equal percentage of members (42 per cent) were raised in more substantial settings. Those who were rural born came from farms enjoying a surplus. Among those born in towns, nearly one fourth of their fathers ran profitable shops or exercised the skills of a craft still in demand; another third were professionals, with a local law or medical practice, or holders of a minor county political post. In any event, these parents offered their youngsters assistance when they reached turning points in their careers. Families were ready to supply the funds for education and to simplify the demands of professional training. They could not, however, pass on established position or power. Success would have to be earned.

A small minority of the Senate, 18 per cent, was born into privileged homes, to fathers rightfully considered part of the nation's elite. Some owned prosperous plantations or conducted an exceptionally profitable business. Over half were professionals, lawyers or politicians, occupying outstanding positions of state or national political power. These families offered their heirs unparalleled opportunities and the means to attain many goals. Schooling was no issue, and introductions to men of influence were no problem. Children would be judged successful if they emulated their fathers' performance and shared their status.

Nevertheless, of only this last group could anyone have predicted that power and prestige would some day be their due. It is true that the percentages of wellborn in the chamber were higher than their corresponding proportion in the general population; America was not an ideally mobile society. But the door to the Senate during the last decades of the nineteenth century was more than half open, not swinging closed. The climb to power in many instances revealed remarkable evidence of social mobility.

In the western parts of the nation, usually designated West North Central, Mountain, and Pacific in the census divisions, the overwhelming majority of senators (94 per cent), even in the 1890's, had early in their careers migrated to the regions they eventually represented. In the older and eastern sections, however, from New England through the South Atlantic and South Central states, the reverse held true; senators were born and raised in the states they served.[2] This geographical differentiation carried important political and social repercussions. More than half the senators elected from the newly settled areas were raised in subsistence families. Those who endured long train rides to the capital over the hot and seemingly interminable plains, in another sense as well, traveled a long road to power (Table 2).

The connections between social and geographical mobility were most apparent in senators' careers begun in the law.[3] Well over half the chamber seats (66 per cent) were filled by attorneys, and access to office was often related to admission to the bar (Table 3). In fact the open quality of the profession in the post-Civil War decades regularly initiated success stories. Future senators, despite a lack of inherited advantages, were able to win their licenses. Thirty-one per cent of New England senators who

Table 2. Senators' social origins, 1869–1901, by region
(per cent)

| Region | Origin | | | |
	Subsistence	Substantial	Elite	Number
New England	31	52	17	(29)
Middle Atlantic	28	44	28	(24)
South Atlantic	28	43	28	(42)
South Central	30	42	27	(40)
East North Central	45	41	14	(41)
West North Central	57	39	4	(28)
Mountain	68	27	5	(22)
Pacific	53	42	5	(23)

Source: See Appendix A.

pursued the law came from subsistence families, while in the West North Central areas the figure jumped to 55 per cent, and in the Mountain states to 87 per cent (Table 4). The widespread opportunity to enter the bar opened political power to men of various social classes.

Education was the first and prime requisite for entering the law, and sons of subsistence farmers, like the descendants of successful merchants, were able to acquire the necessary schooling. Men with the ambition and drive to sustain a rise to the Senate may have been exceptionally persistent even early in life, nevertheless, the availability of education rather than remarkable

Table 3. Senators' occupations prior to election, by decade
(per cent)

| Occupation | Decade | | |
	1870	1880	1890
Law	73	68	57
Business	20	28	24
Agriculture	2	1	8
Other	5	3	11
Number	(117)	(72)	(83)

Source: See Appendix A.

Table 4. Senate lawyers' social origins, 1869–1901, by region
(per cent)

Region	Origin			
	Subsistence	*Substantial*	*Elite*	*Number*
New England	31	54	15	(13)
Middle Atlantic	18	46	36	(11)
South Atlantic	23	42	35	(31)
South Central	31	43	36	(39)
East North Central	50	37	13	(30)
West North Central	55	45	—	(20)
Mountain	87	12	—	(8)
Pacific	42	50	8	(12)

Source: See Appendix A.

sacrifices or extraordinary diligence marked most biographies. Regardless of family circumstances, some sort of primary schooling was at hand. Senator Joseph Brown, born into a poverty-stricken household on the Georgia frontier, attended neighborhood classes at least part of the year; James George, raised in similar circumstances, eked out the rudiments of an education in the "old field" schools of Mississippi. Eastern colleagues even more easily obtained an elementary education.

Nor was it especially difficult to receive some sort of secondary training. Happily, education often proved to be its own reward; funds acquired by teaching in the lower grades supplied the means for additional schooling. Pennsylvania's William Wallace and Kentucky's William Lindsay exploited whatever pedagogic skills they possessed to pay for their own education; by utilizing similar talents, Joseph Brown attended the Calhoun Academy in South Carolina. Part-time labor was always welcome on neighborhood farms, as Senator William Stewart could testify, and Montana's Thomas Carter earned the necessary money by selling books, teaching school, working on farms and on railroads. Tuition costs were minimal and the money was easily acquired. Making one's way through school admittedly demanded hard work, but it was by no means an insuperable task (Table 5).

Perhaps the greatest barrier to education facing men of subsistence origins was the obligation to till the family farm. They were frequently called upon to help feed a large household and sacrifice personal goals for its welfare. Although self-support appeared a simple matter, it also seemed the selfish course. In the all too common event of a father's early death, the eldest son headed the family, surrounded by a flock of brothers and sisters he could not very well abandon. Younger children did not escape responsibilities; unmarried sisters and aging parents often demanded assistance. In this respect, those born into more comfortable conditions held a clear advantage. Prosperous fathers not only simplified the course of schooling; they would not block efforts to achieve private ambitions.[4]

A college degree was still not required for admission to the bar, and would-be lawyers, regardless of financial abilities, were usually content to enter law offices after their secondary educations. Young men from poor homes, their progress slowed by the constant need to work part-time, were understandably reluctant to commence a new and vocationally unnecessary educational experience. However, a surprising number of future senators from even the most humble backgrounds found the time and scraped together the funds to spend some years in college. Nearly half the lawyers from subsistence homes received some such training, usually at noteworthy institutions. Henry Dawes never failed to

Table 5. Lawyers' education and social origins, 1869–1901
(per cent)

| | Origin | | |
Education	Subsistence	Substantial	Elite
College and graduate school	3	13	28
College and vocational training	40	54	56
College	5	11	7
Secondary and vocational training	52	22	9
Number	(63)	(69)	(32)

Source: See Appendix A.

remind his sons, who happened not to be very good students, how he made his own way through Yale while managing at the same time to win honors. And many Washington colleagues probably pressed similar boasts on hapless children.

Some college graduates, particularly those from wealthy backgrounds, enrolled in law schools. Most others joined a law office to gain professional competence. Clerking was a popularly acceptable alternative to formal training, and Chauncey Depew, for example, well able to afford any sort of graduate education, preferred to return to a small office in Peekskill, New York. The intelligent student qualified for a license after three years of reading the law, ending his apprenticeship. In instance after instance, senators' careers gave ample evidence that aspirants, no matter what their circumstances of birth, could complete this course.

Inherited positions, to be sure, affected opportunities. The higher the social origins, the greater the likelihood for outstanding educational achievements. Only 3 per cent of would-be lawyers from subsistence homes attended college and then graduate school, while 13 per cent and 28 per cent of the sons of substantial and elite families, respectively, took this opportunity. Moreover, although 52 per cent of those born into humble circumstances entered law offices directly after secondary schooling, less than one quarter of their wellborn colleagues began specialized training without a college education. Still, such careers clearly pointed to the widespread access to schooling and the accompanying openness of the law. Half the senators who relied on nothing more than their own ambition managed to attend college and then go on to clerk; colleagues from similar backgrounds received at least enough training to qualify for reading the law. The availability of education was of vital significance to the nation because only short steps separated the legal profession from a career in politics.

Although would-be attorneys did not frequently travel beyond state boundaries to receive an education, many chose to leave native surroundings when starting their practice. Not surprisingly, those with no stake or advantage at home most often took the opportunity to move, and migrants were far more likely to be of subsistence origin than peers remaining in the East (Table 4). The young lawyer, license in hand, packed his trunk, stuffed in a few impressive tomes, and set out in search of a suitable office in some county seat. Ideally, the town would be flourishing, progressive, and not professionally overcrowded. With distance no consideration—why not continue another hundred miles to escape stiff competition—communities approximating these standards were not exceptionally difficult to locate. His efforts to attract a clientele were soon under way.

These attempts immediately provoked interest in political life. From the first days of the Republic, lawyers dominated the government service. Since only they could prosecute a case for the county, their talents were in frequent demand. Moreover, professional obligations were admirably suited for part-time work, making attorneys available for public service. Then too, accustomed to jury pleading and oral arguments, they were comfortable on the stump, and even enjoyed it. But beyond sharing these common incentives, lawyers moving westward had even more pressing reasons for entering politics. In fact the impetus was so great that soon after arrival, and at younger ages than their eastern colleagues, they occupied their first offices.[5] The strength of the attraction carried wide significance since physical mobility was, in this instance, the start of social mobility.

Politics was useful and necessary to the newcomer in a growing town. Anticipating only a limited private practice even in the best locations, and anxious at once to earn a living wage and attract prospective clients, the young lawyers quickly turned to local law enforcement positions. The Easterners and Southerners most often began political careers in state legislatures; Westerners preferred to serve as county prosecutors or district attorneys (Table 6). The posts paid small but steady fees. Funds previously earned had gone to schooling; the expense of the trip and the new office probably exhausted any other savings. The income from

Table 6. Lawyers' first political office, 1869–1901, by region
(per cent)

Office	Region		
	East	*West*	*East North Central*
Prosecuting attorney	28	51	41
Local judge	4	9	17
State legislator	48	22	31
Municipal officer	4	5	—
State cabinet	4	9	—
Governor	1	—	—
Congressman	8	4	7
Other	3	—	4
Number	(99)	(45)	(29)

Source: See Appendix A.

official places thus helped feed the beginner while the duties did not interfere with a budding practice. Moreover, these posts were available. Settlers in new areas, as a matter of course, expected their municipal or county organization to duplicate the structure of older areas. Although there may not have been a pressing need for a town prosecutor and assistants, a county attorney and aides, the offices were nevertheless created. No one complained of the tax costs because officials received fees rather than salaries, and few businessmen wished to conduct their affairs without this protection. In most communities there were probably more offices than men qualified to hold them. Attorneys had no difficulty in winning a place.

A county prosecutor found excellent occasions to meet clients and display professional talents. A good court case attracted the curious from miles around; a passionate summation to the jury, a doubtful verdict together with wagers on the outcome sparked excitement and interest. By comparison, performances in the state legislature advertised legal skills poorly. Its meetings were too far away, prospective clients rarely attended, and public attention was only infrequently aroused. The lawyer was kept from his desk for weeks on end, disrupting private affairs. Accordingly, Isaac

Christiancy, having supported himself while studying to enter the New York bar, moved to Monroe, Michigan, upon attaining professional competence and served as the prosecuting attorney for the county for five years. Eventually, he displaced Zachary Chandler from his Senate seat. Similarly, future Oregon senator Joseph Dolph taught school to finance his education and gained his license in Binghamton, New York. After military service in Oregon, he settled in Portland and soon assumed the duties of public attorney. Before entering the School of Philosophy Club in Washington, Charles Manderson practiced law in Canton, Ohio, serving as the city solicitor. Dissatisfied with his progress there, he moved to Omaha where he occupied this same post. For the man who traveled westward, it made more sense to hold local rather than state offices when establishing a practice.

Lawyers in more settled regions also began political careers in local judicial posts, a rare event in the East. Magistrates were not obliged to abandon private retainers—towns could ill afford or were reluctant to provide a living wage—and new practitioners welcomed the added fees. No old functionaries were entrenched in the posts, and again a scarcity of men and a multiplicity of vacancies were common. The duties of a judge possessed limited dramatic potential, but a reputation for honesty and cleverness might easily spread from the bench.

In the last decades of the nineteenth century, the paths from the law to government were simple and direct. Western practitioners were almost compelled to enter office and eastern colleagues maintained traditional connections. The exercise of political power was not confined to a favored few.

Businessmen elected to the Senate first entered politics under quite different circumstances. Their common quality was an extraordinary degree of financial success. Most Senate lawyers (57 per cent) maintained only very ordinary practices. As Herbert Croly, looking back on these years from the perspective of the Progressive era, astutely noted: "Since 1870 the lawyer

... has tended to become a professional specialist and to give all his time to his specialty ... A considerable proportion of our legislators and executives continue to be lawyers, but the difference is that now they are more likely to be less successful lawyers."[6] Legal and political advancement were not linked. In western states attorneys at times headed sizable firms and commanded large retainers without jeopardizing public ambitions; from the start of their careers, public and private interests were more closely linked than for their eastern colleagues. Yet no matter where they practiced, Senate lawyers could not duplicate the occupational successes achieved by the chamber's businessmen. Many entrepreneurs in the chamber (47 per cent) were outstanding figures in key organizations, with incomes in the vicinity of $50,000 a year. Moreover, an almost equal number (44 per cent) were among the nation's economic as well as political leaders (Table 7). In brief, twenty-seven businessmen in the Senate might safely be labeled millionaires.

The chamber's businessmen did not achieve exceptional success because of inherited advantages. They were often (45 per cent) raised in humble circumstances and only a few (10 per cent) shared special privileges. Their educational achievements were

Table 7. Occupational success of Senate lawyers and businessmen, 1869–1901, by region
(per cent)

Rating	Region			
	East	West	East North Central	Number
National Leader				
Law	2	2	10	(7)
Business	24	41	86	(27)
Outstanding				
Law	34	50	42	(71)
Business	68	45	14	(29)
Average				
Law	64	48	48	(104)
Business	8	4	—	(5)

Source: See Appendix A.

more closely determined by families' economic positions; occupational training did not necessarily depend upon formal schooling, and they lacked the impetus of the would-be lawyer. Eighty-two per cent of the businessmen from low social origins failed to advance beyond the secondary level, while 63 per cent of those from substantial households received at least some college education (Table 8). Most successful entrepreneurs could join their colleagues in claiming full credit for success.

Table 8. Senate businessmen's education and social origins, 1869–1901 (per cent)

| | Origin | | |
Education	Subsistence	Substantial	Elite
College and graduate school	—	7	17
College and vocational training	4	26	—
College	14	30	33
Secondary and vocational training	46	33	—
Primary	36	4	50
Number	(28)	(27)	(6)

Source: See Appendix A.

Businessmen typically traveled to Washington from sections offering the greatest and most dramatic opportunities for capturing wealth. They were elected most frequently in the East North Central States (31 per cent), and in the Mountain and Pacific regions (33 and 35 per cent), rich in minerals. They also came from Middle Atlantic states (52 per cent), economically dominated by corporate and financial interests. As these areas continued to develop, businessmen more frequently won seats and in the 1880's made up 28 per cent of all the newcomers to the Senate.

No one particular endeavor was better suited than another for political careers; it was success that mattered. The entrepreneur elected to the Senate was usually the leader in the state's most lucrative and important industry. Among businessmen as well as lawyers, migrants westward were more likely to be of humble origins (58 per cent) than those remaining at home (41 per cent); but the vital attraction here was the area's resources, not a fluid social setting. Mine owners like Nevada's J. P. Jones and William Sharon represented western states, and merchants like Charles Farwell of Illinois came from the Midwest. The Lakes elected James McMillan, involved in shipping enterprises, and Philetus Sawyer, in lumber. One quarter of Senate businessmen made their money in extractive industries; exactly the same percentage profited from transportation and mercantile investments, while slightly fewer (19 per cent) were involved in manufacturing. Their activities accurately mirrored the nation's post-Civil War economic development.

Financial success was achieved only through great effort, and businessmen did not usually enter politics at the young ages so typical of the lawyers. Only a quarter of the entrepreneurs in the chamber found the time or had the inclination to assume a post before reaching thirty, and only a little more than half took this step before thirty-five. Most lawyers (60 per cent) had already gained some political experience by thirty, and 86 per cent of those who would some day sit in the chamber acted in an official capacity before thirty-five. Political involvement was not as logical for the active industrialist as for the ambitious attorney.

A third of the entrepreneurs, usually those holding office earliest, first occupied city council, aldermanic, or other municipal posts. Personal stakes in the future growth of towns and cities often sparked an interest in government. No merchant could hope to prosper in a dying community, and no real estate speculator would see rising values in a wayward settlement. Political decisions, whether to improve municipal facilities or float a bond to attract a railroad, had a vital economic pertinence not overlooked by shrewd investors. Another half of the businessmen destined to enter the Senate opened their careers in the state legislature, although decisions there were not often as immediately significant to personal ventures as in a municipal council (Table 9).

Table 9. Businessmen's first political office, 1869–1901, by region
(per cent)

Office	Region		
	East	West	East North Central
Municipal officer	28	39	29
State legislator	48	50	50
Governor	4	11	—
Congressman	12	—	—
Other	8	—	21
Number	(25)	(18)	(14)

Source: See Appendix A.

Most entrepreneurs, in fact, did not enter politics because of a harmony of public and private interest. Rather, after achieving financial success, they were prepared to devote energy to questions of government. If self-interest had been the ultimate goal of businessmen-legislators, they would have more profitably invested their time in commercial enterprises, and promoted the political efforts of trusted friends or allies. To seek and serve in office was a demanding and economically unrewarding venture. Political interest, not the desire to prejudice government proceedings, led entrepreneurs to state capitals. Having mastered one area, they were anxious to try another.

No single occupation totally controlled access to office. Ten per cent of the senators during these years were neither lawyers nor businessmen. Ranchers and bonanza farmers left the Mountain states to fill a seat, and a few planters and occasionally an ordinary yeoman joined them in Washington. Newspapermen, following an old but fading tradition, left their desks to take a more direct involvement in political life; sporadically, a teacher or doctor caught the fever and began campaigning. But more important, in post-Civil War America the openness of the legal profession, and to a lesser extent the economic opportunities available in business ventures, helped keep membership open to men of all social origins.

Of course, not everyone could become an American senator. Unlike the House of Commons that Namier described, the aspiration and potential to assume a place in the chamber pervaded the society. No member of any class could be confident that his personal ambition would some day be satisfied.

After entering politics, future senators followed several routes to power. At the start they were likely to serve in the state legislature. Attorneys in more settled regions, wisely looked there first, and western lawyers and businessmen in general soon competed for places in the state capitals. The decision was shrewd as well as popular, for the assembly enabled the young politician to grow intimate with party leaders and local citizens. The legislator would soon be called upon to vote for senator, and leaders, vitally interested in the race, were especially anxious to welcome the newcomer. The assemblyman who placed his allegiance in the right quarter found the party contributions to his campaign chest readily forthcoming; others less willing to pledge support discovered well-supported opponents upsetting their plans. In the state legislature members learned the first lesson of politics: the need to accommodate party leadership (Table 10).

An assembly campaign permitted the rising politician to capture a small but valuable constituency. He had little physical difficulty in canvassing the area and meeting the voters. Every friend he made and every vote he won paid immediate dividends and promised future returns, for legislative and congressional districts substantially overlapped. More than one candidate favorably impressed a solid block of supporters and thus began a career that would culminate in a Senate seat. Finally, service in the assembly introduced the novice to the world of parliamentary

Table 10. All political offices occupied by senators prior to election,
1869–1901, by occupation
(per cent)

Office	Occupation		
	Lawyers	Businessmen	Other
Prosecuting attorney	41	—	4
Judiciary	20	1	4
Municipal	7	37	26
State legislator	64	60	59
State cabinet	12	3	7
Governor	14	21	26
Congressman	39	32	33
National cabinet	3	6	—
Ambassador and Vice-President	1	1	4
Party official	21	37	37
Number	(182)	(63)	(27)

Source: See Appendix A.

maneuvers. Debates, rules, roll calls, committee assignments, and caucuses became normal duties and routine considerations.

The House was the next logical step for ambitious politicians. Assisted by party leaders and loyal constituents, and confident that at least the rudiments of legislative activities had been mastered, they were ready and able to take a place in the Capitol. Service there brought additional advantages, with numerous occasions to gain publicity and to earn wide respect and gratitude. Talented members strengthened their position both with state leaders and citizens. Others attempted to gain the governor's chair, and those who attained it were often able to build powerful and trustworthy organizations. Controlling the patronage and influencing the course of legislation, the state executive had ample power and opportunity to secure support. When his ambition overreached state boundaries, he could rely upon associates to repay their debts and return his favors.

Members frequently achieved power through party rather than elective office. The growing complexity and salience of party organization after the Civil War brought a new significance to its administrative posts. The State Central Committee, charged with overseeing and contributing to various election contests, performed vital tasks, and the men dispensing its swelling funds easily promoted personal as well as party strength. Democrats and Republicans also maintained country-wide organizations; the chairman of the National Committee was by no means a national boss but he could, if only infrequently, buttress particular state factions in their contest for supremacy. The winners were likely to remember their benefactors when the second Senate seat became vacant. Diligent efforts on behalf of the party were now regularly rewarded with high public office. A new route to Washington had been plotted.

By the end of the nineteenth century, men painstakingly mounted the political ladder before finally winning Senate election. They went from law enforcement posts to the state legislature, from one side of the Hill to the other. After serving the municipality, they took places in state capitals; upon completing terms as chief executives, they moved to Washington. Senators, in short, were well prepared to wield the authority of their positions. To be sure, colleagues elected in the 1870's were also often familiar with the tasks of government; nevertheless, their successors twenty years later, as a group were even more accustomed to the exercise of power. Sixty-two per cent of the membership in the 1870's were experienced politicians, having served over four years in national office or over six years in important state posts. By the 1890's, however, 78 per cent of the Senate shared these qualifications. Occasionally, a legislator captured an election after short service; when two rivals deadlocked the voting, the assembly might settle on an unassuming peer. And at times a political novice aroused constituents through his oratory and unexpectedly found himself answering to the title of Senator. Still, by 1900 the chamber was the preserve of professional politicians (Table 11).

Table 11. Senators' political experience, by decade of election
(per cent)

	Decade		
Experience	1870	1880	1890
Considerable	29	31	35
Average	33	49	43
Little	33	17	17
None	5	3	5
Number	(114)	(70)	(82)

Source: See Appendix A.

Half the senators elected in the 1870's came to the Capitol after serving exclusively on the state level. A third of them had held national offices and 12 per cent had occupied key party posts. Their successors, however, composed a very different record. Only 21 per cent of the members in the 1890 decade arrived in Washington with nothing more than state experience. Half of the body had already filled some national positions, usually in the lower house of Congress. Moreover, an equal proportion first served the party in some important administrative capacity. These differences reflected fundamental shifts in American political life. In the post-Civil War decades, national legislation began to overshadow state affairs; power, a magnet for ambitious politicians, now centered in Washington. The significance of party also increased beyond the Senate walls as well as within it. With unprecedented regularity, men promoted to the chamber had earlier in their careers helped direct the organization. Not surprisingly, they did not neglect its leaders or its caucus when conducting the legislative business of the nation.

The law was so conducive to political careers that by the 1890's 79 per cent of all attorneys elected to the chamber were politically experienced. And the professionalization of officeholding by the end of the century was nowhere more evident than in the fact that 85 per cent of the businessmen coming to Washington were

similarly prepared. Senate members, regardless of their first occupations, all devoted great efforts to fulfill public ambitions
(Table 12).

Table 12. Senators' political experience, by decade and occupation
(per cent)

	Decade and occupation					
	1870		1880		1890	
Experience	Law	Business	Law	Business	Law	Business
Considerable	26	43	35	20	38	30
Average	39	9	50	50	41	55
Little	31	35	15	25	17	10
None	4	13	—	5	4	5
Number	(84)	(23)	(48)	(20)	(47)	(20)

Source: See Appendix A.

Some distinctions existed to be sure. Lawyers often preferred a
seat in Congress, while businessmen were more likely to serve as
governors and supervise the organizational machinery. The influence of business techniques on the party structure was sometimes direct. James McMillan used the lessons he learned while
accumulating his personal fortune to good advantage when
chairing the Michigan Republican State Central Committee.
Businessmen also entered the Senate at more advanced ages. Over
half the chamber's lawyers held their seats before reaching fifty,
and just 11 per cent came to Washington after sixty. Among the
entrepreneurs, however, only one third took the oath before fifty,
and nearly one quarter after sixty. Having begun the political
course later in life, they were older when completing it.

The popular image of the novice utilizing a financial windfall
to play the part of senator was distorted. It is true that businessmen from eastern sections of the country were more politically
experienced than their western colleagues. (Eighty-one per cent
of the former but only 50 per cent of the latter could point to

eminent records.) Nevertheless, power was almost always reserved for those who had long planned to exercise it. Despite
frequent and exaggerated complaints, only 5 per cent of all
senators elected in the 1890's were newcomers to political life—
a percentage identical to the figure in the 1870's. But the popular
attention devoted to this tiny and insignificant group was disproportionate to its importance. These members rarely influenced
chamber proceedings. There were millionaires in Washington,
but their presence reflected political efforts. No matter who entered the game, winning demanded devoted attention.

Finally, the new structure of the Senate at the end of the
century decreased whatever influence a casual member could
exert. Senate leaders of both sides shared one common attribute:
political experience. Fifteen of the sixteen most powerful members in the 1890's had entered the chamber fully prepared to
exercise the authority of their office. Some were well educated;
others had been content with secondary and vocational training.
Some left very ordinary occupations; others came as leaders in
their fields. But invariably they had devoted many years to public
life, in Congress or in a vital party post. The amateur had no
place in their system.[7]

The preeminence of party helped insure that men from all
social backgrounds would have access to power. In the first years
of the Republic, in the absence of any widespread and systematic
party involvement in the electoral process, the more privileged
classes dominated the offices of government. The social origins of
political leaders in early America has not yet received extensive
analysis, but it would seem that fully one quarter of the senators
serving before 1825 came from elite backgrounds. Men like John
Quincy Adams, Philip Schuyler, Richard Lee, and James Monroe
filled many of the chamber's seats. Not that the new nation witnessed an absolute identification of social and political hier-
archies. But despite Mr. Jefferson's call for an aristocracy of talent

rather than of birth, the wellborn still held the key posts in his administration. No one argued that every citizen was innately fit to administer an office, and the organization that would pay no heed to any other considerations had yet to assume significance.

Andrew Jackson and his supporters first vigorously defended the inherent and natural capabilities of all citizens, regardless of birth or training, to wield authority. "The duties of all public offices are . . . so plain and simple," argued Jackson, "that men of intelligence may readily qualify themselves for their performance." Over the course of the next few decades, practice slowly caught up with creed, and high ranking members lost their favored position. When Whigs and Democrats, from 1840 onward, competed for popular favor and assumed increased significance in elections, senators of elite origins made up only 14 per cent of the chamber, while those from subsistence families composed one third of it. Active political organizations, to be sure, were not the only elements that affected recruitment. Opportunities for education, for entering the law, for succeeding in business, helped keep politics open. But parties, run by workers not aristocrats, provided the mechanism for elevating men of all social origins to power.[8]

In the decades after the Civil War, observers complained that the door to the Senate, like that to so many other institutions in America, was closing. The widespread lament, however, was inaccurate: the chamber was as open in 1901 as it had been in 1869. During these years parties took on new duties, legislative as well as electoral, and continued to pay little regard to circumstances of birth. The subsistent family farm aptly described the origins of 44 per cent of the senators in the 1890's as opposed to 40 per cent in the 1870's (Table 13). Moreover, family connections to politics among members also declined. The fathers of one third of those in the chamber in the 1870's had served in some sort of political post; two decades later the figure dropped to one fifth. These were not times of narrowing political opportunities.

Table 13. Senators' social origins, by decade of election
(per cent)

Origin	Decade		
	1870	1880	1890
Subsistence	40	38	44
Substantial	47	42	34
Elite	13	20	22
Number	(108)	(64)	(77)

Source: See Appendix A.

Party, however, could not erase all advantages of birth. Despite its influence the number of members from humble origins did not increase over these years. Moreover, 13 per cent of the senators in the 1870's were wellborn, but in the 1890's 22 per cent had inherited position and wealth. This increase, however, did not result from a general shift in the types of family occupations; it did not point to a rising influence of businessmen at the expense of farmers. Half of those elected soon after Reconstruction as well as at the end of the century came from agricultural backgrounds; 42 per cent, at both times, were raised by businessmen or professionals. Rather, in the 1890's fathers, regardless of occupations, more frequently ranked with the elite in these various divisions. Then too, slightly over half the members with elite backgrounds in the last decade of the century came from Southern states, where prestige and inherited position continued to carry disproportionate weight.

Despite these qualifications, privilege remained an asset even under party rule. The ambitious and wellborn, from the start of their careers, were able to devote great energies to political designs; free from pressing concerns for funds and closely acquainted with men of influence, they climbed the political ladder with advantages. Henry Cabot Lodge, for example, graduated from Harvard and satisfied his literary whims before giving complete attention to politics in the state legislature and in the House of Representatives; by 1893 he was well equipped to assume Senate duties. Similarly, Boise Penrose, equally fortunate, passed four years at Harvard and studied law before devoting the bulk of his time to politics. In 1897, after thirteen years in the Pennsylvania legislature as the Cameron-Quay lieutenant, he headed the machine and took the Senate seat.

Party did not insure the equal spread of influence to every social class. It did, however, guarantee that regardless of origins, members would have to follow a common route to power. Devotion to party and politics, not family and fortunes, determined success. The wellborn did share advantages, but political organizations at least insured that only the most significant assistance would affect access to office. During these years, as the proportions of members from elite families increased, the number of those from substantial households declined—from 47 per cent in the 1870's to 34 per cent in the 1890's. The help that ordinary town lawyers or businessmen could offer their offspring was not determinative; compared to less fortunate colleagues, they were not especially favored. The system then was not perfect. But it did reward diligence and dedication.

Finally, party also lessened, although by no means eradicated, the significance of occupational success upon political careers. Over half the lawyers elected to the Senate maintained very ordinary practices; only a few enjoyed outstanding legal achievements. Again, it is true that eminent businessmen entered politics more easily than the average shopkeeper and few laborers or mechanics made their way into the chamber. The Senate door was not wide open. Yet the ambitious politician could, and did, make his way in.

Both the Democratic and the Republican organizations in post-Civil War America helped establish this change. There existed no meaningful social distinctions between them; peculiar regional strengths and weaknesses explained whatever differences occurred. Senate Democrats, more often than their rivals, were raised in prosperous or influential families, tended to follow legal careers, and failed to achieve outstanding occupational success. Republican ranks, on the other hand, contained a disproportionate number of businessmen and members of the nation's industrial and financial elite. These variations, however, resulted from a geographical distribution of power and were not evidence of attempts to build an organization on a constricted social base.[9]

The dominance of Democrats in southern and border states and their lack of strength in the newer regions of the country was at the root of these distinctions. Western states most often elected senators from humble origins and usually presented the most dramatic opportunities for financial success. But the Southern-Democratic alliance was the product of war and reconstruction, and was in no way related to social or economic questions. The reasons for the failure of the party in western areas was more complex—new states, for example, tended to support the organization in the majority when they entered the Union—yet they too were unrelated to any particular party prejudice.

These differences disappeared in the states dividing their support between Democrats and Republicans. The wellborn in the Mid-Atlantic and Pacific sections entered one party as frequently as the other, and entrepreneurs were at home in both. Neither organization had a monopoly of the wealthy or the mobile. The increased importance of the two parties did not produce unique social characteristics in either. They both stimulated and were affected by the alterations in American politics during these years.

When newly elected senators recited the oath of allegiance, they were accustomed to the demands of public life. Whether they achieved their reputations in legislative, executive, or party positions, they grasped certain fundamental lessons. During the first years in politics, they learned to accommodate party leadership, and later, to exert authority. Upon arriving in Washington, they were not strangers to power. Senators knew how to give and take orders.

The institution was transformed by the training of its members. Recognizing the value of united action and effective discipline, political professionals appreciated the necessity for leadership and the value of a caucus. Inclined to accept authority rather than contest it, men trained in politics were likely to flatter their chieftains, not denigrate them. Allison, Aldrich, and Gorman faced men attuned to the procedures of party and the likes and dislikes of powerful chairmen. Politicians understood that outstanding assignments went to favorites, that steering committee members were appointed in McMillan's den. They expected influence and not talent to win out and knew the importance of standing well at the throne. Few members inherited a place in Washington and even the wealthiest worked hard and long to achieve position. After these efforts, there was little temptation to turn political maverick. A small minority did enter the Senate waving the standards of rebellion, but it faced a clear-cut choice: it could adapt to the ways of the majority in the hope of exercising power or use the seat to speak to the nation, not the Senate. A new sort of senator now dominated Washington. Ready to follow while eagerly awaiting the opportunity to lead, he helped alter the institution.

☆ V ☆

THE POLITICAL PROFESSION

God made a day twenty-four hours long for the ordinary man
whom he intended to inhabit the earth. For a man who is a
candidate for the United States Senate, a day thirty-six hours
long is required. After a man becomes a United States Senator,
if he still remains honest, he requires a day forty-eight hours
long. All of which conclusively proves that God never intended
any honest man to be ever a candidate for nor the occupant of a
seat in this exalted body.

Albert Beveridge on Senate life, 1899

By the last decades of the nineteenth century political life demanded undivided attention, and only men willing to sustain the
effort reaped the rewards. Fame, prestige, and power were reserved for those who diligently and persistently pursued them. For
Americans outside the perimeter of officeholding, a trip to Washington was a holiday excursion with an opportunity to gaze on
the great barbecue. But officials were usually far too busy to
attend a feast, let alone devour a hearty meal. Government service
left little opportunity for anything else. By 1890 politics was a
full-time profession.

In one of those faded red brick three-story hotels, inevitably
found within three blocks of the state legislature, twice every six
years in the middle of January, a tense and expectant candidate
learned that his ambition was fulfilled. For the next six weeks the
senator-elect received his first lessons in the costs of success. In
short order, he had to arrange food and drink for the legislators,
issue statements to the press, deliver greetings to well wishers, and

somehow find time to settle his private affairs. In March, relieved
and exhausted, the senator finally boarded the train to the capital.
For some the journey offered welcomed hours for relaxation. But
for newcomers to the national scene, it held the excitement and
tension of an adventure.

Senators from northern and western states made railroad connections through Baltimore, and from a window on the Baltimore
& Ohio caught their first glimpse of Washington. Uncultivated but
apparently fertile land separated the two cities, but on the out-
skirts of the capital, the scene suddenly changed. The grim red
lines of the earthworks built for defense still stood out harshly
from the landscape and were immediately followed by the ugly
remnants of the soldiers' camps. The dingy frame houses, bare of
whitewash and surrounded by pools of stagnant water, were now
filled with destitute Negroes, children, and geese. Only some
Southerners missed this tableau; enjoying the pleasures of travel
by boat, they viewed the green shores of the Potomac. Of course,
for many years the very first sight of the city from the water was a
crudely unfinished monument to a late Virginian.[1]

The Washington that greeted a senator in the 1890's scarcely
resembled the town familiar to his predecessors. Visiting English-
men in 1869 had a nasty way of comparing the capital to the
cardboard cities that Potemkin built to please the eye of his queen
as she traveled; they could hardly be blamed for suspecting that
Washington was dismantled once the congressmen departed. Private residences were few, and the great distances between them
were filled with poor Negro dwellings; few whites lived in the
city unless directly involved in national public life. The roads were
muddy and rocky, only Pennsylvania Avenue was paved, and
private carriages were rare. New senators were warned in advance
to leave their good horses and conveyances at home. On a fine
spring day when the wooded banks that lined the Potomac were
in first bloom, Washington could be beautiful; but when it rained
the streets turned to mire, stones jutted out of the earth, and the
capital looked like a poor frontier settlement.[2]

By the end of the century, however, the city assumed something of its modern-day appearance. The long main avenues were laid out and the improvement in municipal facilities was apparent in the sidewalk paving. The population was greatly increased—from 100,000 in 1870 to 279,000 by 1900. The northwest section grew secure in its reputation for fashion, and a few shrewd Senators, like John Sherman, benefited from wise real estate investments. The government also began to sponsor construction. Senator Cole, returning to the capital in 1896 after an absence of nearly twenty years, was struck by the change. Describing the new Post Office, the Library of Congress, and the sumptuous private residences, he enthusiastically told his family how much Washington was improved.[3] The capital had become a city.

Even before inspecting the chamber, newly arrived senators discovered the most important truth about Washington living: its expense. Costly rooms at the outstanding hotels, the Willard or the Arlington, were small and poorly ventilated, a combination bound to dissatisfy men frequently called upon to spend their summers in session. Moreover, the high-priced food was too rich for a regular diet. Families presented further complications. Boarding a wife and children was expensive, and hotel lobbies made poor playgrounds for growing youngsters. The alternatives —to build or rent a house—were beyond many senators' means. Maintaining only a Washington residence was political suicide and the upkeep of two homes was simply too great. Some senators therefore decided to live alone when Congress met. "I wish you would send me," George Hoar plaintively wrote his wife in Massachusetts, "three hundred seventy-five thousand dollars, and seventy-five cents. The seventy-five cents is to pay a washerwoman and the remainder to buy a house to live in in Washington." Louisiana's Randall Gibson preferred to go into debt to build in the capital; at least the family would be together.[4]

Members' $5,000 salaries could not cover living, transportation, and entertainment expenses, and North Carolina's one-time Civil War governor, Zebulon Vance, felt compelled to explain the limits of his average income before taking Mrs. Florence Martin for his second wife. "From my first entrance into public life," the Senator informed her, "I have been placed in the very trying situation of occupying high political positions without the money to live in a style commensurate with their supposed dignity." Yet he made no concessions. If he had money for a carriage, he rode; if not, he walked. "Such has been my manner of life, and if I had believed you to be a giddy woman," he warned, "bent on making a big display as a Senator's wife I should never have asked you to occupy that position." And then wistfully, almost sadly, Vance added: "Not even if you could have brought with you the means for that display."[5]

" 'A Senator's wife,' " mused Blanche Butler over the press notices of her engagement to Mississippi Republican Adelbert Ames in 1870. "Of course it makes no difference what Senator," she lightly added. "It is sufficient that it is 'A Senator.' That sublime word gilds the man, no matter what his deformities."[6] Wives of more experience, however, were often less enthusiastic about their husbands' positions. To some Senate service meant little more than long separations and the priority of public duty. "Disappointed as I felt at your not coming," Olive Cole characteristically confessed to her husband, "I would have felt more to have known you left the Senate when you were needed there." And with genuine concern, George Hoar, upon winning Senate election, revealed to his son: "I feel very deeply how much the action of our Legislature will disturb the comfort of our home."[7]

Letters were often the only contact for families during the sessions, and if historians are thankful for the frequent correspondence of husband and wife—between declarations of love news of Senate politics made its way into these pages—those more personally involved found such communication more frustrating than satisfying. Senators wrote faithfully, at times sitting at their desks and ignoring colleagues' addresses to finish scribbling a note home. The setting, to be sure, was not ideal. J. P. Jones complained to his wife that his Senate seat was a very uncomfortable place for writing to her, especially since there was so much confusion and interruption there.[8] But for lack of time it had to do. Not surprisingly, members made great efforts to predict adjournment dates. Vance took an unusual interest in the close of the 1880 meeting, and when it appeared that business would stretch over the summer, he hastily advised Mrs. Martin: "I am not going to wait until September, I just can't do it. Congress or no Congress I am going to Louisville to marry you in June."[9] The call of politics did have its limits.

Senators' wives in Washington may often have envied their peers back home, for during these years social life in the capital began to make strenuous demands. As the city grew physically more comfortable, it gained social attractions. Bored with New York and Boston society, Madeleine Lee moved to Washington, earnestly hoping to study the power and machinery of government. And Henry Adams' fictional heroine had many real life imitators. When Grant presided at his seven-course dinners, entertainments and obligations encompassed only a small circle, rarely including the wives of public officials. By the end of the century, however, as Senator Henry Dawes observed, "prominent residents, having become an important element" in the city, took a prominent place in society, eventually disputing "the first place with the official circle itself." Washington became noted for its winter season.[10]

Postponing marriage until their careers were well under way, most senators, regardless of social origins, entered families of substance. The matches, like Vance's, may not have secured independent means, but they did assure the rising politician of a mate willing and capable, if not enthusiastic, to carry out an official role. Nevertheless, the demands of Washington life, despite a favored social position, put even the most agreeable wife to the test.[11]

Protocol reflected the institution's importance. Senators' wives, required to call first only upon households that outranked their own, faced a list that was thankfully short: the President, the

Vice-President, and the Chief Justice of the Supreme Court. After the 1886 Succession Act—placing the Secretary of State before the Senate's President *pro tempore* in line for the presidency—wives of cabinet members and the other Supreme Court Justices tried to gain entry into this group; but the Senate, because it confirmed their husbands' appointments, took precedence. Similarly, the diplomatic corps (the Senate confirmed treaties), and representatives (the lower house), also ranked lower in the hierarchy. Every Thursday from one o'clock until six, the Senator's family was at home. Mrs. Henry Cabot Lodge disliked the practice, judging Washington society in no way equal to Boston's. However, she too, for the good of Henry's career, finally agreed to stay put on Thursday afternoons.[12]

Diligent hostesses returned as many calls in person as possible, not content to have a servant simply leave a card. Alice Hill, wife of Colorado's senator N. B. Hill, instructed Mrs. Edward Wolcott who was about to come to Washington: "Every P.M., rain or shine, cold or warm, I make calls from two o'clock till nearly six . . . I have returned [in February alone] over four hundred calls and have three hundred yet to make. Sometimes I find it pleasant, but often get into curious places."[13] No wonder wives were willing to let their husbands go off alone to rule the nation.

Senators themselves found social life more a pleasant diversion than a tedious occupation. Henry Dawes was certain that Henry Anthony "wore himself out in the discharge of duties incumbent on a professional diner-out," but most colleagues welcomed the obligations. Party divisions were usually forgotten after the daily adjournment—the poker game at McMillan's was one notable exception. Republicans were sincerely sorry to see Democrat Calvin Brice return to Ohio, for among his other virtues, his house had been "the greatest social centre ever known to Washington." Earlier the Whitneys had set the pace, but the Brices, constantly offering splendid entertainment, left them "out of the running."[14] To his close friend, Thomas Bell, James McMillan confided:

"Our life in Washington you would say was very gay but as we do not go out to large gatherings except at the White House we do not think so. We give one or two dinners a week and go out three or four times."[15] Perhaps it was not very gay, but the McMillans dined socially practically every night of the week.

Capitol Hill was not as drastically altered as the city, but by the last years of the century senators enjoyed new comforts and conveniences designed to help them work more efficiently. Space was a perennial problem. Few of the vast unused areas of the Capitol building were suited for occupancy and designers hesitated to tamper with a national monument. "An architect has told us," Henry Dawes complained to his colleagues, "that it would not be according to true taste to put outside windows on our committee-rooms, and we have surrendered . . . We cannot have any committee rooms because some architect saw once in England just such a place."[16] In the 1890's, however, the Senate rented the nearby Maltby Building with its eighty-odd rooms. At the price of a short walk, newcomers were assured decent working conditions. Moreover, the Senate provided every member with a secretary, at $1,500 a year, and a new typewriter. The staff and equipment, although not abundant, usually proved adequate.[17]

Ventilation in the chamber had always been notorious. "The weather has been very hot," complained Benjamin Harrison in the spring of 1881, "and the sessions of the Senate held in a chamber that has no window opening outdoors makes a stay of six hours in it very oppressive."[18] A decade later, however, the system—ducts under the senators' chairs—was modernized; at the same time electricity replaced gas lighting, and despite all the facetious remarks on the temperature of senatorial oratory, the chamber became cooler. If appearance was never made subservient to utility, at least the Capitol and its environs were impressive sights. A broad expanse of green now led up to and encircled the building, and inside the chamber a dark green carpet set off the mahogany desks. The Ladies Reception Room was bedecked with inlaid tiles, satin upholstery, and olive and crimson draperies.[19] All in all, the setting was pleasant, if not always conducive to work.

Freshmen members appreciated every comfort since the first few months in Washington were challenging and difficult. Senate initiation was never easy, even for those most familiar with political life, but by the 1890's the formal political structure made the process still more laborious. New senators diligently attempted to master the procedures, not permitting any interference with their education. "If after examining the matter," Ben Tillman informed a constituent, "I think it wise to introduce a bill I will do so; I am too busy now with other more important matters. And above all, I have to learn the ropes before I can be of much service or use."[20] Petty obstacles often seemed unsurmountable. "I shall never learn to know these Senators by sight if I live here a century," Hoar despairingly informed his wife. Questions of greater importance provoked even more anxiety.[21]

Most newcomers were preoccupied with power and influence within the institution, scrutinizing leaders for signs of favoritism with all the intensity of Calvinists examining omens for salvation. John Spooner hoped to win his place through hard labor, convinced that "a new man must demonstrate his ability and willingness to work in order to acquire status in the Senate."[22] Albert Beveridge, leaving nothing to chance in his climb to success, worried almost pathologically about his progress. At Mark Hanna's daughter's wedding in June 1903, Aldrich suggested that Beveridge come by to discuss pending financial legislation. Hearing nothing more definite by the end of July, the Indiana Senator grew frantic. "I want to get into the harness," he whined to Orville Platt, and decided to dispatch a telegram to the Senate leader. Beveridge read and reread Aldrich's response until he finally concluded that it was not sufficiently cordial; and he was beside himself when Platt was requested to arrive at the Senator's home on August 6,

United States Senators, 43rd Congress, 1874

United States Senate, 55th Congress, 1898

while he was not asked to attend until the tenth. Only Platt's constant support enabled him to regain some composure, and he went off to Rhode Island ready to do whatever Aldrich demanded.[23] The stakes of the game, after all, were high and senators were understandably anxious about the outcome.

Constituents and the state press carefully watched their representatives' Washington progress, but new men could hardly satisfy immediate expectations. N. P. Hill resolved to be in his seat for all Senate sessions, to try and pave the way for important legislation affecting the state, and to look after local interests; nothing more could be expected from freshmen senators, he informed his critics. "So much is expected of me both in South Carolina and outside," Ben Tillman explained to his wife, fearing he would be unable to meet the demands.[24] Veterans' efforts to ease the rigors of initiation were appreciated. "I always take an interest in helping a new Senator to start right," Spooner declared. "I know how a new man in the Senate feels and how nice it is to have someone take an early interest in you."[25]

Nevertheless, freshmen were still intimidated by their surroundings. Tradition decreed that newcomers not deliver any speeches in their first session, but they were usually too frightened in any case. A "feeling of awe oppressed me so heavily all the first years I was here," admitted Timothy Howe in 1868. "I had been trained all my life in such encounters and yet I never knew anything like timidity or awe until I came here."[26] And his successors, regardless of their preparation, shared his sentiments. The unfamiliar quality of the work combined with a desire to impress leaders and constituents drove freshmen senators to the peak of their energies. "I have never worked harder in my life," claimed Hill, and Beveridge concluded: "For a man who is a candidate for the United States Senate, a day thirty-six hours long is required. After a man becomes a United States Senator . . . he requires a day forty-eight hours long."[27]

Timidity and exhaustion alternated with anxiety and apprehension when members first entered the chamber. After years of service, some tensions decreased, but other concerns invariably replaced them. As senators grew older and their children prepared to leave home, separation from family became more painful. "I am at an age now," Senator Richard Coke informed Texas governor James Hogg in his letter of resignation, "when, if ever I am to have any pleasure with my family I must have it. My reasons are purely domestic for desiring to be at home."[28] Those remaining in Washington faced the persistent pressures of reelection, and even the most obliging senator tired of filling constituents' requests. "I am continually beset by individuals, newspapers, socialities, churches and the like for more money than I have got," Francis Warren impatiently notified his friends. "I am also bedeviled with all the enormous wants of everybody in Wyoming. . . . I am tired of having everybody think I am to be robbed because they suspect I want another term in the Senate . . . They can take their Senatorship and stick it in their— pocket."[29]

Other senators became aware of the implications of success. "The higher you get," philosophized Matt Ransom, "the more danger of falling and the longer the fall. Of course all this fills me with trouble, and sometimes the consciousness of doing all your duty does not sustain you." Senate routine also took its toll, and after some thirty years of service, J. P. Jones admitted that sitting all day in the chamber had become tedious and tiring. Soon, with great enthusiasm, he declared himself free, emancipated from Senate duty.[30]

Daily meetings wore thin the patience of the most tolerant men. "It would be a capital thing," acknowledged George Hoar, "to attend Unitarian conventions if there were not Unitarians there, so too it would be a delightful thing to be a United States Senator if you did not have to attend the sessions of the Senate."[31] As party leadership and caucus work swelled in importance, sessions became more tedious; fewer speeches were made for the purpose of swaying votes, and attendance turned into a dull but half-necessary chore. Members excluded from the party's inner circle, deprived of good committee assignments and positions of influence, found political life increasingly unrewarding. "It is becoming more and more evident to me," Henry Dawes despondently wrote to his wife in 1890, "that I am 'lagging superfluous on the stage' and that I had better 'bring home my trunk' with me."[32] Outsiders did not reap many satisfactions.

Most comment was prompted by the great burden of work. Working in obscurity on tangential committee duties was irksome, and the methodical or ambitious senators who performed these tasks publicized their travail. "I thought I knew something of hard work in my profession," observed one-time lawyer Daniel Pratt in 1870, "but it was little in comparison to what I am called upon to perform now." And a fellow attorney, Matt Carpenter, confessed three years later: "I am on four committees and the result is I do not have a moment to myself from one end of the week to the other."[33] The weight of Senate labors increased in the next decades and the incentives to fulfill them also heightened. Francis Warren, somewhat prone to complaint, did not exaggerate when declaring in 1891: "The calls that are made upon a public servant, if conscientiously attended to, leave a man no leisure or peace. There is always something to do." His own schedule provided an appropriate illustration: up early attending department and committee meetings at least four times a week, in the afternoons sitting in Senate sessions, every evening answering twenty to one hundred letters.[34] And Warren was fortunate; Wyoming constituents rarely bothered him with Washington visits. After many years of service, John Sherman still objected to the routine, and Spooner never tired of recounting the multitude of tasks he performed without thanks.[35] By 1890 the senatorship was often a tiring job.

"As a matter of money and getting along," noted Francis Warren, "no man can keep even in politics. I cannot live within my means depending upon political income. I find everyone else in the same fix."[36] Unhappily, for their families at least, not everyone could fall back upon the large private income that the Wyoming Senator received from the Francis E. Warren Livestock Company. When Donelson Caffery simply told his wife: "You know the [Senate] salary doesn't support us," the alternatives they faced were less clear. The need for supplementary income was pressing, but by the end of the century Senate duties were so time consuming that members commonly shared the most ordinary of worries: how to maintain a family in dignity.[37]

In 1871 Timothy Howe informed his niece from Washington: "I have been studying law for the past week . . . so I have given but little attention to the legislature."[38] Ten years later J. P. Jones, busily winning and losing mining fortunes in Nevada, would have been pleased to emulate Howe's example, but he enjoyed less liberty. Jones found, as he worriedly told his wife, that his absence from the chamber had become a topic of discussion and remark among his colleagues; it seemed clear that in order to maintain in the future the position of influence achieved earlier through his friendship with Conkling, he would have to stay at his post and dutifully fulfill the responsibilities of the office. There was no mistake here. Absenteeism, Jones concluded, was now regarded as a lack of appreciation for the Senate, even an indication of contempt for it.[39]

John Spooner, campaigning for a seat in 1890, pledged to a party caucus that if elected he "would have no client but the people of Wisconsin." Convinced that "no man can faithfully serve in the Senate, and practice law," he kept his word. There was hardly enough time for both professions.[40] Nevada's William Stewart discovered the same truth. "I have been living in hopes of being able to find time to attend to some private business," he recounted to his brother, "but it has been truly impossible . . . I am literally overwhelmed with matters connected with my office as Senator." To a friend in Butte, Montana, he confided: "I am not worth a cent for private business now. You know it is said that it is impossible to serve two masters. The public service is the Deity that

I am now serving, and although I have not lost my love for Mammon, I have neglected that individual in the most shameful way."[41] William Vilas, Spooner's Democratic colleague, finding that "public cares and obligations interfere with the proper consideration of private business," began to turn away clients. "I shall have either to quit politics or quit everything else," moaned Zebulon Vance, and George Hoar feared that he would have to abandon the practice of law altogether if he "would succeed as a Senator."[42]

The conflicts between private careers and the political profession were well understood by those in and out of public life. Would-be officeholders and senators were warned in advance of the difficulties. "The path of the politician," J. Scott Harrison lectured his son Benjamin, the future senator and President, "is at best a rugged one, full of thorns, and but a few roses, and before treading it, a man should accumulate enough of this world's goods to fall back upon . . . Were I in your place I would not enter the arena of politics until my private fortune would justify taking a *final* leave of my profession."[43] Newspaper editor Frank Munsey also counseled Albert Beveridge to give first attention to the law. He told Beveridge that Senator Stephen Elkins wisely promised his bride, "not to go into politics until he had made his fortune, and he kept that promise." L. T. Michener, veteran Indiana politician, seconded the recommendation. Senators' law practices were ruined during terms of office, and members had to begin "from the bottom of the ladder," after Washington service.[44] Ideally, concluded Francis Warren, "a man ought to keep out of politics as a business."[45] But by the 1890's this alternative barely existed.

For some the incompatibility of Senate duty and business demands was so great that they left public life. Stephen White had spent fifteen years working his way up to win the California senatorship in 1893, but as his first term neared its end, he wondered whether to seek re-election. "The duties of the place," he admitted, "are exceedingly pleasant to me," but the expenses were too onerous. "When I came here," White told interested supporters, "I enjoyed a very good practice and notwithstanding my absence from home I have been able to keep matters in very good shape. Still I cannot expect to do this indefinitely . . . Clients will not stand the absence of their attorneys for a very great period, and it is unreasonable to expect them to do so." Calculating that he would turn forty-six when his term expired, that "the best business years of my life will be those immediately to follow," the Senator determined not to emulate the example of men who gave their lives to their country and died to "leave their families almost penniless."[46] In 1899 White left politics for the law, and during the next two years provided for his family before suffering a fatal heart attack.

Senators taking less pleasure in public life ended Washington careers more easily. Nevada's James Fair, having accumulated a fortune in the Comstock mines, entered the chamber after a brief political apprenticeship; however, he never found the duties of the position appealing and consistently neglected Senate affairs. He soon informed Johnson Camden, another colleague torn between the call of politics and business: "It was impossible for me to return to the Senate for another term without a great personal sacrifice . . . And to tell the honest truth, strange as it may appear, I really had no desire to return to the Senate for another six years." When Camden himself left office a year later, Fair happily remarked: "You and I have too many other cares to be bothered with the Senate . . . I am glad you are troubled no more with that hateful Senate as I know you will be much more happy."[47] Another Comstock millionaire, William Sharon, was tired of Washington after one term. Senator Sharon, observed J. P. Jones, seemed as uncomfortable in his seat as a fish out of water. West Virginia's Henry Davis, after twelve years at the capital, announced in 1882 that he would not stand for reelection. "Business is more agreeable to me than politics," he told the press, "and I am now engaged in lumbering, mining, banking and farming . . . My ambition is to make a success of these enterprises."[48] Politics was too annoying and distracting.

Most members, however, attempted to satisfy both ambition and appetite. Lawyers worked at a frantic pace whenever the Senate adjourned. Albert Beveridge devoted every spare moment to his office, and since no one fulfilled Hoar's daydream by willing him a legacy like Cicero's, he spent the summers diligently at practice.[49] "I am not wedded to my place here in the Senate," Benjamin Harrison explained to his supporters. "With my ideas of the responsibilities and the duties connected with it, it is a laborious place, and the pay is so small that I am compelled to fill my vacations with hard work to supplement my income."[50]

During sessions, many attorneys like Harrison, relied upon associates, and Stephen White, for one, trusted to his secretaries; businessmen, for their part, frequently brought sons into the firm, or also expected partners to carry the enterprise. Yet these arrangements were never fully satisfactory. "If by any chance I am re-elected," Harrison promised C. C. Henry, "I may have to devote my time to passing a bankrupt law to pay your debt that way. I will not for another term impose upon my law partner to show profits when I can't show work."[51] Stephen White prepared briefs in Washington but realized that clients would not wait much longer; the senior McMillan wanted his son to enter the business but understood that at this juncture the young man would profit more from an independent venture.[52]

Francis Warren's trusted associates carefully supervised his ranching interests, but nevertheless, the Senator was incessantly complaining of being "entirely at sea," and all too often without "advice from home." "I want to hear very often," he endlessly reminded subordinates, "even if there may seem to be nothing to write about." And the constant refrain of "keep me advised," pointed to the frustrations encountered in attaining the goal.[53] Convinced that profits came only to those who "watch out closely and attend strictly to business," Warren found geographical separation from his company exasperating, and his reaction was not atypical. "Everything seems to be at loose ends," Senator Charles Fairbanks complained to his brother in Indiana. "I have no information . . . I am in ignorance of my own business . . . I cannot stand it to have matters go on as they are."[54] Such were the penalties of public service.

The Senate did offer some opportunities to further particular business interests—not by the roundabout effects of legislative decisions but by contacts made through chamber membership. When Johnson Camden first ran for a seat, he was fully cognizant of its many uses, both for West Virginia's economic development and his own enterprises. "The easy access which it opens up to make the acquaintance of the men you want to know," was a valuable attraction.[55] And William Allison, in his early years of service, performed crucial labors for Iowa's entrepreneurs in the eastern money markets. Moreover, senators profited from the successes of their colleagues; men of great wealth were more than generous with loans and tips for needy friends.[56]

Nevertheless, most senators in the last decades of the nineteenth century remained in office despite economic circumstances, adjusting as best they could to any hardships. "From the financial standpoint," declared John Spooner in 1897, "I ought not to go back to the Senate," and a good many peers could truthfully have uttered similar sentiments.[57] Stephen White, extraordinarily concerned for his family's welfare, left public office, but those who remained had somehow to rationalize placing public life over other obligations. The problem was more widespread than outsiders imagined, for senators labeled millionaires often fell very short of the mark. J. P. Jones, for example, was as concerned with his income as any of his colleagues, and on these grounds his wife frequently tried to persuade him to return to private life. Convinced that he would be happier and more independent there, she feared that the worries of business added to those of politics would prove to be too heavy a burden for her husband term after term. She was not exaggerating the tensions, but nevertheless Jones remained in Washington, missing economic opportunities while hoping to accumulate a fortune.[58]

Political careers demanded too much time and energy for anyone primarily dedicated to furthering financial enterprises. The chamber did not deserve to be popularly known as a club. The misnomer implied a leisure and comfort that few senators ever experienced.

The compensations of office, the opportunity to exercise the power inherent in a Senate seat, enabled most members to tolerate all the accompanying frustration and anxieties. The inconveniences could not weaken its attraction for professional politicians. Announcing his decision to seek re-election, New England's Joseph Hawley unhesitantly declared: "That is the only political ambition that I cherish without concealment or reservation. Suggestions concerning anything else I treat with respect, but they do not disturb or divert me." And Justin Morrill had long since decided that "whatever future public service I may render will be in the Senate . . . There is no gift, no office to which I could be appointed, that I would accept in preference to a seat in the United States Senate."[59] John Spooner, for all his financial worries, agreed that a seat in the chamber "is the best position I think in the United States." No other post held any appeal for William Stewart, and Idaho's Fred Dubois stated unequivocally: "There is no office I would have except that of Senator."[60] The Senate was the place for anyone whose greatest satisfaction was political life.

Johnson Camden thought himself "much 'fonder' of business excitement than political excitement," but not long after leaving Washington he regretted his decision and thought to return. "My business matters are now all in good shape," he notified potential supporters, "and in condition to be taken care of by others . . . I like to work out problems of development, and moneymaking, but don't care much about either after it is accomplished." Friends insisted that his private affairs could not stand "the conflict between them and the incumbency of a political place," and warned that his interests were entirely too large and in their present shape require too much . . . personal supervision and care."[61] But Camden ultimately followed the advice of fellow businessman William Thompson. "What have you been getting money for all this time?" demanded Thompson. "What are you going to do with it? How much of it are you going to take to the Other Shore? How much advantage is it going to be to your children to heap up their mounds . . . My dear fellow, money is simply the exchange medium for what you want." And Camden soon returned to political life.[62]

Of course, after several years of service, members often felt ill-equipped or ill-disposed to take up former occupations. "I do not know," Henry Dawes told his wife in a typical mood of discouragement, "what I can do for a living after these long years of work here." And so despite a fringe position in the Senate, he ran for re-election. Vance complained of heavy political demands but to any suggestion that he leave office, he simply replied: "I don't want to practice law any more."[63] The frustrations were at least familiar.

As for other political offices, the governor's chair and a House seat, unable to compete with Senate attractions, were stepping stones rather than resting places for aspiring politicians. Francis Warren fondly recalled that the governor held "the whip hand as an Executive, whereas one is not much of anybody as one of 88 Senators," but he, like most state heads, came to Washington as soon as possible. Constitutional restrictions on gubernatorial re-elections often forced incumbents to look elsewhere and then too, as one Southerner noted, the typical $3,000 a year salary was so small that he "was financially unable to continue in the office."[64] Stephen White, invariably conscious of money matters, refused to run for the place, fearful that, if elected, his "practice would nec-

essarily be destroyed or rather lost." Some tired of life in a pro-
vincial capital and others soon found state boundaries too narrow
for the grandeur of their political programs. After all the vital
decisions affecting the nation were shaped in Washington.[65]

Although some members of the House steadfastly defended the
honor of their body and never would admit that entering the
Senate was a promotion, in post-Civil War America, Senate election was, as James Blaine put it, "a call to go up higher." Virginia's John Daniel, sensitive to the pride of the House, referred
to a congressman's Senate election as a "translation." "I will not
say 'promoted' to the Senate," he explained to a New York
audience, "as members do not recognize that as the proper word,
until after their translation has taken place."[66] The Senate offered
longer terms, greater prestige, more opportunity to impress national politics. "House discussion," recalled Henry Dawes after
service in both bodies, "had little deliberation in it. One had to
watch his chance, be instantaneous in seizing it, and then, with
eyes on the clock delivering what was possible within two given
spaces . . . On the other hand, no one jumps to the floor in the
Senate, but deliberately rises when he is moved to speak."[67] Addresses were as long as necessary and sometimes longer, but at
least members had their full say. Moreover, senators almost
always exercised greater power within the state, determining the
fate of congressmen's ambitions. For good political reasons, few
representatives during these years neglected the opportunity to
enter the upper chamber.

Once elected, the greatest temptation to leave the Senate was a
cabinet post offer. Members, however, frequently rejected the
invitation and their reasons highlighted the appeals of Senate life.
The lofty and unfettered quality of the service came first to mind
as they pondered alternatives. J. P. Jones flatly informed his wife
shortly after Arthur became President that he would not consider
entering the cabinet. He much preferred the Senate position, judging it to be more dignified and independent.[68] John Spooner ex-

plained his preference for the chamber in even greater detail. "It is a place of much more independence, and of much greater dignity," he told supporters. "A Senator is elected for six years, and his tenure is not subject to the power of the President." A cabinet officer, on the other hand, felt innumerable annoyances and pressures. "He is subject to the whim and caprice of a President, and may have his life made miserable by the jealousy and intrigue of other members of the official family."[69] Edward Pierce warned his friend Charles Sumner that the cabinet threatened "uncertainty of tenure and a measure of insubordination," while the Senate possessed the virtues of "fixedness and independence." And Congressman James Clarkson reminded Allison that the shift meant "going from a place of power to one of dependence."[70]

Most colleagues were also certain that the Senate offered greater political responsibility than a cabinet post. Spooner, for his part, dreaded the administrative duties of an executive post, "almost infinite in detail."[71] Then too, a cabinet invitation usually went to the chamber's leaders; already occupying positions of maximum influence, they were not likely to accept the subordination demanded by a President. Wondering whether to accept McKinley's 1897 cabinet offer, Allison recognized that in the Senate he possessed "a power and influence to wield just now which no other man on the Republican side could possibly wield." Advisers did not even believe that the cabinet could further whatever presidential ambitions the Iowa Senator held and Congressman Jonathan Dolliver took great pains to convince him that "the Cabinet has long ceased to be a stepping-stone" to the White House. It entailed too close an identification with the President; the officer shared all the responsibility for the administration's failures, received very little of the credit, and at the same time was alienated from his constituents. After performing laborious tasks, he was likely to be a "back number in politics," when the term expired. No one was surprised when the Republican caucus chairman preferred to remain in the chamber.[72]

All these advantages notwithstanding, some senators in every administration moved over to the cabinet. The opportunity to serve as *the* Secretary of State rather than as *a* senator was enticing, and national figures, like James Blaine or John Carlisle, unable to achieve power within the chamber, welcomed the change. Nevertheless, the independence and influence of the Senate fixed most members to their seats.[73]

Positions on the Court or in an embassy were even less attractive. Both places usually ended political careers and neither offered compensating rewards. Senators did not enjoy "searching through records and writing opinions," and the Supreme Court salary of $10,000 a year, with no opportunity to earn further remuneration, was not in itself any temptation.[74] Not many members had the funds to fulfill ambassadorial duties, and in any event, they valued a seat in the chamber more highly. "I suppose," speculated George Hoar when turning down a McKinley offer, "there never was a Minister to England who would not have eagerly exchanged his place for that of Senator if the opportunity had come to him."[75] The vice-presidency was universally regarded as a sinecure; as L. Q. C. Lamar put it, a spot to gain "four years of rest and a good income."[76] Senators judged election to the White House a promotion, but they were too dedicated to the exercise of power to seek any other position.

During these years, about a dozen senators left the chamber for different posts, and Benjamin Harrison went on to become President. Senate service, however, satisfied most political ambitions. Only death could dislodge many occupants from their places; Morrill, Hoar, Platt, Hale, Quay, Hanna, Allison, McMillan and Gorman died in office at ripe old ages. Others voluntarily retired, too old or too tired to fulfill its burdens. After leaving politics, George Edmunds enjoyed a Philadelphia law practice, and Philetus Sawyer passed long peaceful days in Oshkosh, Wisconsin. Younger and less fortunate men, defeated in the legislature, were often unwilling to return to county seats after years in the capital. Some lawyers moved to New York or continued their practice in Washington. Other colleagues frequently sought quieter surroundings. "I doubtless would be as much disappointed as every public man seems to have been with retired farm life," confessed L. Q. C. Lamar, "but the delusion is strong upon me that I would be happy on a farm."[77] Still others desired the comfort of the familiar, more or less content to follow old occupations in native regions. Those unwilling or unable to return to former pursuits often qualified for a political sinecure, subsisting on the steady, if small income.[78] In any event, after leaving the chamber, members usually withdrew from the excitement and challenge of public life. The Senate was the peak of their careers.

By the last decades of the nineteenth century, only men devoted to politics found Washington life tolerable. The rewards of business were everywhere apparent, and not without forethought had senators determined to pass by financial opportunities. They made their decisions fully aware that political life demanded sacrifices. To accuse them of coming to the Capitol for the express purpose of making money was unfair; there were countless other paths more appropriate to that ambition.[79] Politics was not a detour, a short-cut worth trying. It was an entirely separate trail, with its own pitfalls and delights. Professionals now plotted the routes and faithfully followed its turns and twists. For better or for worse, the day of the amateur was over.

THE STRUCTURE OF STATE POLITICS

Just now it may seem a long time before the next campaign, but it is easier to maintain an organization than to create one. Organization is half the battle. When party organization is perfect, campaigns are more easily conducted and victory more certain.

Observations of Senator James McMillan's
state party manager H. C. Tillman, 1888

"It is useless for anyone to boss the politics of a state," Jerome Chaffee, one-time Colorado senator, informed John Logan, his former colleague, in 1886. "It may do for once but the people won't take it for a steady diet. A leader must give the people the greatest latitude or they will rebel. How anybody can expect the patriots of a state to stand such practices as in Pennsylvania I can't see. You and I would be the first to rebel."[1]

Had Chaffee observed the conditions of government ten years later, he would have been even more astonished at the diet of his countrymen. Pennsylvania did not rebel; Senator Matt Quay was more invincible than his predecessors, Simon and Donald Cameron, and Boise Penrose patiently waited his turn. Tom Platt commanded in New York, and across the Hudson Senators James Smith and William Sewell were in firm control. New England Senators Aldrich, Hale, and Gallinger belied Chaffee's expectations, as did Senators Martin in Virginia, Elkins in West Virginia, and McMillan in Michigan. In 1896, despite Chaffee's optimistic prediction, Democratic and Republican chieftains efficiently superintended the course of state politics.

Effective leaders rarely dominated the pre-Civil War parties. Webster, Clay, and Calhoun enjoyed great prominence, leaving indelible marks on Washington, but they did not systematically attend to the narrow and detailed concerns of Massachusetts, Kentucky, and South Carolina politics. There were times when several vigorous Whig county bosses joined together or the head of a Jeffersonian city machine united with two upcountry politicians; but these alliances were usually designed to secure only local control.[2] In the post-Reconstruction decades, however, a new pattern transformed state affairs: centralized power became the norm, not the exception. Party heads and their subordinates exerted consistent authority that reached into isolated hamlets as well as into the populous capitals, into rural counties as well as into city wards. By 1900 the monarch had displaced the feudal princes.

The chamber's sturdy leather chairs were plush thrones for the new party bosses. During the last years of the nineteenth century, would-be leaders contested Senate elections, and the victor won party power as well as the trip to Washington. The coincidence was not surprising. The senatorship satisfied a politician's grandest ambition, and state authority was at once a prerequisite for and a guarantee of a place in the chamber.

Each state party nominated a Senate candidate in caucus, and the majority then elected its choice in formal session. This system compelled Senate hopefuls to exert wide influence. The more supporters in the caucus, the better the opportunity for nomination; the larger the numbers in the assembly, the greater the chance for election. To make their position secure, aspirants vigorously courted the ward captains, the county chairmen, and the convention presidents. They had ample time to marshal forces and distribute favors for commitments in the Senate race were almost as well known as party labels. Constituents demanded that a candidate for the legislature declare his allegiances well in advance, and state laws often compelled him to respect the pledge.

Invariably, the Washington contest entered every election district.

Would-be senators regularly linked private ambitions to the party's welfare. In the first place, it made no sense to win the endorsement of a perennial minority. Moreover, no one could risk antagonizing a substantial portion of the membership; dissidents might ally with the opposition, turning victory into defeat. Under these circumstances, candidates relied upon the organizational machinery to smooth over animosities, confident that it could forestall any bolts. In Maryland, Arthur Gorman always asked the Democrats to convene in caucus to approve his re-election, even when the meetings became empty formalities, and in Rhode Island, Charles Brayton, Nelson Aldrich's clever manager, followed identical tactics.[3] The reasoning was straightforward: any mechanism that consolidated and harmonized party ranks was to be carefully maintained. Thus, from the start of their careers, senators encouraged caucus action to promote unity. They would retain the habit long after coming to Washington.

Political observers could predict the outcome of January Senate elections once the November ballots were counted. Factional squabbles might occasionally confuse matters, but a party chieftain was usually in firm control. In Wisconsin, for example, the 1896 Republican majority prepared, without debate or dissension, to send John Spooner to the Capitol. With equanimity, Spooner noted: "No other name has been mentioned."[4] The state leader also frequently dictated the choice of junior senator. With Aldrich's approval, George Wetmore ended his worldwide traveling to join the Philosophy Club at McMillan's. New York's Chauncey Depew satisfied an old dream because Tom Platt finally consented, and West Virginia's outstanding glass manufacturer, Nathan Scott, came to the chamber when Stephen Elkins approved his candidacy.[5] Such efforts were not always successful. Indiana's Republican senior senator, Charles Fairbanks, owned one place but he could not prevent the extraordinarily eager

Albert Beveridge from grabbing the other.[6] In most instances, however, a close friend, obliging partisan, or potential heir accompanied the head of the party to Washington. Order now characterized Senate elections as well as proceedings.

Senators, through their own efforts or by carefully delegating responsibility, exercised unprecedented state authority. As professional politicians dedicated to the needs of the party, they ruled their organizations. Always prepared to meet and satisfy the most burdensome political demand, they would not hesitate to undertake a long and tiring campaign to win votes. When tact would cajole opponents, they exercised it, and when the party chest was low, they energetically set about filling it. As a result, centralized control defined the structure of state politics at the end of the nineteenth century.

This new type of leadership often originated with the Republican organization. In fact, a few of the men who led the young party to its first victories still retained and exercised power forty years later. Justin Morrill, the first Republican congressman to be elected from Vermont, opened his fourth campaign for Senate re-election in 1891 by promising to withdraw from the race should any opposition develop. Having issued a similar pronouncement six years before, he knew full well that no one would challenge his carefully maintained organization, and talented young men like Redfield Proctor understood the necessity of waiting their turn. So long as Morrill held the reins, Vermont's politics remained orderly.[7]

Some party leaders of the 1890's inherited power from their predecessors and systematically managed to increase its scope and intensity. Their organizations were machines but they did not deteriorate in time. Succession was not always as evident as when Simon Cameron, furious with newly elected President Hayes, resigned his place in favor of his son, Donald. Grenville Dodge, in greater privacy, selected William Allison to run for senator. Yet both men consciously and successfully named the party's future chief. The procedure could assume biblical overtones: Mark Hanna took his seat from John Sherman just as the crafty Jacob snatched his blessing from an aging and near blind Isaac.[8] In each instance the political heirs fulfilled their tasks even more skillfully.

Party chiefs often increased their stature by prudently settling disruptive and lingering factional disputes. New York's Roscoe Conkling informed Simon Cameron in 1871 that the "party had never been so united in this state, never in better fighting order," but within a decade the Republicans were divided into two warring camps and Conkling's career terminated because of the split.[9] By 1890, however, Tom Platt securely controlled the organization, bringing a new authority to New York politics.

"There is nothing more singular in political history," Chauncey Depew recounted to a fascinated President Harrison, "than the strange mixture of antagonisms in the reorganization of the party . . . I write this bit of history because it shows how little is left of the ancient feuds." The old guard that surrounded Conkling in the 1870's, Chester Arthur, Alonzo Cornell, and Tom Platt, had long since disbanded. "After Arthur's election and the defeat of Conkling's efforts to return to the Senate," recounted Depew, "they quarreled, and the feud became so bitter that neither Conkling, Arthur, Cornell, or Platt spoke to each other." Joining the anti-Arthur forces, Platt was soon identified with the anti-Conkling wing. "The two most prominent leaders of the anti-Conkling forces were Hiscock and General Merritt. Now again Hiscock and Platt are together and Merritt has for some years . . . taken no part in party manipulation. Again, while I led the fight in the Senatorial contest which ended in the retirement of Mr. Conkling," Depew concluded, "the most enthusiastic and devoted of my friends at Chicago [the national convention] were the immediate friends of Mr. Conkling."[10]

Platt's reward was commensurate with the difficulty of his task: "Four-fifths of the legislators at Albany would have no wish" except to record his wants. And for many years, he dominated the most powerful organization in New York's history.[11]

Similarly Philetus Sawyer, the Wisconsin lumber millionaire, rose to command the state's Republicans. In the early 1870's the Madison Regency, as the State House ring was known, engaged in typical court intrigues as feuding leaders switched alliances and maneuvered for position. Selecting his allies prudently, Sawyer defeated Elisha Keyes, the one-time undisputed boss, for party control and for the Senate seat. Naming John Spooner his co-senator, political lieutenant, and heir apparent, Sawyer ruled the organization until his voluntary retirement in 1893. Without losing momentum, Spooner took over the reins.[12]

Most often, however, dogged hard work accounted for political success. The state's first Republican senator and boss, Zach Chandler, was not a novice in leadership; and having earned two million dollars in Detroit mercantile and real estate investments, he unquestionably possessed the wherewithal to run an organization. In fact Hamilton Fish considered Chandler not a bad fellow but too much the political manager. Nevertheless, dissident Republicans defeated his re-election bid in 1874 and he could not recapture power.[13]

James McMillan, on the other hand, suffered no such reversal; his efficiency ably protected his position. Emigrating to Detroit from his native Canada, McMillan began his business career unpretentiously as a purchasing agent for a local railroad. Advancement came quickly, however, and after managing a freight car manufacturing concern, he joined with John Newberry, a leading admiralty lawyer, to extend the scope of his interests. Shipbuilding, railroad construction, and steamship lines were part of their investments, and the firm of McMillan and Newberry earned the two partners millions. McMillan's political apprenticeship was equally commonplace but after serving in municipal office, he successfully managed Newberry's 1878 congressional campaign. Soon consenting to serve on the Republican state committee, he became its chairman in 1886. The Michigan millionaire then extended his control over the party, and no one was astonished when he was elected to the Senate three years later.[14]

Exercising the skills that had earned him a fortune, McMillan captured control of the Michigan party; and his 1889 campaign for the chamber seat admirably illustrated that the techniques of effective management could be valid in politics as well as in business. In his capacity as state party chairman, McMillan dispatched letters to Republican legislators running for election, enclosing anywhere from $25 to $750. The state committee expended some $34,000 on the campaign but it allocated only a small proportion to the assembly contests; McMillan himself raised and sent out those funds. "A check sent to me will be used in the proper way," he assured prospective donors and they took him at his word.[15] Between June 16 and November 1, 1888, McMillan contributed $7,000; his future colleague, Francis Stockbridge, gave $8,700, and retiring Senator Thomas Palmer presented $5,000. The money was quickly dispatched to needy legislators, with McMillan's best wishes for success invariably appended. If the sums proved insufficient, he somehow managed to send more.[16]

Hugh McMillan, James' younger brother, was the chief aid in this and other endeavors, and utilizing his privileged position to the fullest, the manager clarified what the candidate thought it best to insinuate. Assuring a victorious legislator that they were delighted with his good fortune, Hugh added: "You may be sure my brother will not forget his friends when the proper time comes."[17] The successful candidate would surely remember McMillan also when the right moment arrived.

In November 1888 the McMillans were busy with the mechanics of bringing out the vote. Hugh made sure that miners and loggers in the northern regions were transported to the polls by specially scheduled trains; with one typical arrangement, he guaranteed "two hundred votes we might not otherwise get."[18] After such devotion to detail, the Republicans carried Michigan and, as might be expected, the proceedings in the two Houses the following January became formalities. The credits the McMillans had scattered were now gathered. Hugh selected the men to nominate his brother and instructed others to deliver seconding speeches. The caucus quickly chose McMillan, the legislature duly elected him, and Michigan's next senator prepared to take his seat. The carefully constructed organization was, of course, not dismantled. Party successes continued and, as McMillan was informed:

This result shows most conclusively what quiet work and an active continuance of party organization can accomplish . . . Just now it may seem a long time before the next campaign, but it is easier to maintain an organization than to create one. Organization is half the battle . . . When party organization is perfect, campaigns are more easily conducted and victory more certain.[19]

But there was no need to tell the architect that his building would stand.

The merger of competing business interests at the close of the nineteenth century sometimes helped to consolidate the state party leadership. Events in New Hampshire exemplified the process. The coalition that united the Republican party there during the Civil War disbanded in the following decade and left various factions competing for supremacy. The state's old and viable tradition of rotation in office plagued many successful incumbents. But the most important barrier facing any potential leader was the competition between the Concord Railroad and the Boston & Maine. When one company endorsed a candidate, the other automatically sponsored a rival, disrupting the majority organization.[20]

Into this turmoil stepped William Chandler. The one-time railroad lobbyist, National Republican Committee Chairman, and Secretary of the Navy, was appointed in 1887 to fill an unexpectedly vacant Senate seat. When he ran for re-election two years later Jacob Gallinger, congressman and chairman of the state Republican Committee, challenged him. Gallinger championed the Concord Railroad, regularly urging its claims before the legislature, while Chandler, long absent from the state, was not identified with either line. The Boston & Maine, preferring neutrality to certain enmity, backed Chandler's candidacy and their efforts, together with his experience, brought victory. But in these peculiar circumstances, Chandler could not dominate the party and Gallinger carried on the struggle. In 1891 the Concord man captured the second Senate seat and factionalism continued to split the Republican ranks.[21]

In 1895 the Boston & Maine merged with its competitor, and the political repercussions soon became evident. Gallinger was easily re-elected in 1897, but in 1900 the newly consolidated railroad set out to defeat Chandler. The former lobbyist had recently delivered long harangues on the illegal use of passes, the corruption of the legislature, and the nefarious powers of the corporation; the lines responded by resolving to remove him from the Senate.[22] Convinced that defeat was certain unless the company ended its hostility, the unpredictable Chandler changed tactics. He dispatched letter after letter to anyone who might carry influence with the road's president, Lucius Tuttle. Eugene Hale suggested contacting his co-senator, William Frye, a director of the Maine Central which was part of the Boston & Maine network; but Frye could only state that Tuttle revealed no sign of antagonism. Vermont's new senator, Redfield Proctor, sent his sympathies but little more, explaining that in his state the roads were too competitive to undertake joint action.[23]

Chandler finally persuaded Aldrich to call on Tuttle; the Rhode Island Senator, however, reported that Tuttle had promised to continue in the future as he had in the past and not interfere with the election. Despite these assurances, Chandler recognized that Tuttle's "subordinates all over the state are as busy as the devil in a gale of wind nominating Senators and Representatives whom they believe will be hostile to me and whom they can control. The railroad and the money machine in New Hampshire is against me and it may not be possible to divert its assaults."[24] His fears were valid. The 1901 legislature turned down his bid and Gallinger gained undisputed control. The moral seemed clear: one railroad, one political leader.

The powers of a great corporation also proved to be invaluable assets for other state chieftains. Donald Cameron inherited the Republican organization from his father, but the rights to his patrimony did not go uncontested. When he tried to capture the second Senate seat for a loyal partisan in 1881, a revolt broke out; aggrieved Republicans hoped to ally with the Democratic minority and select a more acceptable candidate. The Democrats, however, under the authority of William Wallace, refused to join the dissidents, rejecting the opportunity to elect one of their own men. Wallace's solicitude for Cameron's welfare seemed unusual only to those who did not understand their mutual allegiance to the Pennsylvania Railroad. When the Democratic leader faced a similar challenge some years before, Cameron had secured Republican neutrality. Wallace was now pleased to repay the kindness.[25]

Events in New Hampshire and Pennsylvania were not typical of the nation; elsewhere, the concentration of business enterprises, by itself, did not smooth the way for leadership. Professional political skills rather than economic connections usually stabilized state power.

The mine owners of Colorado often shared a harmony of interests; nevertheless, politics remained faction-ridden for several decades. In the 1870's and 1880's Henry Teller, a successful Central City lawyer and investor, competed with Denver's Jerome Chaffee for dominance of the territorial Republican party. As the capital swelled in importance and the gulch towns died, Chaffee gained the advantage. When statehood came, he captured the first

Senate seat and authority over the organization. His control, however, was weak and short-lived. He could not prevent his rival from also winning election, and when Chaffee soon lost interest in politics and neglected its duties, Teller's influence immediately rose.

Nevertheless, succession to power was still not easily accomplished for Teller's ambitions were quickly challenged by Nathaniel Hill. The Brown-educated chemist had come West and made his fortune by devising an inexpensive process for extracting precious metals from their ores. Despite common stakes with Teller in mining enterprises, Hill continued to oppose him. The contest was balanced and funds were no problem for either man. Eventually, Teller's superior political skills determined the outcome. Consolidating the younger members behind his candidacy, he defeated Hill for the 1885 Senate vacancy. Conscientiously rewarding his followers, Teller proceeded to rule the state until well into the twentieth century.[26]

Politics in Nevada followed similar lines. J. P. Jones, one of the first Comstock millionaires, in alliance with William Stewart, an outstanding mining attorney, exercised extensive authority in the Republican party. But William Sharon, still wealthier from his holdings, together with his nephew, Francis Newlands, forcibly opposed their leadership.[27] Only through the most strenuous efforts did Jones keep power. The demands were extraordinary; long, tiring rides through desert country alternated with stump speeches in dry, hot towns. The Senator grumbled to his wife when it came time to start still another political campaign in Nevada, telling her how much he dreaded it. Invariably, however, he went out to meet his constituents and deliver his talks, conscious of the need to maintain his popularity. The omnipresence of mines and an oligarchy of owners did not simplify the duties, and Jones' income, often fluctuating, was of small benefit in the campaign.[28] Political authority had to be sustained through political efforts.[29]

Party chieftains, utilizing every prerogative at their disposal, ordered the politics of a majority of states. By the 1890's they dominated organizations in California as well as Rhode Island, in Iowa as well as New York, in Wyoming as well as Wisconsin. Nevertheless, the Democrats could not generally match the authority of their Republican rivals. The differentiation was not the result of two fundamentally distinct political styles but rather reflected the fact that southern parties did not regularly duplicate the national pattern. The Democrats were by no means untouched by the movement. David Hill in New York, Calvin Brice in Ohio, Henry Davis in West Virginia, Arthur Gorman in Maryland, Thomas Martin in Virginia, William Vilas in Wisconsin, and George Hearst in California effectively administered their organizations. But for peculiar reasons, many southern states followed a unique course.[30]

The divergence began with Reconstruction. Although the Republicans temporarily suppressed rival parties, they could not harmonize their own ranks. The paths to political power were diverse, running through the Florida Freedman's Bureau for Thomas Osborn, the Collectorship of the Port of New Orleans for William Kellogg, and the military governorship of Mississippi for Adelbert Ames.[31] In state after state two contending factions divided the organization. Native Republicans, favoring moderate Reconstruction policies, competed with more radical newcomers, prepared to enact punitive measures. Ames, a native of Massachusetts, opposed James Alcorn, a local and conservative planter; Alabama's Willard Warner held much milder views than his recently arrived antagonist, George Spencer. The contests invariably came to a deadlock and each faction's leader took one of the chamber's seats. In Washington, Ames served alongside Alcorn and Warner sat beside Spencer.[32]

Even after the Democrats returned to power, two opposing camps continued to divide the Senate places. In the course of serving the Confederacy and throwing off Republican rule, generals and redeemers gained fame and popularity. Not surprisingly, these advantages were often used to win Senate elections; in typical fashion, Augustus Garland in Arkansas, Wade Hampton in South Carolina, and Richard Coke in Texas directed Democratic efforts, served short terms in the state capital, and then began long careers in Washington.[33] Despite the invaluable advantages of medals and heroics, these leaders could not unite southern parties. A basic cleavage still separated them. Politicians receptive to industrial advancement competed with colleagues more devoted to traditional ways, and no one was able to bridge the gap. In the end a member of each school shared party control and a Senate seat. North Carolina's popular and agrarian-minded Zebulon Vance served with Matt Ransom, a New Departure sympathizer. James Barbour satisfield Virginia's capitalists and John Daniel pleased her old-fashioned citizens, while Mississippi's Edward Walthall and L. Q. C. Lamar maintained an identical balance. In Alabama, John Morgan faithfully corresponded with his mentor, antebellum senator C. C. Clay, and his colleague, James Pugh, kept in close touch with Birmingham's businessmen.[34]

New Departure senators, unable to overcome the appeal of the past and the rural political bias, rarely exerted undisputed authority. But traditionalists, boasting impressive military and government records, were in a better position to capture the organization. The one-party system in the South, however, decreased any potentiality for harmony; elsewhere, the contending factions might have supported different groups. Even more important, the traditionalists, devoted to strict constitutionalism, rarely approached politics with such modern goals as efficiency and organization. Enjoying personal popularity and the assurance of Senate re-elections, they did not direct their talents and ambitions to the orderly exertion of power. They contentedly gave rivals their due and shared the honors.[35]

Friction between the two camps heightened during the last decade of the century. The Populist threat strengthened the rural wing of the Democratic party and agrarian spokesmen in Texas,

Kentucky, Georgia, Tennessee, and South Carolina grew more powerful. Nevertheless, clear-cut victories even during the 1890's were unusual; most organizations remained divided and leaderless.[36]

The structure of southern politics complicated Gorman's tasks as chairman of the Senate caucus. The customary distribution of the chamber seats between opposing factions made his efforts to achieve national unity especially trying. Disharmony was built into the process of election, and Gorman was forced to exercise every talent for compromise to offset its effects. On the other hand, Allison and Aldrich faced Republican colleagues with no such obstacles.

The western states admitted to the Union between 1889 and 1897 also failed to emulate the political development of their more mature predecessors even though territorial government encouraged effective party leadership. The office of governor, federally appointed, and Territorial Delegate to Congress, popularly elected, possessed unusual potentiality for power. Governorships were filled in Washington, and party men with excellent connections usually received the posts. National influence, together with a large amount of local patronage, helped chief executives like Wyoming's Francis Warren and Idaho's George Shoup to build up dependable followings. After statehood, both men translated their control into Senate elections. Delegates, for their part, occupied the most significant positions available to the territory's inhabitants. The campaigns brought invaluable prominence and the opportunity to perfect dependable organizations. After this apprenticeship, South Dakota's Richard Pettigrew and Wyoming's Joseph Carey traveled to Washington.[37]

The divisive issues of the 1890's and the concomitant rise of the Populists, however, soon ended the brief authority of western leaders. By accommodating silver sentiment, Francis Warren survived as head of the party, but his good fortune was unique. George Shoup stood out against currency expansion and suffered defeat, while his colleague, Fred Dubois, joined the Silver Republicans only to be dislodged by an alliance of Democrats and Populists. Pettigrew remained in office as a Silver Republican, but the 1900 victory of the regulars destroyed his power.[38] In a less tumultuous era, the new states might have maintained centralized party organizations.

Finally, the Populists were less affected by the tendencies of these decades than either major party. Like the Southern Republicans during Reconstruction, they too divided into two factions. Moderates, with particular grievances and concrete reforms, confronted radicals, determined fundamentally to alter American society. The competition was intense, and without effective leadership, Populist attempts to elect senators often ended in disgust, confusion, or failure.

When the People's party, for example, gained a small majority in the 1891 Kansas legislature, the moderates predominated numerically over a highly vocal band of radicals led by Jerry Simpson and Mary Lease. Republican incumbent John Ingalls, famous for his frequent speeches vilifying the Democrats, made a desperate attempt to gain Populist support; but despite his Senate proposal to outlaw all speculation in agricultural commodities, the Simpson-Lease wing vetoed his candidacy. The moderates, more frightened of the radicals than of the Democrats, settled on William Peffer, an undistinguished conservative editor of the *Kansas Farmer;* in case the left-wingers bolted, Democratic votes would probably secure his election. The stopgap proved unnecessary since all the Populists remained loyal; yet because of party divisions, a lackluster and untalented senator went to Washington.[39] Similarly, Populists carried Washington in 1896, but unable to agree on a candidate of their own, they promoted Silver Republican George Turner. Richard Pettigrew could not control the South Dakota organization in 1897, and Mark Hanna persuaded enough Populists to elect James Kyle; the new Senator, in return, promised to vote for Republican organization in the chamber.[40] A new party could anticipate factional difficulties, but the Populists proved extraordinarily untractable.

The southern branch performed just as poorly, frequently passing over fellow members to elect Democratic senators. Despite a Populist majority in the 1891 Florida legislature, Democrat Wilkinson Call captured the seat. Unable to resist Zebulon Vance's appeals, the North Carolina Populists returned him to the chamber; Vance promised his sympathy but refused to agree to a major platform proposal, the sub-treasury plan. And the election by Georgia Populists of John Gordon, a Civil War veteran and hapless investor in less than reputable schemes, was even more of a blunder. Vance at least had a reputation for supporting farmer demands.[41] Election procedures were intricate and the Populists could not usually master the techniques. Not surprisingly, direct election was prominent in their list of reforms.[42]

In post-Civil War America, Senate contests were so vitally linked to state leadership that they assumed unprecedented importance. Elections usually proceeded with efficiency and dispatch; but at times the significance of the outcome was the cause of delay and obstruction. Between 1893 and 1899 nine legislatures, caught in a deadlock, were unable to select anyone to go to Washington. The public and the press blamed the silver sentiments of a determined minority; yet even in 1899, after the movement waned, four states were unable to complete the electoral process. Currency agitation, in fact, accounted for only a few of the incidents. Gold and silver factions thus divided the Democrats in Kentucky and the Republicans in Washington and Oregon. Wyoming's Populists, holding the balance of power in the 1893 legislature, refused to ally with either party.[43] In most instances, however, personal ambitions, unrelated to the silver question, blocked action. In Pennsylvania, John Wanamaker, the mercantile king, feuded with Matt Quay, preventing any election in 1899; Delaware Republicans split their support between John Addicks, a newcomer and millionaire, and Anthony Higgins, an old party regular, and no one was chosen. William Clark and

Marcus Daly disrupted Montana's Democrats, internal divisions stymied California's Republicans, and both states lost full representation. But factionalism, not rival ideologies, separated Wanamaker and Quay, while individual designs, not political principles, kept Higgins and Addicks apart.[44] When states could not elect a senator, personal designs were usually at fault.

This was not the first time in American political history that factionalism disrupted party harmony, yet theretofore, deadlocks did not characterize Senate elections. For example, when the Liberal Republicans bolted in 1872, they joined with Democrats in the state legislature to elect acceptable candidates; in Minnesota, Samuel McMillan replaced Alexander Ramsey and in Michigan, Isaac Christiancy succeeded Zach Chandler. Even during the silver controversy, partisans formed suitable alliances, circumventing barriers to election. In the 1890's, however, the traditional recourses were no longer appropriate or applicable. The Senate race had become the battleground for party leadership. There were no issues to attract the opposition, no incentives to prompt interference. Unable to distinguish among antagonists, the minority was frequently just as pleased to see the state's seat vacant as to have another vote cast in the chamber against its national party.

Moreover, Senate contestants rarely solicited outside assistance. Support by a rival party settled no questions of power and ostensibly gave credence to charges of disloyalty. Stalemates were overcome when one candidate gained dominance within the organization. Eventually, Warren won out over Carey, Quay defeated Wanamaker, and Wyoming and Pennsylvania were once again represented by two senators. The stakes were high and the parties autonomous. Fierce competition was sometimes bound to end in a draw.

The rule of Senate party leaders affected the political process in scattered capitals as well as in Washington. When state chieftains turned their attention to national affairs, they often delegated local control to trusted subordinates; from the perspective of Capitol Hill, management for its own sake seemed a minor accomplishment. Of course, party victories and personal ascendancy had to be assured for the tickets to Washington were not one-way. But there was no sense in over-extending the capacities of the organization. Prudence and caution rather than dreams of a monopoly of state power determined the course of action. Moreover, secure in their position at home, senators carried few debts as they entered the chamber. National party spokesmen, from the President to the chairman of the campaign committees, and vast economic interests, from steel to sugar, would not, or could not, undermine their authority. As ambassadors from sovereign states, senators surveyed the chamber.

State bosses utilized their powers with discrimination, not attempting to dictate every aspect of politics. Attentive to men and offices rather than to the legislative work of assemblies, they still preferred not to intervene unless some important personal interest was at stake. James McMillan, for example, kept clear of the gubernatorial contests of 1890 and 1894. Publicly, he announced that party success rather than individual advancement was his primary concern; privately, the genial host confided to his son that it was unwise to meddle in contests except against an avowed enemy: disappointed office-seekers could form dangerous combinations. After his election, McMillan continued to avoid too prominent a role in state gatherings and disliked serving as chairman of the central committee.[45] Other colleagues also preferred to distribute honors widely and often purposefully abstained from serving as delegates to national or state conventions. The skills of leadership demanded that the limited ammunition be fired only on the proper occasions.[46]

Among the various state offices, senators devoted much attention to the selection of the speaker of the state assembly. By controlling the committee assignments, he was an invaluable ally when canvassing support; with the bait of fine places, friends could be rewarded and new supporters attracted. "I tell you," Grenville Dodge advised William Allison as they attempted to capture the chamber seat and state party, "if you want Harlan [the incumbent] defeated it is necessary to get an anti-Harlan man for Speaker, for, as is always the case with a Speaker, there is no end to the amount of influence he will wield."[47] Mark Hanna warned Senator Sherman that their enemies hoped to capture the speaker and sway "members who are selfish enough to consider their own interests as of first importance."[48] Wisely, most leaders tried to link their designs to the ambitions of others.

The governor's office posed tactical difficulties. Potential opponents, emulating the careers of many senators themselves, could build up strength in the state capital; but party chieftains' frequent interference here might bring disagreeable publicity as well as unwanted factionalism. McMillan suffered no inconveniences for his restraint, but in Ohio, Governor Joseph Foraker gained enough influence to alarm Hanna and secure a Senate seat. Decisions demanded the most skillful exercise of power for the line between negligence and foresight was difficult to discern.[49]

The election of state legislators posed far less complex issues. The risks in any one race were small, and the rewards, a vote for the Senate, were considerable. "If I were you," Richard Pettigrew instructed Idaho's candidate, George Shoup, "I would put a man in every single legislative district and have them report to you every day. They can assist the men in their election in the district. These fellows, so elected, will stay by you in the legislature."[50] Stephen White, the masterful California politician, told friends: "I am more than ordinarily interested in the nominations made for the assembly; first, to see that they are strong men, and second, that they are not personally inimical."[51] Interference was expected and not at all dangerous. Even so established a person as John Sherman prodded his managers to secure him a unanimous caucus nomination; it would "strengthen me in my position in the Senate and enable me to do what I so much desire to do." The successful candidates, knowing whom to thank, customarily gave a party for the legislators, and in January, Sherman promptly complied with the custom. But always the astute politician, he reminded his lieutenants that "in deference to the public sentiments in Ohio," liquor had best be omitted.[52]

Senators invariably helped select their junior colleagues for the difficulties of serving with an active rival in Washington were patent and to be avoided at all cost. They also supervised the legislature's choices for other, more abstruse, reasons. In many states powerful customs dictated a geographical division of the chamber seats, and senators did not wish to see anyone elected by chance from their particular region since that would only complicate their own re-election. Detroit, as McMillan well knew, enjoyed the rights to one senatorship, but not both. Similarly, precedent allowed Omaha, Indianapolis, and St. Paul one place, and the rural sections the other. According to statute, one senator was to be elected from eastern and one from western Maryland, while the mountains that bisected Vermont provided her apportionment. Despite cogent arguments that sectional divisions were irrelevant since senators labored for the entire state's welfare, the divisions were usually maintained.[53] Leaders therefore respected these considerations with typical prudence, directing their efforts, here as elsewhere, to securing re-election, not revolutionizing political practices.

Senators conscientiously supervised state organizations to protect their authority. Consequently, they could act freely in the capital, without fear of reprisals from the national party. Insofar as organizational needs were concerned, tact and caution were most necessary in local affairs. In Washington, a senator's independence, at worst, could cost him influence within the chamber; but his authority at home would not necessarily be diminished. No national figure, from the President to the National Committee Chairman and the head of the caucus, could seriously threaten him. State leadership brought political immunity.

Presidents in post-Civil War America preferred to avoid the entangling webs of state politics. When John Logan campaigned for Illinois' 1879 Senate place by openly and resolutely attacking the policies of Hayes, W. H. Smith, a good friend of the President, moved to retaliate. "You may be sure," Smith advised the Chief Executive, "that if Logan is elected, he will make life a burden to you if he can do it."[54] Nevertheless, Hayes, unwilling to take a part, refused to sanction his plans. Two years later James Garfield utilized every strategy to force his New York nominations through the Senate over Conkling's opposition; but when the Senator abruptly resigned his seat and attempted to win a vote of confidence from the legislature, the President pulled back. "I have fought the assumption of Mr. C[onkling] against my authority," he scrawled in his diary, "but I do not think it best to carry the fight into New York."[55] Grover Cleveland shared less of this reluctance; still McKinley entered the executive offices and revived the habits of his Republican predecessors.

James Blaine, as Garfield's Secretary of State, revealed the potentialities of presidential power to effect state decisions. Garfield hesitated to attack Conkling in New York but Blaine shared none of his reservations. "Everything possible or impossible must be done to beat those fellows at Albany," he instructed his friend and ally, Stephen Elkins. "Do what you can, but don't go to Albany," he concluded with more than usual circumspection.[56] The limitations of travel proved minor. According to J. P. Jones, partisan but still in a position to know the details, offers of federal posts of every sort were made to the New York legislators if they would vote against Conkling's re-election.[57] And not surprisingly, the New York Senator lost his bid. But such systematic and effective exercise of the federal patronage was rarely duplicated by Garfield's nineteenth-century successors.

Presidential unwillingness to wield the leverage of the patronage paralleled its diminishing importance. In the years immediately following the close of the Civil War, the distribution of federal offices could determine factional disputes. Conkling headed the New York Republicans after Grant gave him, and not Reuben Fenton, patronage control; similarly, Simon Cameron and Henry Anthony profited from the General's favoritism. By the 1890's, however, state leaders were no longer overly concerned with particular executive decisions; only a vendetta would provoke their retaliation. Senators possessed sufficient resources within their own organizations to obviate any simple dependence upon the whims of the White House. Usually entering the chamber after having consolidated state power, they infrequently needed reinforcements to bolster tenuous positions.

The distribution of federal offices now often appeared bothersome and hardly worth the effort; for every ally attracted through some sinecure, ten others went away angry. So keen a politician as Stephen White told Theodore Roosevelt, then chairman of the Civil Service Commission, in all honesty: "I do not believe that you will find me hostile to the reformations which have been inaugurated with reference to the Civil Service." Hoping to extend rather than curtail the system, White observed: "At present, members of Congress and Senators are annoyed from day to day by the persistent demands of persons for place, and it is a question whether we were elected to legislate, or procure employment."[58] To lighten the burden, state senators of the same party split the offices down the middle. Nevertheless, at the start of each session members devoted their correspondence to answering the innumerable applications and complaining that patronage was a deadly plague.[59]

Perhaps the greatest advantage to controlling the offices was the assurance that no rival could benefit from them. State leaders would not permit a contending faction to feed and grow on the patronage and should a hostile President disagree, they were not without protection. Senatorial courtesy could be invoked against an overactive executive, and usually, if not invariably, the chamber supported any beleaguered colleague. David Hill headed the

New York Democrats despite the machinations of Grover Cleveland, and the Senate assisted him by rejecting several appointments.[60] Members were rarely forced to retreat to their defenses but in any event they were adequately insulated from the power of the President.

The national committees, organized to help in election contests, exerted minimal influence; their efforts were sporadic and temporary, and their occasional victories, rarely durable. With their assistance, a senator might win one trip to Washington but he would not capture state dominance.

Democrats and Republicans vigorously contested Senate elections in the 1890's, for party strength in the chamber was so evenly divided that the outcome of any one race could determine majority and minority status. As margins grew slimmer, the national committees increased their labors. The National Republican Committee Chairman, Mark Hanna, knew the value of travel. His first circuit through the South pinpointing Republican delegates had helped secure McKinley's nomination and in the autumn of 1896, after working for the party victory, he undertook a second journey to capture the Senate for the incoming President. The confused political conditions of several states invited his skills and where Republicans had not won outright majorities in the legislature, he effectively arranged alliances. The election of Senator Kyle over the protests of Populist leader Richard Pettigrew was a typical success. Hanna owned no monopoly of intrigue, even if James K. Jones, his Democratic counterpart, was usually less adroit. But for all their energy, national interference remained haphazard. They tackled a specific assignment, be it in Delaware or Idaho, and then turned attention elsewhere.[61]

The Senate could not select its members. The constitutional right to judge senators' qualifications and the legality of their elections was rarely abused. During Reconstruction, the authority was sometimes exercised for partisan purposes, but by the very next decade judicial evaluations were again the rule. Despite a Republican majority in 1899, Matt Quay was denied his seat; paying no attention to party lines, the chamber voted that governors could not appoint a senator when legislatures failed to elect one. The institution gained no political influence through this constitutional prerogative.[62]

To be sure, senatorial associates often aided one another. Colleagues serving in high party positions would tap national committee funds for an extra sum; some money from the congressional campaign fund was available, but it had to be distributed nationally to House and Senate hopefuls.[63] Wealthy senators donated liberally to friends' campaigns. When Allison ran for re-election in 1892, the ever generous McMillan sent $500 in August and promised another check in September. Others, less affluent, composed letters of praise. John Spooner, for the edification of Kansas Republicans, described the very ordinary senator, Preston Plumb, as "one of the most remarkable men of my acquaintance. He is a man of wonderful qualities of mind, a really great debater, and one of the few great leaders of political thought and action in this country today."[64] Exaggerations, after all, were expected. Moreover, members took the stump for each other and willingly contacted any influential friends, confident that the kindness would be well repaid.[65]

These services, however, were tangential; McMillan's $500 would not fill Allison's campaign chest and Plumb would not win re-election because Spooner labeled him a remarkable man. Still Senate leaders, as well as less powerful members, could only supply petty favors. No matter how avidly Allison, Aldrich, or Gorman would have wished to affect the selection of chamber members, they too, through letters and speeches, could accomplish little. They did enjoy one advantage: the right to distribute preferable Senate positions. A legislature conceivably might hesitate to replace someone who brought preeminence and appropriations to the region, and national stature made effective campaign oratory. But Allison and Gorman could, at most, help established colleagues, not would-be senators, and by 1900 not many new arrivals in Washington depended upon this sort of assistance. The efforts of the caucus chairmen, like the President's, were not often decisive. No monarch yet ruled in the capital.[66]

Senators also enjoyed a great deal of freedom from economic as well as political pressures. During the last decades of the century, business interests frequently meddled in state affairs, but insofar as Senate elections were concerned, their achievements were not often notable. The influences they exerted were balanced by the strength of political organizations, and party leaders were not compelled to defer to their demands.

It is not always easy to uncover the part that corporations played in electing senators, but in most instances their authority was limited. Companies were unusually reticent to discuss their efforts at the polls. Thomas Kimball, an agent for the Union Pacific Railroad, told investigators in 1888 the full details of his lobbying techniques; yet when asked about attempts to influence the choice for senator, he would admit only to individual, not company, activities. Political involvement, alleged Kimball, was "a right I exercised as a citizen and not as a representative of the Union Pacific."[67] Corporation executives ostensibly participated in campaigns simply as ordinary Americans.

Soon, however, business leaders dropped this dubious distinction and acknowledged what everyone already knew: companies were involved in the political process. Henry Havermeyer, head of the largest American sugar refining enterprise, explained his policies to an 1894 congressional board of inquiry. The organization, its president declared, distributed state campaign contributions, although none of the funds went to national races. "As we look upon it," added Theodore Havermeyer, partner and brother, "we are simply large real estate owners." The corporation supported good government because efficient police and fire facilities were essential to its welfare.[68] No special favors were asked and none were expected. "I have long since learned," one business official told his questioners, "the truth of the colored man's version of: 'Blessed are dem what 'spects nuffin, den dey don't get disappointed.' " Donations were not even intended to secure "fair treatment," for that would have been forthcoming in any event.[69] Every economic interest tendered contributions, Havermeyer complaisantly concluded. Sugar only followed the popular example.

Despite its few concessions, such testimony was an inaccurate and incomplete guide to the political roles of the corporation. For one thing, the differentiation between state and national campaigns was not firm; to elect a legislature was to affect the selection of senators. Moreover, a company's interest obviously extended beyond the requirements of good government. Without question it wished to see receptive and well-meaning representatives serving in the Senate. The corporations were not as innocent as their public statements would have it. But that is not to say that they could effectively prejudice the course of politics.

There can be no doubt that in a few states, such as New Hampshire, Pennsylvania, and New Jersey, a company dominated the assembly so completely that promoting friendly members to the Senate was not very difficult. Yet this control was exceptional. In most states a wide range of interests tried to influence the power structure, and no one group could be confident that its demands would be favored. In New York, Ohio, Wisconsin, Michigan, California, and Oregon, all sorts and sizes of manufacturing, transportation, banking, mining, real estate, mercantile, and agrarian enterprises took some active part in politics; and their aims were by no means identical. Manufacturers and suppliers did not always agree on tariff questions, mine owners and railroad operators frequently divided on questions of transportation regulation, and merchants often disputed bankers on fiscal policy. Moreover, particular corporations could not effectively direct politics in more than one or two capitals; no business was so vast that it could command the sympathies of a substantial minority of the Senate by manipulating state politics. Even giant insurance companies, for example, preferred national regulation to state control because the difficulties of dealing with several legislatures were too burdensome.[70] As a result of these limitations, corporations had to resort to more indirect methods to try and insure favorable treatment in Washington. Campaign contributions thus became typical in post-Civil War America.

Several considerations combined to limit the influence that companies could exert through their political gifts. In the first place, corporations hoped to win the regard of the men who actually gained power; accordingly they distributed their monies as broadly as possible and all possible winners received part of their largess. The practices of railroad president C. P. Huntington were common. "Some of us," he instructed his Republican-minded partners, "ought to act with the Democratic party. I think there is little difference between them now; it is only the seven reasons: the five loaves and the two fishes." The logic was clear. The railroad "cannot afford to be too openly for the man that loses."[71]

When one party firmly commanded a state, gifts were not squandered on the minority. "Wherever there is one dominant party," Havermeyer affirmed, "that is where we give the contribution." Otherwise, corporation funds were readily forthcoming to both political organizations.[72] Sometimes the internal corporate structure encouraged this tactic; directors, divided in their political loyalties, would not permit the exclusive support of one organization.[73] In other instances the threat of reprisal neutralized favoritism. The Union Pacific may have preferred to support John Thurston for senator from Nebraska, but his competitor, Charles Manderson, was not without powerful friends. John Gear, chairman of the Senate Railroad Committee, informed Grenville Dodge, a Union Pacific associate, that the road had better refrain from action. There were some vital matters to be adjusted in Congress and Gear threatened that "they will be held up if the

U.P. people are going to put anything in the path of Manderson. Of course," he instructed Dodge, "you can put it on the ground that you are intimate with some of the Committee especially so with myself, the Chairman."[74] Undoubtedly Dodge relayed the message.

Then too, companies were not necessarily efficient in their attempts to gain power. Politics was an intricate business, and outsiders were not always familiar with its complexities. Friends informed Senator Henry Dawes that Massachusetts' manufacturers "do not give the attention to the primaries they ought; the management of the caucuses is (therefore) in other hands." The companies might try to influence the legislature on Dawes' behalf in January, but "businessmen," he was warned, "neglect as a rule their political duties in all preliminary matters."[75]

Campaign contributions usually entered politics after the fact, adding their weight when the balance was already tipped. Party leaders did not require the talents of money raising, for corporations spread their gifts widely. Then too, the era of exorbitant election costs was still in the future and funds seem to have been available in more or less of an adequate supply. Complaints on this score were rare, and from all indications, the problem was minor.[76] Moreover, the size of campaign chests did not decide political contests. Wanamaker and Quay were both well provided for, as were Addicks and Higgins, Clark and Daly, and Jones and Sharon. Availability of funds did not distinguish David Hill from Tom Platt, John Spooner from John Mitchell, Leland Stanford from George Hearst, or Charles Faulkner from Stephen Elkins.

Rather, enlarged treasuries facilitated expanded political efforts, helping to extend and entrench the power of party chieftains in all parts of the state. Campaign contributions meant that the election costs of friendly legislators could be more easily paid, trains could be ordered, speakers dispatched, and leaflets distributed. Organizations, buttressed by funds, were more secure in power—and thus, less susceptible to external control. Money was a tool for the political artisan and he used it artfully.

The heightened power of party forced corporations to seek favors as supplicants, not as patrons, proving their good will by giving rather than receiving donations. Appeals for action were couched in terms of party welfare. James Swank, for example, representing the American Iron and Steel Association, asked William Allison to try and treat the group well for they had pledged large sums and were likely to respond again. "Human nature is human nature all the world over," Swank noted. "We would not for one moment think of using any improper means to secure the favorable consideration by your Committee of the steel rail duty. But our friends on the Committee are Republicans striving for the success of our party in the coming election. I beg you, therefore, to make it easy for me . . . to secure . . . additional collections."[77] As Swank realized, senators gave first allegiance to the party, and its organization shaped the vital political decisions. The party's importance made contributions necessary. Yet at the same time, its power restricted a donor's influence to a minimum. More than equal to particular economic interests, Republicans and Democrats could safely ignore any specific demand.

Centralization set the tone of post-Civil War state politics, and local politicians, senators, businessmen, and reformers recognized the change. Contemporaries offered explanations, but their interpretations were usually confused, contradictory, and misleading. Most observers, like Moisei Ostrogorski, related the movement to the other portentous event of these years: the rise of the corporation. Monopoly, Ostrogorski asserted, had its counterpart in political unity. In those states "where capitalistic interests were concentrated," senators ruled the party on their behalf. As company hirelings, bosses dominated every facet of local government and followed its bidding in Washington as well. This sort of analysis was popular for the two frightening innovations were related and, at the same time, a solution was proposed. Break up the trusts and the bosses will disappear; eradicate the party and the corporation would disintegrate.[78] The neatness of the formula, however, did not validate it.

Even those most certain that monopolies prompted political centralization could not consistently define the relationships between these two spheres. Economic interests, first stated Ostrogorski, "equipped and kept up political organizations for their own use, and ran them as they pleased, like their trains." This argument conveniently fitted into his scheme and yet he was soon forced to conclude: "It was with them [the politicians] that the corporation now had to deal, whether they liked it or not, by purchasing their support or by submitting to blackmail."[79] The confusion was inevitable, for during these years party unity occurred in states lacking monopolistic business interests and failed to mature elsewhere despite their presence. Political leadership was a political development.

The economic changes that followed the Civil War were not irrelevant to this process, but they did not establish it. Progressive spokesman Herbert Croly rather than Moisei Ostrogorski perceptively grasped this distinction. "Just as business had become specialized and organized," wrote Croly in *The Promise of American Life* (1909), "so politics also became the subject of specialization and organization . . . But to consider the specialized organization of our local politics as the direct result of specialized organization of American business is wholly to misunderstand its significance." Political efficiency, Croly maintained, demanded the boss. He is "an independent power who has his own special reasons for existence. He put in an embryonic appearance long before the large corporations had obtained anything like their existing power in American politics; and he will survive in some form their reduction to political insignificance. He has been a genuine and within limits a useful product of the American democracy; and it would be fatal either to undervalue or to misunderstand him." The industrial leader, Croly accurately concluded, did not create the boss, although through his support "he has done much to confirm the latter's influence."[80]

The skills and strategies of Republican and Democratic leaders then, not the appearance of the trusts, altered state parties. Professionals devoted full time to its concerns, investing it with a new authority. When men trained in business, like James McMillan and Mark Hanna, achieved political success, it was testimony to personal genius for administration and meticulous attention to organization, not to the firms of McMillan and Newberry or Mark Hanna and Company. Private wealth may have smoothed the first steps but it was not ultimately responsible for power. J. P. Jones complained but he toured Nevada again and again; McMillan composed individual notes to every Republican legislator. Leadership was never grasped or maintained without the devotion of unrelenting effort.

By 1900 party chiefs were secure against defeat and would not be effectively challenged until the Progressive revolt. Their surest protection was a statewide power. Losses in one district barely affected over-all control; reverses in one ward were matched by victories elsewhere.[81] Only a counter-organization able to strike with uniform strength over an entire state could threaten their dominance. Understanding that organization was essential to politics, that the Platts, Allisons, and Gormans could be beaten only with their own techniques, the Progressives first made the necessary effort. Hiram Johnson in California and Bob La Follette in Wisconsin proved capable of attracting and administering large political followings. The leaders of 1900 were often defeated a decade later, but only after setting the future course of state politics.[82]

Secure in power, chamber members were not dependent upon national party organizations for their future careers. And since senators, unlike the members of Parliament, were free from the danger of reprisal, it is no wonder that discipline in the Senate never equaled the standard set in Commons. But perhaps more remarkable, independence did not make these ambassadors to Washington cantankerous. The chairman of the caucus could not bolster or weaken their authority at home and yet he frequently welded diverse members into an effective chamber party. The very dedication to organizations that rendered state leaders impervious to external threats also made them good party senators. Trained in the virtues of the binding caucus, they understood the necessity for discipline. Devoted to the exercise of power, they were willing to pay obeisance in order to share in it. They were professional in Washington as well as in Albany or Sacramento, and could no sooner play the maverick in one capital than in another. To be sure, Allison and Gorman resorted to flattery more often than intimidation. Nevertheless, they stood before a caucus filled with politicians ready to compromise for the sake of party. The Senator from Iowa and the Senator from Maryland knew how to manage this sort of gathering.

☆ VII ☆

THE BUSINESS OF INFLUENCE

Just as the plaintiff in a lawsuit may properly employ an attorney
and barrister, so a promoter may properly employ a lobbyist.

James Bryce, *American Commonwealth,* 1888

It would be unreasonable to deny to corporations having large
interests at stake the right to be represented before committees
of the legislature, and the right to pay proper compensation of
money to those who represent them.

United States Pacific Railway Commission,
"Report," 1888

Various interest groups in post-Civil War America attempted
to manipulate political power. Although laissez-faire doctrines
undoubtedly carried some appeal, still, as James Bryce remarked
in 1888: "The lamentations with which old-fashioned English
thinkers accompany the march of legislation, are in America
scarcely heard and wholly unheeded." Americans, he believed,
customarily welcomed "the action of government into ever-widen-
ing fields."[1] In fact the people were probably too busy devising
intricate schemes for the legislature to spare the time for complaint. Laissez-faire theories notwithstanding, the voters assumed
that abstract intellectual commitments would not prevent an institution like the Senate from acting, provided the pressures exerted were great enough.

Although various associations appeared in Washington during these years, the business groups rather than the farmers, or
the laborers, or the consumers most diligently attempted to in-

fluence politics. Their efforts, more than any others, at once shaped and were affected by the place of party in government. Since no particular enterprise could wield power in several state legislatures and campaign contributions did not guarantee favorable action, companies turned to other expedients, especially lobbying. Still the results were not to their liking; corporations could not dictate political decisions. As the most relentless pursuers of power, their fate clarified some of the implications of the Senate's transformation.

In the 1870's, when party did not yet superintend the course of Senate affairs, lobbying for the first time became a vital element in government. In initial appearance, however, lobbyists were careless and haphazard, neither especially benefiting nor endangering Senate proceedings. The cause of the disorganization rested not with the agents but with their chief sponsors, the railroads. Transportation companies were by no means unique in their Washington practices—many midwestern towns with a creek hoped to promote a canal that would empty into the Mississippi— but they were lobbying's most devoted patrons. Some lines energetically tried to capture congressional appropriations while others were equally determined to maintain privileges. But whatever their goals, they could not systematically pursue them without help.

The railroads in the 1870's were critically short of money. Collis Huntington, president of the Central Pacific and the Southern Pacific, lacked sufficient funds to fulfill numerous construction plans and still he was far wealthier than Tom Scott of the Texas & Pacific. The need for capital in business ventures left little room for political expenditures just as it made government assistance all the more necessary. Begrudging every cost, executives frugally doled out their money and intently watched for the return on their investment.

The results of the railroad's economies were apparent in the early career of William Chandler. After the Civil War, the New

Hampshire Republican opened a one-man lobbying firm, without an office or staff. Typical of his profession, Chandler accepted employment from a startling number of companies and even from competing organizations. Until the mid-1880's he served as chief lobbyist for the Union Pacific Railroad. "You will report frequently," charged Grenville Dodge, head engineer and sometime lobbyist, "to the proper officers of the Company, and will, of course, consult and advise on important matters, with any associate counsel . . . but in the absence of direction otherwise . . . your action will be authoritative."[2] While exercising this warrant, Chandler accepted retainers from the Baltimore & Ohio, the Kansas Pacific, and the Atchinson, Topeka & Santa Fe, paying no attention to one company's friendships or another's rivalries.[3]

Soon after the Northern Pacific was incorporated, Chandler also sought to take a part in its affairs. "Of course, we do not want you or anyone else to be antagonistic in this great work," responded the head of the line, Jay Cooke. "I am not willing to deprive you of a good fee, if our Company had no objections." Chandler was hired and soon intervening for Cooke's interests in Union Pacific affairs.[4] Finally in 1873, when Tom Scott began his long but unsuccessful attempt to win congressional underwriting for his railroad's bonds, Chandler joined his old friend Dodge as a Texas & Pacific lobbyist. Although the Union Pacific did not always smile on Scott's enterprise, he readily served both companies.[5]

Lobbyists accepted numerous and conflicting retainers, for few employers paid satisfactory fees. In 1869 Chandler received only $5,000 in return for several years service on behalf of the Union Pacific, and in 1870 he was forced to accept stock when the road could not, or would not, pay cash.[6] Estimating his total 1871 income from lobbying at a meager $3,000, Chandler furiously denounced Union Pacific president Oliver Ames for begrudging the agents every cent of their salaries. Moreover, financial prospects did not improve in time. "I am $5000 dollars worse off than

I was one year ago," he complained to Dodge in 1873,[7] and it was small consolation to learn that the line was niggardly with other lobbyists as well.[8]

Collis Huntington and other company presidents would not divulge political expenses, lumping them under "legal costs" on the books,[9] but the scorn they heaped on the lobbyists was unlimited and unconcealed. "The damned strikers are so numerous," lamented Huntington to his partners in 1870, "that if we should endeavor to put the matter [of purchasing government property in San Francisco's harbor] before Congress this session I have no doubt it would cost us more than it would be worth . . . The Strikers, or Third House members, are very quick and hungry in Washington this winter."[10] Seven years later conditions and attitudes had not changed appreciably. "It seems as though all the strikers in the world" were gathered in Washington. "If we are not hurt this session," Huntington irritably contended, "it will be because we pay much money to prevent it, and you know how hard it is to get it to pay for such purposes."[11]

Nevertheless, when the Southern Pacific and Texas & Pacific were urging rival proposals before Congress, Huntington was afraid to forego help. Partner Mark Hopkins suggested hiring a certain lobbyist, and the railroad president immediately agreed. "I should not want to pay him a great price for I do not believe Scott can pass his bill," he lamely added, "but I think it of so much importance to us that I do not want it to fail for any lack on our own part."[12] In fact, Charles Crocker, another associate, found Huntington overcautious. "I would not spend a dollar to beat Tom Scott," he told his colleague in 1878, "for I think he is already beaten without it. You are there, where the lobby has access to you, and their bread and butter depends upon their making themselves seem necessary to the success of any movement."[13] Of course, matters were not very different for Tom Scott. One would-be lobbyist was informed that although he could be "of great service to Scott's Texas railroad bill . . . money is scarce everywhere." The company, however, would "allow . . . $50 per week for expenses, for a month anyway, possibly for the session."[14] Employers were even more trying than congressmen.

Lobbyists also required substantial sums to cover their costs. "There [are] a lot of Press fellows here who are after us unless we pay," Richard Franchot, a Southern Pacific agent in Washington, noted frankly in 1872. Hotels, entertainment, cigars, and champagne were other drains, especially when supporters traveled to the capital and defended the corporation before Congress.[15] Expenses climbed higher since Huntington, convinced that elected officials were attentive to constituents' telegrams and letters, detailed men to arrange writing campaigns. Then too, county and state resolutions could be still more effective. When the railroad president discovered that Scott, spending liberally, "gets every little gathering in the South to pass resolutions favoring the Texas & Pacific bill," he immediately set out to emulate him. Naturally, efforts in Washington often had to be duplicated in state legislatures. Federalism insured that all attempts to influence politics would be extraordinarily expensive.[16]

The narrow-minded president of the Southern Pacific devised three special categories for public men: the clean, the commercial, and the communists. Huntington's finest compliment was to label a politician clean. "Sargent has done all we have asked, and is an able and honest man," began his description of the California Congressman who subsequently won election to the Senate. "He is a very clean man and will do the right *all* the time."[17] Short of capital and loathe to spend it, the California entrepreneur highly valued any senator who would consistently do the right without seeking favors in return. For these very select few, he reserved the title clean. Next, but lower, in his estimation were the commercial —officials whose support was purchasable. "Scott is working mostly amongst the commercial men," Huntington informed head lobbyist David Colton in 1876. "He switched Senator Spencer of Alabama and Walker of Virginia this week, but you know they can be switched back with the 'proper arguments' when they are wanted."[18] Proper arguments called for the expenditure of funds, but at least commercial politicians were tractable. Huntington despaired only of the communists. They combated his pet projects incessantly and could not be dissuaded by the strongest of arguments or the handsomest of gifts.[19]

The handful of clean senators were not neglected by their admirer. "If you could," the railroad man instructed partner Leland Stanford on the subject of Roscoe Conkling, "arrange something out of which he could make some money (something handsome). You will have to be very careful how you do it, as he is very sensitive, but, of course, like the rest of us, has to eat and drink." Because the New Yorker was "so straight he leans backwards," he was not to be "deprived of this world's goods."[20] Senators William Stewart and Samuel Pomeroy were also gratuitously rewarded, and as for Sargent, "he is," proclaimed Huntington, "our friend, without doubt, but we must take care of our friends."[21] Even when John Conness, a "good and true friend" of the enterprise was defeated for Senate re-election, he was not abandoned to his own devices. "He has a large family of children . . . and I think we should do something handsome for him," the company president instructed his colleagues. "He should have something handsome; something worth from six to ten thousand dollars a year . . . He is not the man to beg of us or any one else, but I think we owe it."[22]

These supporters, of course, were thanked without any direct cash expenditure. Conness was tendered a job with the company, Conkling was offered "an interest in some city or town property on the line of the road," Sargent received company stock, and Stewart was granted "fifty thousand acres of land of average quality of the lands along the line of the road." Although such gifts might hopefully insure the steadfastness of a loyalty, Huntington did not intend to corrupt public officials. In fact, he instructed his partners not to inform Conkling and Pomeroy of the arrangements, for "they would take nothing from us while they are in Congress."[23]

In December 1883 the alleged corruption spread by the railroads provoked a public furor second only in its intensity to Credit Mobilier. After the death of chief lobbyist David Colton, his widow, dissatisfied with her property settlement, sued the Southern Pacific. She introduced Huntington's letters to his top Washington contact into evidence, and straightway they were reprinted prominently in the country's newspapers. When reporters interviewed him about the correspondence, Huntington, without embarrassment, expressed amazement at the excitement. "Where's the evidence of corruption in these?" he demanded. "I've been in business fifty years and practiced the usual methods known among business men to accomplish certain objects, but I've never bought votes or bribed men directly or indirectly."[24] The materials themselves lent some support to his contention, and a later congressional investigatory board exonerated him from the charges. In 1876, during the fierce battle with Scott, for example, Huntington confessed to Mark Hopkins that he might have won over certain congressmen to the road "had they not been offered large sums" to vote against him. "You know our rule is never to buy a vote." He also expressed similar sentiments to Colton himself; Scott promised to pay huge sums, but "you know I keep on the high ground."[25]

Although the Southern Pacific president halfheartedly denied in congressional examinations that "commercial Congressmen" designated men willing to be bribed, he ultimately conceded the venality of some officeholders. "Eighteen hundred years ago," Huntington reminded his questioners, "the best man that ever lived selected twelve men and 16⅔ per cent of them were 'short weight.' " A few politicians might be influenced by money, "and while it is very likely that there have always been such men in Congress," still it never helped to traffic with them.[26] The dangers of discovery and scandal were great, and buying two or three officials drove away ten honest men. He might have added, but it demanded too much candor, that a vote purchased by one bidder could easily be won over by another; then too, the strategy was too expensive to adopt as a habitual practice. Occasionally a supporter could be picked up with a generous gift—short weight men we have always with us—but economic interests did not influence the political process through bribery.

Most senators did not fit into any of Huntington's ingenious classifications, and corporation presidents perceived that an overwhelming majority of the chamber was neither steadfastly in favor of, nor unalterably opposed to, their pet projects. A few determined supporters and detractors were often on hand; nevertheless, the fate of legislation rested with a large, diverse, and uncommitted membership. On this unattached bloc, the companies exerted their funds and energies, compelled to convince individual senators of a proposal's validity. Despite the great cost of the effort, the results remained unpredictable.

The purpose of lobbying, declared Huntington, was to gain a full and sympathetic congressional hearing; since elected officials were most attentive to a constituent or an acquaintance, business interests thought it most effective to locate and retain men "whom he [the congressman] would allow to talk to him." If a single agent could have fulfilled the corporations' purposes, they would willingly have allowed him a satisfactory retainer. But the California entrepreneur and his rivals were required to hire part-time, one-session lobbyists who, having access to one or two congressmen by some chance, for a fee were willing to expound the virtues of a particular design. Huntington accurately estimated that in the winter of 1876–77, Tom Scott employed some two hundred lobbyists in Washington. Each would corner a few politicians and explain Texas & Pacific contentions. No one particular salary was large but the size of the payroll made the total outlay enormous.[27]

As Scott discovered, a flock of agents was no guarantee of satisfaction; his line never did win congressional backing. Arguments could be countered; the men lobbyists exhorted were soon visited by rivals.[28] To bring a measure of stability to the chaos, companies often attempted to capture good will as well as intellectual agreement. An obligation might be repaid with a loyal vote. Although bribery was neither permissable nor desirable, there were other methods for bestowing favors on potential supporters.

Corporations willingly advanced loans to men in office. The maneuver was legally defensible, albeit on weak moral grounds; more important, the funds did not necessarily determine the borrower's actions. When California first sent Cornelius Cole to the Senate in 1865, Huntington, convinced "he is much the best for us," was happy with the choice. Within two years, however, he altered his opinion. "There is no good feeling in Cole," he bitterly warned his colleagues; "his heart is cold and his blood is white and I do not nor cannot like him."[29] Yet Cole owned a vote and when he requested a loan, the railroad agreed. Cole had promised to "do all that he could for us," the president now assured his partners. Still the Senator did not reliably support the road; the favor did not secure his loyalty. When Cole was finally defeated for re-election in 1873, Huntington quickly wrote to Hopkins: "Herewith I send you account and some notes against Cornelius Cole. He has often promised to pay them . . . [but] he did not. You will collect these notes and accounts, if you can do so." When Cole was tardy with his payments, Huntington wished to sue him.[30] At least *one* bad investment would be recovered.

The Texas & Pacific followed identical practices with as little success. When Georgia senator John Gordon needed $5,000, he turned to one of their lobbyists, Sam Barlow; two others admittedly had offered him the money, but, he told Barlow, "you would not consent to my taking the loan from either as long as I am in the Senate, did you know the sources."[31] Gordon believed that he could take funds from the Texas & Pacific lobbyist with impunity, and when the Scott bill was raised in the chamber, the Senator informed his benefactor: "I cannot vote for it. There is nothing as you know which I could do consistently, at which I would hesitate to oblige you; but not only my convictions but my constituents are against it . . . I know you would not have me guilty of a shadow of turning from my convictions on any matter of legislation."[32] Good will did not always insure roll-call support, and many senators were willing to accept gifts precisely because they did not feel bound to repay them on the Senate floor. Corporations' best laid plans often found their proverbial endings.

The distribution of railroad passes to congressmen began as another stratagem to win supporters, but demand soon overwhelmed willingness to supply, and business organizations found themselves making more enemies than friends. The roads were expected to issue passes, and recipients felt no obligation to repay the favor; but, at the same time, those denied the courtesy took offense. Since they could ill afford to provoke more antagonism, company heads were as opposed to the system as any Granger legislature. "When in Washington," Huntington informed Mark Hopkins in 1869, "I had to give out many passes, mostly at the request of Senators and Members of Congress, and since Congress adjourned I think we have averaged six letters per day from Senators and Members of Congress asking for passes over the road. I refuse many, and I give many. This giving free passes is all wrong."[33]

Nevertheless, the pressure continued unabated. Vowing in 1870 to refuse passes to all "except those that I am quite sure can and will help us," Huntington angrily reminded Stanford five years later that the Central Pacific had carried 6,186 deadheads, "which is a fearful number to carry free on a road like the Central . . . I think we made a mistake three times out of four in issuing passes."[34] But many senators' requests, not very subtly, mentioned the speed and generosity with which a rival line met their demands, and companies would not allow competitors even the most dubious advantages.[35] Passes remained bothersome and expensive, not effective corrupters of public officials.

Railroads also sold congressmen stock at very attractive prices and placed their relatives in sinecures somewhere on the payroll.[36] Yet even those most handsomely treated repeatedly failed to back the organization at the crucial times. Aaron Sargent was one of the few "clean" public men, at least until 1875 when for no obvious reason he turned "very cross and bitter against the Central Pacific Railroad people," and resigned his strategic position on the Senate Railroad Committee. "His going off," observed Huntington, "looks as if he did not care to help us or harm us much."[37] During the next year, Sargent became even more "bitter, and very active," and "if necessary," it seemed, "would sit up all night to do us harm." With bewildering inconsistency, however, he once again shifted course, and in 1877 Huntington gleefully reported: "I have had a talk with Sargent. He will be all right and I think we would be better off with him in the Senate than with almost any one else."[38] Senators, corporations discovered, were not loyal allies. They deserve rebuke for accepting the companies' gifts, and the companies deserve censure for having offered them. Yet it must not be forgotten that whatever corruption existed did not settle the fate of legislative questions.

Despite significant expenditures and efforts, from the most legitimate to the most questionable, business interests could not efficiently prejudice the legislative process. Their methods were too haphazard. Reviewing the events of these decades, Huntington confided to a California friend: "We have never had any men in Congress—either branch—with the exception of three, that have been worth anything to the State or to ourselves."[39] And a lobbyist, named Taylor, for the Texas & Pacific, told Sam Barlow that the road's failure to win its way in Congress was due to a want of organization and to misdirected ventures in Washington. "The measure had every element of success, equity, sectional feeling, local interests, hostility to Huntington and Gould, politics." But because of ineptitude, "all have been frittered away." The numerous lobbyists so frequently worked at cross purposes and accomplished nothing that Taylor despaired of the whole system. "There should be one man here with full powers who should have no dealing save with Senators and Congressmen," he recommended. "It is a waste of money to attempt anything in the future without an organization inside of both Houses of Congress. Lobbyists are positively detrimental." The company had squandered "time and money after shadows."[40]

These judgments by Huntington and Taylor were not official cant designed to mislead a naive public. Rather, they represented considered and accurate opinions. Lobbying, as its practitioners fully understood, was not an effective political tool. The costs were high and the returns unreliable. Other methods did not guarantee any better results. Companies were by no means scrupulous in their dealings, but dishonesty was not necessarily rewarded. Loans, gifts, jobs, and railroad passes did not effectively determine political decisions.

It is no simple matter to explain why a legislature acted as it did. In light of the public's reaction against the railroads, for example, congressional legislation in the 1870's might have been more drastic. But although the government did not cripple the lines, it certainly did not deal with them generously. Rather than capturing new land grants, companies faced forfeitures, sinking fund requirements, and rate regulation. These decisions resulted from a long series of congressional estimates and deliberations; they were not simple reflex actions to the hammer of business interests. The corporations' efforts were too muddled and their agents too unskilled to deserve any credit—and the companies themselves shared this conclusion. Lobbyists frequently warned their boss to "get your house in order," for it might well "snow or hail or rain." If corporations manipulated congressional politics so effectively, why did company presidents celebrate adjournments, thankful that the enterprise had survived?[41]

Business interests during these years faced a Senate of individuals, not of well organized parties, and the dispersal of energies heightened the confusion. Political consolidation would soon reorder the institution, but the alterations would only increase the difficulties.

In the last decades of the nineteenth century, when congressional legislation became even more pertinent to a multitude of economic interests, the early defects did not curtail the use of lobbying. Tariff and currency rather than railroad policies now attracted the agents to Washington, and their numbers and importance swelled visibly. The common use of the epithet, the "Third House of Congress," recognized their new stature.

Despite intense public criticism, lobbyists performed legitimate functions in Washington. By the 1890's they devoted almost all their time and attention to public officials already sympathetic to their position, occasionally detouring to convince the doubtful but invariably ignoring known opponents. Agents typically answered the inquiries of interested senators, explaining the various proposals on the calendar and clarifying the pertinent but dull details of intricate bills. With regularity, they supplied information that only representatives of particular organizations could gather. Helping members of Congress to understand the increasingly technical legislation that came before the chamber, lobbyists became the experts in an era of specialization. /

When Wyoming's Francis Warren set out to defend the high wool tariff on the Senate floor, he, like his colleagues, first contacted a pressure group. No sooner would he open his speech, Warren told Dewey, Gould and Company, than Senator Vest, a noted free trader well versed in the details of wool, "will cover me up with all sorts of figures." Therefore, insisted Warren, "I want *facts* to build up my arguments." American and foreign costs of wool production, the difference between distinct grades of wool here and abroad, selling prices of the various grades—even Warren, the largest sheep grower in Wyoming, would not have these figures on hand.[42] For their part, the agents expected to fill the gap. "Before the sugar schedule should be reached," lobbyist

John Searles convincingly proposed to Allison and Aldrich in 1888, "come to New York and go through one or more of our refineries in order to inform yourselves thoroughly on the subject;" Searles was quite pleased when they acceded to his request.[43] As *amicus curiae,* welcomed assistants, lobbyists achieved influence in the legislative process.

The congressional investigation of the sugar interests' role in the formation of the 1894 tariff schedules revealed the essentially pedagogic quality of the Washington lobby. Henry Havermeyer, president of the American Sugar Refining Company, and his representatives more frequently bored than tempted the chamber members. Havermeyer untiringly traveled about the capital gripping a large sample case full of small boxes of crude and refined sugar, including pieces of all the sugars grown anywhere in the world; only a senator on the witness stand would think to call it "a most interesting exhibit." After considerable efforts to gain personal introductions and at every possible opportunity, Havermeyer produced his satchel, spread the specimens, and launched a tedious analysis of the varying grades of sugar, the tests to differentiate them, selling prices, costs, and the equity of ad valorem rather than specific duties.[44] "How can a Senator know about a great question," volunteered Theodore Havermeyer, "unless he keeps himself informed by those who have devoted their lifetime to it and have a lifelong interest in it?"[45]

The accuracy and reliability of the statistics were beyond doubt. "A man who has big interest at stake, does not dare to tell anything except the truth," asserted the president's brother and partner, "because if he did not tell the truth it would be found out the next day, and his evidence would not be worth a snap."[46] Moreover, Senators' inquiries were penetrating and to the point. Henry Reed, head of Revere Sugar, divulged confidential price and production data to James Jones, in charge of the Democratic tariff, despite his concern that rivals might see the figures;

Jones had wanted the accountings in order to formulate sched-ules.[47] The Senator also diligently examined Havermeyer on "the methods and costs of refining, and as to the yield of refined sugars from the different kinds of raw sugar." When Havermeyer claimed he did not know, Jones testily left the interview.[48] Sen-ators expected lobbyists to supply the necessary facts.

Personal relationships with public officials were considered so vital that lobbyists would not bother to contact men they did not know. Herbert Terrill, agent for the sugar refiners, explained that he discussed rates only with friends; with others "I presumed my views would not have had much weight." Texas senator Horace Chilton contended that corporations disliked great turnovers in office; their representatives could not form stable connections among constantly changing members.[49]

The lobbying profession soon became an appropriate occupa-tion for defeated or retired senators. Republican George Spencer informed William Chandler soon after the Democrats regained control in Alabama that he would make an effective Washington agent. "I think I could utilize the 12 years of Senatorial life to good advantage," he confided.[50] Recognizing that ex-senators had access to friends who remained in office, corporations regularly hired them. The practice became so widespread that Eugene Hale proposed in 1897 to alter the rules governing visitors' rights to the chamber floor. As a traditional courtesy, all former members were permitted to enter the Senate and mingle with their old as-sociates. But because of the prevalence of one-time colleagues among lobbyists, argued Hale, only those "who are not interested in any claim . . . or directly in any bill pending before Congress," should have the prerogative. The restriction would "prevent ex-senators from enjoying the privilege of the floor of the Senate for the purpose of urging or opposing claims or bills in which they are employed as attorneys." Nevertheless, rather than afford equal op-portunity to all lobbyists and spare itself possible embarrassments, the chamber maintained its custom. Corporations naturally continued to hire former senators on the strength of their old connections.[51]

The services that lobbyists performed were welcomed by those of like mind, and senators willingly trusted the tasks of research and speech writing, as well as of general counsel, to men sharing similar outlooks.[52] Members, welcoming the publicity and prominence, encouraged pressure groups to distribute their speeches. After delivering a long attack on Cleveland's free-trade policies, John Sherman solicited the support of American Iron and Steel. "I have your letter," secretary James Swank immediately replied, "suggesting a subscription from our Association to aid in the circulation of your speech. Please put us down for ten thousand copies."[53] A few senators were wary about accepting the service; George Hoar once returned a $10,000 check to Andrew Carnegie, noting that he never assumed the task of mailing his addresses and did not take funds for the purpose. But most colleagues willingly procured and accepted such aid.[54] Ever anxious to impress constituents, senators also cooperated in sending out associations' educational tracts and pamphlets. They gladly supplied long mailing lists, including the names of friendly local postmasters to see to a proper distribution.[55] Senators and lobbyists customarily joined together for their mutual benefit.

Loans were still readily available for the right senators in the 1890's, but bribery was the particular province of ridiculous and insignificant adventures. The 1894 sugar investigations highlighted one typical case. Charles Butz, suffering from some sort of physical paralysis with a history of mental illness, was accused of offering Populist senator James Kyle $1,400 to vote against the tariff and proposing that the son of Democratic senator Eppa Hunton instruct his father to oppose the pending bill. Butz, not affiliated with any company and earning a meager livelihood by occasionally seeing a private claim through Congress, conceived a farfetched money-making scheme. He would line up some senators against protective tariffs and then sell his services to a group of English free traders; with their funds, he would make his payoff and keep the rest for profit. Kyle and Hunton naturally gave Mr. Butz no attention; the country was not imperiled by his activities.[56]

/ As lobbying became an integral part of American political life, its practices were clearly and unashamedly defended. In an 1888 report, a majority of the Pacific Railway Commission, after questioning Huntington and other officials, expounded the rationale. "It is impossible," they explained to Congress, "for the railroad companies to avoid expending considerable sums of money in causing their interests to be properly represented . . . It would be unreasonable to deny the corporations having large interests at stake the right to be represented before the committees of the legislature, and the right to pay proper compensation of money to those who represent them."[57] Corporation spokesmen echoed the theme: business was so complicated that without technical advice, Congress could not justly legislate. Elected officials "must represent the material interests" of their constituents, and lobbyists clarified these needs.[58] Senators, in private action and public statement, also voiced agreement. "It is of the utmost importance," avowed Nelson Aldrich, "to manufacturers and to members of Congress . . . to have in existence some representative organization whose officers or agents can speak with authority on the various complex questions constantly arising."[59] The Third House of Congress was an important adjunct to the other two.

/ Lobbying, therefore, was never a term popular with corporations or their Washington employees. Invariably, without regard for degrees or licenses, agents were referred to as attorneys, and their salaries labeled retainers. According to sponsors and practitioners, lobbyists resembled the members of the bar for they too presented arguments before a constituted authority. Lawyers pleaded a client's case to its best advantage, always within ethical limits, and ostensibly lobbyists put forward the company's position as best they could. Government faced no danger from the practice, they argued, for senators, like judges, heard several sides of a case and were free to choose among them. The political process was as honest as the court's routine.[60]

The defense of lobbying had some appeal and validity, but the system unfortunately was not free from serious flaws. Senators did not always possess the judicial virtue of disinterestedness. "Congressional lobbyism," proclaimed Thomas Bayard in 1882, "has become a feature in American government," establishing the doctrine that a senator may "vote upon a question involving his direct personal interest," or "bring into Congress schemes and plans which should put money into his own pocket, under the color of exercising his power and duty as a representative of the public." Such behavior, lectured Bayard to his colleagues, discredited the institution. "There is no doctrine more accepted everywhere in courts of justice than that a judge, even when a mere relative is interested in the result of his adjudication, is disqualified to sit in the case, much less in his own case."[61] But few men who heard Bayard, regardless of their contacts with lobbyists, could testify to a career free from personal economic activity. Lawyers kept up a practice, and businessmen did not sever company affiliations. Senators bore no resemblance to Plato's model counselors; their hands frequently touched the worldly metals.

Although the chamber's members could not systematically promote their private welfare during congressional sessions because of the press of public business, they were able to snatch scattered moments for personal affairs. Their random and brief attention turned naturally to various sorts of speculation, and at times the Senate resembled the floor of a brokerage house. Wealthy colleagues were often able and willing to recommend a highly profitable investment, and appropriately, West Virginia's Henry Davis became a favorite among his peers. The son of an enterprising but unsuccessful town site speculator, Davis began his career as a brakeman for the Baltimore & Ohio. Enjoying regular promotions and marrying well, he was able in 1858 to devote full attention to a mercantile business among the Piedmont farmers. The Civil War stimulated the enterprise. The Union needed the region's foodstuffs and lumber, and Davis accumulated the capital to expand his real estate holdings. Political success paralleled business advances, and in 1871, ready to develop the great coal and timber regions of the Cumberland, Davis was elected senator.[62]

Political friends in Washington were now brought into his projects. Not long after arriving in the capital, the new senator and his marriageable daughter met New Mexico's Territorial Delegate and most prominent real estate speculator, Stephen Elkins, and Davis acquired a son-in-law and extraordinarily talented business associate.[63] To tap the area's resources, Davis set out to construct the West Virginia and Pittsburgh Railroad, and heading the list of directors was a not too distant relative from Maryland, Arthur Gorman. James Blaine, Thomas Bayard, Connecticut's William Barnum, and Maryland's other senator, William Whyte, also soon joined; Johnson Camden, one of West Virginia's leading oil refiners and allied with the Rockefeller interests, was included as well. Stock in the popularly designated "Senatorial Railroad," was publicly issued at forty dollars per share, but Davis' Senate associates made their purchases at twenty dollars. Few who were asked turned down the opportunity.[64]

Davis was no narrow partisan. Frequently crossing the chamber's dividing aisle in search of business associates, he included Republicans Jerome Chaffee, William Windom, and William Allison in his coal ventures.[65] His colleague, Johnson Camden, was more narrow in outlook, but Democrats James Fair and George Vest, as well as Arthur Gorman, were offered lucrative proposals.[66] Nor did prosperous members disregard less fortunate senators. Gorman generously advanced loans to Zeb Vance and John Morgan, while Davis readily satisfied Matt Ransom's needs. And borrowing from friends carried unique advantages; the West

Virginia entrepreneur, after the slightest of hints, unceremoni-
ously tore up Ransom's IOU.[67]

Republicans were not dependent upon Democratic munifi-
cence, for the School of Philosophy Club offered not only fine
poker games but excellent investment and loan opportunities as
well. Allison and Aldrich were partners in business as well as
politics, and McMillan was as genial a banker as he was a host.
Frequently looking after his friends' portfolios, he gladly sold
Allison $5,000 worth of Detroit Electrical Works stock, "so as
to have him make something."[68] The Michigan Senator was also
prepared to lend needy colleagues substantial sums, although as
a businessman he felt compelled to collect 6 per cent interest.
Fellow club member Charles Manderson borrowed $5,000, and
William Washburn, $15,000; even Senator Chauncey Depew,
one-time president of the New York Central, was in McMillan's
debt.[69] These practices were not confined to the inner circle. The
aloof John Sherman, for example, was also known to give an
occasional real estate tip.[70]

The public implications of senators' investments varied greatly.
Some activities presented few dangers; stock ownership in Davis'
railroad, for example, assured members of profitable returns without impinging upon their official duties. Buying stock in an enterprise did not necessarily mean that the public welfare would be
ignored. Businessmen, after all, had not come to Washington to
further their fortunes, and for most of them the trip entailed
sacrifices. Nevertheless, there can be no doubt that private and
public interests at times collided. And the results could be un-
fortunate.

Members sometimes confused public and personal responsibilities. Since they often passed upon questions with a significant
bearing on their personal ventures, senators turned political in-

sights to the service of their companies. Francis Warren, the Wyoming woolgrower, judging that the 1897 Senate tariffs would not adequately protect wool, presumed a drop in prices; with this advance knowledge, he confidently instructed his brokers to keep his goods off the market for another year.[71] McMillan advised his son in 1901 that since Cuban annexation was imminent, investments in the American beet sugar industry should not be expanded. "You can use this information for your own benefit," he prudently added, "but do not connect my name with it."[72] Johnson Camden, for his part, sent oil magnate Henry Flagler important official government documents on eastern storage requirements.[73] Senators, unselfishly, helped family and friends as well as themselves.

The actions of a fractional minority of the chamber bordered on the criminal. When John Patterson, Reconstruction senator from South Carolina, was chairman of the Railroad Committee, he attempted to sell political information for private profit. Convinced that the Kansas, Missouri & Texas bonds were climbing solely on the basis of rumors that his committee would soon recommend government aid to the road, he instructed a close friend, William Grant, to contact Sam Barlow. "He assures me," Grant informed Barlow, "that the bill will not be taken up," and advised we "go short" on the bonds. Of course, Patterson "will expect to be benefited by any sale you may make."[74] Southern Democrats were often no more scrupulous. John Gordon also tried to turn some inside knowledge into a profit on state bond speculations. Even the most prudent senators, however, inadvertently leaked helpful data. An acquaintance of Thomas Bayard once related how he earned a handsome sum by anticipating a gold price rise. Although not a frequent investor, he knew what to do when Bayard remarked in passing that the inflationists held a slight majority in Congress.[75] Political information and financial acumen were a profitable combination.

Despite Bayard's unfair and simple-minded accusations, congressional lobbyists did not originate the problem of conflict of interest. Senators did not have to await the bribes of an interested corporation in order to own stock; through colleagues' advice and their own good sense, they were often able to build up bulging portfolios. Banning lobbyists from the Capitol would not solve the dilemma. The difficulties were more intricate and less amenable to control.

The introduction of corrective legislation was one Senate response to the danger. In June 1886 Kentucky's James Beck moved to forbid senators from accepting "employment or payment for services from a railroad company or any of its officers which had obtained its charter or grant of land or pecuniary aid from the United States Government." Beck reminded his colleagues that while senators were forbidden to appear professionally before the Court of Claims or any other government department, statutes outlawed few other private activities. Although the principle was identical, there was still no prohibition against accepting a retainer from a railroad that had business before the Congress. It was obviously time to modernize the law.[76]

However, the obstacles to conflict of interest legislation were immediately apparent. Why single out transportation, inquired Orgeon's John Mitchell, a close friend of railroad builder Henry Villard. Logically, retainers with every company involved in interstate commerce should be banned. Furthermore, why limit the laws exclusively to attorneys? The businessmen sitting in the chamber should be enjoined from handling goods liable to government taxes or tariffs. William Evarts, the brilliant New York lawyer, extended Mitchell's reasoning. There existed no valid rationale for discriminating against the defenders of the roads; surely the opponents warranted disqualification.[77] Moreover, interceded George Hoar, Congress exercised jurisdiction over the District of Columbia; following this logic, senators ought not to be allowed to purchase land in the capital. Beck, in frustration, accused his colleagues of making a burlesque of legislation. But, in fact, they were purposefully clarifying the impossibility of curing these evils by statute. Senators, as lawyers or businessmen, took a part in financial enterprises. To enact an equitable code would require prohibiting all private economic activity.[78]

Many members, not convinced that personal business connections posed a threat to duty, contended that economic involvement did not dictate legislative decisions. When some colleagues questioned the propriety of owning mines and voting on coal tariffs, Henry Davis heatedly replied: "I suppose I am interested personally to the extent of one ten-thousandth part of the coal mined in this country . . . and yet Senators speak as if that would have any weight with me . . . as if coal was the thing above all others; as if some little personal feeling actuated me." With equal vehemence, Thomas Bayard answered references to his railroad retainers. They were strictly limited to service in the law courts and had no relation to his votes in the chamber.[79]

Other senators argued that multiple interests improved rather than corrupted legislation. "It is not the theory of this government," expounded Henry Teller, "that the men who sit in this Chamber are to be divorced from all business . . . [or] from all private interests. They are to participate in the general business of the country, and thus become acquainted with the interests and wants of the people."[80] George Hoar, deserving his reputation for probity, reiterated the contention:

We do not want our legislators . . . monks. The theory of our government . . . is that that is the best legislative body which contains the representatives of all the great interests of the country; that men are fitter to legislate who have by personal experience . . . that personal knowledge which comes only from close interest in the things in which the people of the country or of the state they represent are interested.[81]

Observers also contended that senators should be at liberty to enter all court cases, "for no one ever supposes that a lawyer is a party to his client's cause . . . In fact it is the duty of judges and lawyers alike to see to it that a full representation of both sides of every case be had." To restrict members' freedom would only injure justice and government.[82]

Despite the confidence of these assertions, the issue was not summarily dismissed. By the last decade of the nineteenth century, a heightened sensitivity to conflicts of interest characterized the attitudes of most public officials. The problem was by no means resolved, and serious ambiguities remained to plague incumbents and citizens; but the first tentative and broad guidelines were set down. The question, after all, was of recent origin, for in antebellum America industries rarely crossed state lines. Senators, at most, owned limited interests in specialized and local companies, and decisions in Washington only tangentially affected their affairs. In the post-Civil War decades, however, national corporations which extended beyond state boundaries, and stock issues which covered the nation, were common phenomena; and at the same time congressional legislation assumed a critical pertinence. Only then did senators' personal finances, frequently and significantly, encroach upon their official actions.

To be sure, no new moral code was promulgated during these years. The men occupying public office did not hold standards differing from contemporary ones, and only the most facile exercise in historicism could absolve dishonest officials from responsibility. The ethic of not judging one's own case was at least biblical in origin, and as familiar to those traveling to Washington in 1870 as in 1900 or in 1960. Rather, as the dimensions of the problem swelled and novelty no longer obfuscated its implications, senators scrutinized their actions with prudence and caution. The public also grasped the significance of the altered economic conditions and reacted crudely but consistently, damning every business affiliation regardless of its particular importance. Convinced that stock holdings necessarily determined voting behavior, they forced their representatives to grow even more responsive to the issue.[83] Moreover, the changes coincided with the increased professionalization of political careers and the overwhelming demands of Senate life. To the sins of absenteeism were added the dangers of conflict of interest. Extended private financial involvements now began to lose some of their attractions.

Public life, however, was never financially feasible without some sort of nonpolitical occupation. "I know," affirmed Teller as the chamber debated these matters, "that if some of the Senators sitting in this body were compelled to refrain from any kind of business by which they could add to their incomes, and [had] to depend entirely upon the salary paid them as Senators, they would be compelled to leave the public service." Since a $5,000 stipend could not support a senator and his family, and the people, despite strict opinions, were not "willing to say that their public servants shall do nothing but attend to the public interest," outside incomes remained indispensable.[84] By 1900, however, members often selected their clients and investments with more than monetary returns in mind.

The new attitudes were widely evident. When recounting the

career of Allen Thurman, Ohio's long-time senator and Cleveland's running mate, the Democratic campaign literature in 1888 apologetically noted that Thurman actually devoted little attention to his law practice, "save in about a dozen important cases in which his relations could not be violently sundered."[85] William Stewart informed a would-be business partner that same year: "I am pleased to learn that petroleum has been found in our state. If it is on an Indian reservation I could not be personally interested in it. I have made it a rule under no circumstances to have any personal interest in any measure or question that can possibly come before Congress or any of the Departments."[86]

John Spooner also explained to prospective clients that he "would not become interested as an attorney in any matters where the influence of my position as Senator would be valuable to a client." Lawyers, like Thurston of Nebraska, resigned railroad retainers before running for national office, and businessmen, like McMillan, retired from railroad directorships before coming to Washington.[87] Senators grew wary of owning newspapers and even more prudent about the sorts of legislative information they released.[88] New Jersey's wealthy senator, John McPherson, did not believe that sugar stock ownership would, in any way, affect his vote; yet he would not himself own, or permit his son to purchase, stocks whose values might be altered by Senate action. Matt Quay righteously told investigators: "I do not feel there is anything in my connection with the Senate to interfere with my buying or selling stock when I please." Still he, too, sold his shares of sugar—at a loss—so as "to vote [on the 1894 schedules] without having any interest in the stock"[89]

The declining use of railroad passes reflected part of the

change. The Interstate Commerce Act of 1887 prohibited passes for national lines, and states often enacted similar laws. "When I went to Yellowstone Park," Spooner related to former cabinet member Daniel Lamont, "I paid my fare and was glad to do so." Spooner returned his Northern Pacific card, and many of his colleagues duplicated the action.[90] Managers, as expected, were pleased with the measure, often revoking privileges already granted.[91] But the system was so harmless that although the letter of the law was usually respected, strange schemes were often devised to break its spirit. The most ingenious and popular technique was to become a railroad official, for the law specifically excused the officers of carrying companies. Senator Pettigrew always began his pass requests with the statement: "I am President of the Sioux Falls Terminal Railroad, ten miles of standard gauge." And he shared his good fortune with less well-placed colleagues. "Elect Charles F. Manderson . . . Vice President of the Company," Pettigrew instructed an associate, and "then get out some letter heads showing his name."[92] Accordingly, Senator Manderson became eligible for free transportation.

With no exact formula available for determining when a senator resembled a judge sitting in his own case rather than a responsible representative, a wide range of morality existed within the chamber. Many members would not accept retainers or purchase stocks that could conceivably conflict with their public duties; but others carried on diverse economic activities with impunity. Discipline was out of the question. Without clear-cut demarcations, no consistent judgments were possible. Moreover, the arguments of Teller and Hoar favoring senatorial involvement in the general business of the country were respectable and could not be disregarded. The public, for its part, could not effectively redress any wrongs at the ballot box. Senators' financial holdings were often well-guarded secrets and other, more important, issues customarily determined electoral decisions. Then too, members' key holdings were frequently invested in the state's leading enterprise; who was to judge whether Henry Davis supported high coal duties for his own good or for the good of West Virginia? Officeholders were usually immune to reprisals, and the sanctions that existed were internal. Neither the Senate nor the voters could assume the role of brother's keeper.

Ambiguities remained, but when lobbyists entered the Capitol in the 1890's, they recognized that certain practices were beyond even the vague boundaries of acceptability. Corporations could not expect to affiliate public officials, through bonds or retainers, when pertinent measures were due for consideration. No one would now believe the defense that stocks were pedagogic devices rather than corrupting influences. Senators, in fact, could no longer dare accept such offers, and companies, anticipating rebuff or scandal, feared to initiate them. The implications of a member's twenty-year company affiliation, begun long before his political career, were complex; but the meaning of a sudden offer of a stock option was not. Corruption still came to light as congressional investigations reminded senators and agents of the proper limits. Individual failings, however, and not a rotten system were at fault. Lobbyists had not prompted the dilemma of conflict of interest. Still, the wariness that now often typified Senate conduct circumscribed their behavior.

The relationship between politicians and lobbyists at the end of the nineteenth century was also testimony to the strength of parties. The image of Henry Havermeyer, president of America's largest sugar refining corporation, seeking out a senator in order to open his satchel and display his specimens was a valid indication of the balance of power. The unity of Senate parties stood in direct contrast to the fragmented concerns of business enterprises. Economic interests revealed little evidence of general harmony. Sugar growers battled sugar refiners just as wool growers combated wool manufacturers. What benefited one railroad, injured another; and when Tom Scott was pleased, Huntington complained. Merchants and importers, in search of low tariffs, opposed manufacturers seeking protection. Silver mine owners prospered while creditors lamented, and large city bankers urged proposals that their small town brethren denounced. Even monopolies within industries did not promote political unity. They only served to increase the size of the contestants.

Politicians, on the other hand, entered the caucus ready to compromise for the welfare of the organization; no matter if sugar rates and coal duties were not exactly to their liking. On both sides of the aisle the message was clear: take some bitter medicine or sacrifice the whole thing. In this setting, party welfare superseded any senator's commitment to a particular proposal. Party men, not businessmen, composed the only real community in Washington.

The competition for party favor did not guarantee the protection of the national interest. George Edmunds confidently announced: "One bias offsets the other and the general outcome is the good of the Republic."[93] But his optimism was excessive. Politicians did hear several sides of an argument but many voices, belonging to the farmers, laborers, professional groups, minorities, and consumers, were still absent from Washington. The preeminence of party did not simply mean equal justice for all. Still, by 1900 a forum to which various interests could appeal had been created. Business groups were the first to take advantage of the opportunity; but in the next decades other interests would also organize their efforts. The post-Civil War years did not represent the acme of corruption. Rather, it witnessed the start of the modern system by which pressure groups vied for government support.

☆ VIII ☆

IN DEFENSE OF PARTY GOVERNMENT

No permanent good ever was or ever will be accomplished by instrumentalities of government except party government. You may say that there have been instances of despots who have made great improvements. But either the good they did perished with them or they made changes in the constitution tending toward freedom, that is tending to substitute party government, which is freedom, for despotic or oligarchic government which is slavery.

Senator George Hoar, in reply to a civil service reformer, 1895

The changes in political life after 1870 did not escape comment. Men in high office and students of government, from the perspectives of Capitol Hill or the university library, explored the implications at length. For the first time detailed texts examined the structure of American parties. Pre-Civil War studies did not offer acceptable descriptions of political organizations, and between 1870 and 1889 only six works devoted to these questions were published. However, in the following decade, there suddenly appeared no fewer than seventeen pertinent volumes.[1] Moreover, politicians as well as professional scholars scrutinized and questioned their allegiances and obligations with a new intensity. They offered a perceptive and appreciative, if less formal, account of the party and its machinery.

These able commentaries have suffered a curious neglect. Recent political scientists have not ignored the substance of their predecessors' arguments but they have isolated it from the context of time and place; few have wondered why this rather remarkable discovery occurred in the 1890's, or speculated whether it reflected significant alterations in government practices. The declarations by public officials have attracted still less attention. Historians, sympathetic to Mugwump sentiments, customarily have disregarded or dismissed arguments vindicating the political system. The inattention, however, was not warranted. The defense of party at once reflected and reinforced the modern structure of American politics.

Senators, like most Washington officials, were not prone to systematic analyses. Nevertheless, their scattered speeches and writings, taken together, offered one of the first thorough and intelligent appreciations of party's contributions to democracy. More important, these notions helped strengthen Democratic and Republican organizations. Senators more willingly disregarded personal opinions to accept caucus compromise when they judged party to be vital to government. They balanced any inclination to break ranks by considerations of party welfare, and organizational needs won out with regularity. The defense of party helped buttress its place in American politics.

Politicians before the Civil War did not often devote sustained attention to the subject for there was little impetus to abstract generalizations. Occasionally a noted leader expounded on some of the virtues of loyalty, but his was a minority voice. Most commentators, when they discussed party at all, argued that it existed only to further certain well-defined principles; alliances were to achieve specific goals and then disintegrate after enacting the platform. The place of party in democratic government was essentially transitory. In fact the political realities of these early years reinforced popular attitudes. Party mortality was strikingly high, and obligations were not very demanding or vital; factions joined together soon to disappear and allegiances shifted freely. Most Americans readily supported several organizations in the course of their lifetimes.

In the chamber, senators did not often cite the organization's welfare or the caucus' need to defend their actions. At the polls, they labored for partisan victories; yet they usually limited their oratory to the personalities and issues of the day. Campaigns did not customarily include appeals to party regularity or fervid homilies to the label on a banner. Even those most committed to the survival of democratic institutions paid little heed to the fate of particular groups. The passage of specific measures was important, but the demise of an organization prompted no fear for freedom's future in a one-party state. There were few incentives to investigate the performance of party government when its virtues and significance sparked only brief discussion.[2]

Liberal Republicans in 1872 confirmed the assumptions of antebellum America. With the passage of the Fifteenth Amendment, their spokesmen insisted, the Republicans had fulfilled their purposes; the Union was saved and the Negroes' rights secured. The party ought to disband now that its principles were enacted, and a new organization, devoted to contemporary issues, could then come into power. "What the country now stands most in need of," announced Carl Schurz, "is parties without records."[3] When it became apparent that the older organization possessed a strong hold on the people's affections and did not intend to relinquish it, Liberal Republicans grew frantic. The country was endangered for Republicans would continue to rule with their own existence the sole goal of survival. "Political bummers acting in the name of party," would control elections, lamented Lyman Trumbull, and with no great issues to bind the membership, principle would disappear from politics. Party loyalty would imprison good government, and spoils and petty interests would serve as the shackles.[4]

Convinced that the survival of an organization lacking clear and unambiguous policies was a most serious perversion of the political process, Liberal Republicans lost all sense of perspective. Despite real weaknesses in Republican authority when

Grant was inaugurated, they exaggerated the scope of the discipline. "The great evil that we will have to overcome," Schurz frantically warned Charles Sumner, "is that great party spirit which turns everything to selfish advantages and has created a sort of terrorism to which but too many submit."[5] True to doctrine, they bolted to run their own ticket, and although the slate was easily defeated and soon forgotten, the ethic was not. Mugwumps and their allies periodically repeated similar sentiments to a large and appreciative audience.

Nevertheless, an alternative perception of party's role in government soon won recognition. Its formulations, although not very popular, were appropriate to the actualities of American political life. Liberal Republican attacks called forth immediate rejoinders, but the first brief replies revealed few innovations. Oliver Morton and other prominent Republican spokesmen proclaimed party an indispensable instrument in the salvation of democratic government; still, they based their appeals exclusively on the historical fact that Republicans had protected the Union and would best safeguard the accomplishments of the war. Having preserved the nation, party was designated the savior of freedom.[6]

A decade later, however, more outright appreciations of party, not bound to a peculiar circumstance, were voiced. Senators explained to constituents that principles could only be fulfilled through the efforts of political organizations. "I may be a good deal of a partisan," announced John Sherman, "but I think I can be a partisan and patriot at the same time. I believe that where a man has strong convictions of public policy, and that policy is represented by a party, the best he can do is to aid and advance the interests of that party."[7] Other colleagues were even less circumspect in their statements. "Political parties," Senator John Reagan confidently informed the Texas press in 1896, "are unavoidable in a free country like ours as necessary means of adopting and enforcing principles which will secure the rights, promote the welfare, and protect the liberties of our people."[8] And Senator Lyman Casey instructed North Dakota's inhabitants: "Parties are a necessity to popular governments . . . Great principles can only be maintained by a conscientious union of those who hold them."[9] The defensive tone of Sherman's pronouncement—a constituent would best be advised to affiliate with a party only after it favored a specific measure— was quickly disappearing. Parties were not an alternative but a necessity.

The argument soon extended far beyond any simple identification of organization and principle. Party in itself was vital to American government. Confessing that he was "not of those who believe in non-partisanship in politics," John Ingalls informed his colleagues that "political parties, energetic, vigorous, and well-defined are indispensable to the success of free popular governments. Wherever the life of States is freest and more irrepressible, there party spirit is most active and aggressive." Warning his countrymen that "when parties perish this government will expire," Ingalls explained that "in this country the only government is the party in power. Here is no dynasty, no ruling family, nothing corresponding to the functions of government under other systems except the party."[10]

Senator William Evarts offered a similar exposition. "In this country, as by necessity under free and representative government, government must be carried on by party and its power must be sought by the methods of party . . . Party ties and party duties are the only mode in which free institutions are carried on in representative government." The New York attorney contended that "steadfast and intrepid adhesion to party is a merit," otherwise government degenerated into "force and fraud." Even if issues were temporarily muddled or obscured, betrayal and desertion were still inappropriate. Party deserved continued loyalty. Its machinery promoted the just exercise of power and the benefits of progress.[11]

When in 1895 Dorman Eaton, the avid civil service reformer, completed an historical survey of Massachusetts politics, he dispatched a copy to George Hoar. Fearing that the Senator might miss the all too obvious and belabored analogy, in an accompanying letter Eaton asserted that colonial Massachusetts exhibited the most common and significant failings of party rule: it could not correct its own evils. "If the theory is sound," the reformer smugly concluded, "I am sure you will agree to look in the future more to public opinion and less to party opinion."[12]

Annoyed with the communication, Hoar penned a lengthy reply three days later. The Senator first skillfully took the would-be historian to task for equating the parties in the pre-Revolutionary Bay Colony with contemporary national organizations. "I think you might as well call the combination of the serpent with Eve party government," he reproved Eaton, "as apply that name to the ruling power in Massachusetts." Turning next to the functions of the present day organizations, Hoar explained that the party enacted legislation essential to the public welfare. "No good principle or measure can ever be carried out in a free government otherwise." In fact the only alternative was "oligarchic, monarchic or despotic government." An organization at times might succumb to dangerous influences, but ultimately there was "less of evil in party government than any other, and in party government the remedy is swifter and more easily applied than in any other." Hoar had no doubts that "the man who doesn't belong to a party, who doesn't unite with other men . . . by proper organization and combined effort, is always useless and commonly mischievous. The most mischievous person that I know in politics, is the man who says he votes for the best man without regard for party."

The Massachusetts Senator ended his argument by firmly insisting that "no permanent good ever was or ever will be accomplished in human affairs by instrumentalities of government except party government." The successes that despots occasionally achieved either perished with them or became part of a

fundamental change toward freedom, "that is, tending to substitute party government, which is freedom, for despotic or
oligarchic government, which is slavery."[13] This equation, a notable contribution of the post-Civil War decades to American
political thought, helped alter the character of the Senate.

The new appreciation of party dignified the virtue of partisanship. Eulogies delivered in the chamber frequently included some
mention of the member's steadfast loyalties. When one-time
caucus chairman Henry Anthony died, Democrat George Pendleton thought it proper to state: "His fidelity to party organization
was inflexible and pronounced. His appreciation of a like fidelity
among his opponents . . . [was] equally conspicuous."[14] Similarly, William Evarts eulogized Thomas Hendricks, his colleague
from across the aisle. "He is entitled," the New York lawyer declared, "to the credit of having been a consistent, an intelligent,
a prudent, a patient, and a courageous statesman in the service
of the Democratic party, which he espoused and to which he
unflinchingly adhered."[15] Even in the most solemn circumstances,
partisanship was now celebrated along with more traditional
attributes. As John Spooner put it: "Honest partisanship is honest
citizenship."[16]

Yet at the same time, spokesmen assumed that party loyalty
promoted the natonal well-being only in a two-party system. "The
history of our country," announced Senator Henry Davis, "is that
two great political parties are necessary to free government and
the nearer equal the better for the people."[17] A minority organization, persistently supported, was essential to the political process. Of course, before such statements could command general
agreement, the sentiments excited by the war had to lose force.
During the conflict and for some years later, the standard Republican posture toward the minority resembled the attitude of
Cato to Carthage. They labeled Democratic efforts to reconcile
North and South short of union as sedition, and marked any
sympathy for the Confederate aims as treason. Judging their

rivals traitors, Republicans hoped to destroy, as well as defeat, the party. Democrats answered in kind, the highly vocal Copperheads capturing most headlines. Republican war legislation, they charged, subverted the basic form of government and threatened the survival of freedom. The notion that a majority and minority were vital to democracy found few supporters in 1869.[18]

Attempting to win popular favor, Democrats and Republicans incessantly returned to these arguments, and sectional harmony was slow to affect political life. Still the memory of the war gradually blurred, and common ties reunited the economic and social order. The issues of the 1860's lost prominence and campaign orators stopped punctuating their rhetoric with cries of treason and subversion. Soon the values of a two-party government gained unprecedented approval.

Election contests were invested with a new importance. "I know by no instruction of my observation, nor by anything I can draw from history," contended William Evarts, "any other mode of conducting the debates of great and free people except by means of great and firm parties."[19] John Ingalls maintained: "It is by the conflict and collision of political parties that the latent and richest powers of the state are made manifest." Campaigns clarified the issues and alerted the public, insuring that full discussion preceded government decisions.[20]

More important, minority parties checked any inclination to tyranny. "A minority is absolutely indispensable to the preservation of liberty in any country," insisted Henry Teller. "If there was not a minority party in this country, there would be little prospect for the maintenance of American liberty."[21] New York senator David Hill concurred: "An honest and patriotic opposition party was necessary to check and prevent excess on the part of the party in power."[22]

Two-party politics also limited the corrupting nature of power. "The difficulty of self-government in a free country," warned David Turpie, long-time Indiana senator, "has often taken the form of inability to maintain an opposition of sufficient strength and numbers to curb and control the factious spirit of power." Wisely, "the people in a republic, almost instinctively, make from time to time a change in the administration." When a party assumes office without effective opposition, when "there is no actual check or curb upon their power, they assume that there ought to be no other restrictions upon its exercise." Irresponsible government was bound to follow.[23] "Is there anything on earth," Kentucky's John Williams asked his peers, "that corrupts men like long possession of power and the temptation incident to it?" Professing great admiration for the part of the Lord's Prayer which reads, "Lead us not into temptation," Williams would have liked to add for the sake of politicians: "Nor keep us exposed to it too long."[24]

/ Partisan purposes often prompted statements of the doctrine, and Democrats, usually out of national office, often spoke of the need to transfer power. Yet the Republicans, despite long tenure, also accepted the premises of two-party politics. Some members, for example, admitted that Cleveland's election in 1884 would probably benefit, not threaten, the nation; one party had controlled the government long enough.[25] Others used the argument to rationalize Republican efforts in the South. "The minority party," Garfield told a national convention, "can exercise an effective and wholesome restraint upon the party in power. Without such restraint party rule becomes tyrannical and corrupt." John Sherman echoed his words in the Senate: "If either party prevails in any one of the Northern states, it makes no great difference, for the time being; any mistake is corrected by the changes of political parties; but in the South," he informed his listeners, "you have but one party, you allow no other."[26] The need for political competition was clear. /

Moreover, senators now commended a host of other qualities essential to the proper functioning of the party. They lucidly defined and explicitly endorsed the value of organization, of unity, and of leadership. When Thomas Bayard complained of the "absence of that high conscientious, self-respecting tone, all of which is comprehended in that good word, gentleman," among his peers, he professed sentiments more appropriate to his father and grandfather, senators from Delaware in their day. But the younger Bayard was far more mindful than his forebears of the preeminence of organization in politics. "I am sensible," he confessed to the mild-mannered lobbyist, Sam Ward, "of the necessity of correspondence and co-operation to effect organization— no one is more impatient than I of the selfishness which marks insubordination and the short-sightedness which fails to discern that no great object . . . can be achieved without the suppression of much individuality of will and judgment."[27] For the sake of party, organization took precedence over ambition and independence.

Other members learned the same lessons from contemporary events. "A free government can only be administered through party," Newton Booth instructed California Republicans. "The moral triumph in the war of rebellion . . . [was] due, not to any unorganized, vague sentiment diffused at large, but to the powerful organization of that sentiment in the Republican party."[28] West Virginia Democrat Frank Hereford pointed to Reconstruction days. "Through party organization and discipline," he lectured a would-be bolter from the state convention, "we came into power and broke the chains of tyranny that had hitherto bound us. And only through that same party organization can we retain power."[29] Senator Francis Warren counseled his supporters: "Organization is everything in politics and it must be kept up." Zebulon Vance gave similar instructions to the North Carolina farmers, noting: "It is peculiarly an age of organization."[30] And all this emphasis seemed just and proper, for as Texas Democrat Horace Chilton declared: "Organized thought is as necessary as free thought to advance a country. Free thought is sometimes radical—organized thought is nearly always conservative."[31]

Party unity was not only essential to the enactment of proposed legislation, it promoted the meaningful competition of two organizations for power. David Turpie explained that when the parties, "unbroken and undivided," debated a political question, the people could express their preferences at the ballot box. "But when one of the two parties in such a contest has been beaten by its internal dissensions, there is no such verdict or judgment; the only thing decided . . . is the truth of the adage that a house divided against itself cannot stand."[32] Two-party politics, contended William Evarts, demanded "great and firm parties," and George Hoar praised the "tenacity and consistency" of their members.[33] Disunity was the worst possible fate. "When you have defeated the Democratic party—torn it into fragments, what then?" Horace Chilton asked potential dissenters. The answer was obvious: "Chaos." Vilas described the fragmented Democrats as "mere opposition, not a party . . . carping at our adversaries, picking flaws to excite popular feeling, but not at all a great, united, cohering party." Without unity, men were "mere critics who proffer nothing."[34] Democracy required more from its parties.

Finally, leadership, by encouraging organization and unity, assumed heightened significance. "The people must remember," announced South Dakota's Richard Pettigrew, "that this is a government of political parties, that these parties are organized, have their machinery and manage the business and are really a great political and governing organization inside of the government, shaping its affairs and dictating its policy. It requires men of great ability to manage these party organizations, ability to adapt the sentiments of the people, ability to adapt means to ends and accomplish results." Unfortunately, the Senator conceded, constituents revealed no understanding or appreciation of the leaders' efforts.[35]

Academicians, professors of government and political science, published the first methodical studies of party practices, and the

numerous volumes that appeared in the last decade of the nineteenth century reflected, in part, their scientific aspirations. As
universities sponsored graduate programs and as departmental
chairs of government were divorced from moral philosophy,
scholars increasingly preferred to investigate the political process
rather than speculate on the good society. Eagerly probing for
the real forces in democracy, they settled on the parties; here was
an unparalleled opportunity to survey the actual rather than the
moral side of government. "Political phenomenon are observed,
classified and generalizations are made from data thus collected,"
explained Professor Henry Jones Ford of the new discipline. "Instead of considering first what ought to be, the aim is to consider
first what is." And Frank Goodnow, in his preface to *Politics and
Administration*, announced his desire "to get back of the formal
government organization and examine the real political life of
the nation."[36]

More significant in promoting this new fascination, however,
was the realization that political parties, in fact, dominated the
affairs of government. By the 1890's observers perceived that in
Washington, as well as in state capitals, party maneuvers were
inseparable from political events. It became axiomatic to declare:
"In recent times . . . every advanced people has come to look to
party—to an extent already great and everywhere increasing—for
government." And Lord Bryce's observation was an equally acceptable, if somewhat contradictory, introduction to a volume on
the American parties: "In America the great moving forces are
the parties. The government counts for less than in Europe, the
parties count for more."[37] At the end of the century students often
stated with the air of having grasped a great truth the not very
remarkable conclusion that America had always been governed
by parties. More sophisticated colleagues, however, understood
that there was "as little resemblance between the parties of the
Federalist period and their compact, highly disciplined successors of to-day, as between the feudal levies of the crusading

period and the armies which established the unity of the German empire."³⁸ |

Scholars in earlier eras, although not blind to the existence of political organizations, still paid them little attention. Tocqueville, for instance, wrote two volumes evaluating the quality of democracy in America and practically ignored the subject. His unwillingness to link party and democracy was apparent at the outset of his chapter, "Parties in the United States." "Parties," he informed his readers, "are a necessary evil in free government." Their deleterious qualities, not their valuable functions, occupied his attention, and he never clarified precisely why these organizations were in any way vital to democracy. In common with his American contemporaries, Tocqueville defined party in terms of principles; rather than discuss the scope of influence or the sources of power, he divided organizations into two types. The great ones "cling to principles rather than to their consequences; to general and not to special cases; to ideas and not to men." On the other hand, the minor ones agitated society but did not lead revolutions, employing only wretched means to gain despicable ends. "America," concluded Tocqueville, "has had great parties, but has them no longer," and so summed up politics through Jackson's first term.³⁹

| American parties were not only unprincipled but also transient. | The French visitor had little cause to investigate their functioning for, insofar as he could tell, they came to power only to disappear soon after. Created by great spurts of energy and ambition, they were liable at any moment to fracture or splinter; there was no basis for discussing permanent structures or inherited powers. Accordingly, Tocqueville, in common with his hosts, devoted few pages to party. More agreeable and significant topics demanded exploration.

Sixty years later, however, another foreign author, James Bryce, gave over a substantial portion of his two volumes on the American Commonwealth to party practices. He and his contemporaries could not ignore the subject. "The spirit and force of party in America," wrote the Englishman, "has become as essential to the action of the machinery of government as steam is to a locomotive engine." No satisfactory account could omit a thorough analysis of the driving power. Moreover, the parties were stable; by 1900 few doubted the survival of either the Democratic or Republican organizations. Party structure was set, suitable for investigation, and its powers were ongoing, capable of survey. "Though the books and articles dealing with the public life of the United States may be counted by hundreds," observed Bryce as he started his second volume, "I know of no author who has set himself to describe impartially the actual daily workings of that part of the vast and intricate political machine which lies outside the Constitution."[40] He and his peers soon remedied that defect.

Despite an intention to scrutinize only the actualities of politics, scholars rarely refrained from judging the efficacy and desirability of the party system. Yet perhaps their eager dedication to the "real forces" of government was as responsible as detached intellectual appraisals for the common belief that in a large and populated state party alone could administer a democratic government. Two-party politics, argued Woodrow Wilson during these years, was the most effective arrangement for assuring governmental responsibility. "The more power is divided," he insisted, "the more irresponsible it becomes . . . Power and strict accountability for its uses are the essential conditions of good government."[41] Harvard's A. Lawrence Lowell extended the catalogue of party virtues; only its organization could link America's scattered and mobile population to the government. Princeton's Henry Jones Ford emphasized its pedagogic role, the ability to stimulate citizens to ponder the issues.[42] Moreover, it could best unite the various branches of government in a constitutional structure that made separation of power a fetish. Finally, party rule contained "a principle of conservatism, inasmuch as it must always seek to keep faction within such bounds as will prevent it from jeopardizing party interests."[43]

Students of government, like men in public office, consistently welcomed organization, unity, and leadership. "The far more extensive duties assumed by party organization in this country," declared Ford in 1900, "make it so intricate . . . that it can be managed only by those who are trained to it as a business." Probably "when history comes to reckon the achievements of our age, great party managers will receive an appreciation very different from what is now accorded them."[44] Others, like Professor Anson Morse, echoed the theme. "For however large the number of those who think and feel alike may be, they cannot, until organized, do anything noteworthy in support of their common interests." The implications were clear and Morse did not shrink from them: "Of course, the control of a party naturally gravitates into the hands of those who are best able to promote its real or apparent success. It is because organization has come to be so very important . . . that the man who can organize has risen to the high position in party management which he now holds."[45]

Although these opinions did not differ from the declarations of the men serving in the Senate, distance from Washington added a crucial perspective. Investigators were usually critical of party's actual performance. Wilson, Lowell, and Ford agreed that organizations were not sufficiently united in Congress or adequately responsive to constituents. All too often devotion to details of management took precedence over concern for effective policy, and the public welfare was ignored for the sake of political intrigue. Nevertheless, Wilson and his colleagues argued for an increase in party strength and power. Contemporary organizations were too weak to fulfill essential duties, to provoke debate, to prevent corruption, to link the various segments of government. America required more, not less, party authority.[46]

There were, to be sure, dissenting voices to the defense of party government. Mugwumps in 1884, disgusted with Republican rule, repeated the Liberal Republican arguments of 1872. In traditional phrases, they criticized the parties for enforcing discipline to destroy individual conscience and responsibility. "If he enters a party," declared noted Massachusetts attorney Morefield Storey, "and especially if he is dependent on obtaining and holding office, he ceases to be a free man."[47] Charles Francis Adams, in typical Adams style, asserted that independents should avoid forming third parties. "We do not want more organization, more discipline, 'more machine' . . . I don't want a third party. I don't want any party; there will always, in this country at any rate, be enough of those who will act with parties, but under present conditions I want to stand on my own legs."[48] Parties were to represent only specific principles, and Mugwumps looked to the disintegration of established organizations. They sadly witnessed increasing strength and stability.

The Populists presented a similar critique, but more determined to enact a program, they could not offer consistent declarations. "One of the great evils of representative government," announced party chairman Marion Butler, "is that it soon develops into a government of parties and this throws legislation into the hands of party leaders." When partisan sentiments and pressures dominated the legislative process, deliberate judgments were impossible. Butler concluded that the Populists, unlike their rivals, were dedicated to principles, not "merely party ends."[49] The new group, however, took pride in its organization and platform. "If the party is going to scatter, if there is no cohesion for success," complained William Stewart, then all efforts on its behalf were wasted. And Marion Butler, speaking "with the authority of my party," informed fellow senators that "we are a distinct organization, acting in perfect accord and harmony." Butler unashamedly cited the necessity to "push forward the cause of the party, and to strengthen and build it up," justifying the effort by pledging "the inauguration and maintenance of great national policies."[50] Presumably the dangers of party rule to democratic government passed when one's own organization gained control.

In times of great excitement and tension, normally quiescent senators often hurled epithets of "blind partisan" at opponents, be they party colleagues or rivals. The passions generated by a fierce chamber debate induced participants to wrap themselves in a cloak of principle while accusing their antagonists of wearing the party yoke. When Democrats resented Republican efficiency in framing a tariff bill, they immediately denigrated the lash of discipline; and Republicans replied in kind when circumstances were reversed. The dialogue took on something of a comic quality by the end of the century, but nevertheless, the habit persisted.

The strength of the party caucus inhibited any tendencies to independence, and members who broke ranks naturally endowed their stance with great dignity. They became defenders of principle, and their opponents, disciplined hacks; they labored for the nation, adversaries stood only for the organization. Despite lengthy writings on the vital place of party in democracy, George Hoar indulged in breaking ranks. Disapproving of Republican legislation to annex the Philippines, the Massachusetts Senator informed supporters: "I know too how many men in the Senate feel constrained by mere party fidelity . . . to vote for the treaty, [although they] loathe and abhor it as much as I do . . . Have I a right, without violating the constitution, to surrender my opinion to that of a majority of the party?"[51] Under calmer circumstances, senators viewed the contrast of party with patriotism as unreal. When discussions followed more theoretical paths, members admitted that only political organizations could transform patriotism into more than an abstract commitment. But passions often overcame sound intellectual judgments, and party served as a convenient scapegoat.

Nor did more professional observers unanimously agree on the value of party government. Moisei Ostrogorski, for example, diligently tried to substantiate the argument that party inherently violated democratic precepts. Although dedicated at first to principle, organizations soon degenerated into self-seeking oligarchies. "As soon as a party, were it created for the noblest object, perpetuates itself," declared Ostrogorski, "it tends invariably towards power, and as soon as it makes that its end, its master passion is to maintain itself against all opposition, with no scruples as to its means." The compelling force behind this inexorable movement was the full-time party manager. "To win or hold power, the party is obliged to provide itself with a permanent organization. This cannot be formed or kept up without the help of professionals." Leaders, to protect their power, instilled mechanical cohesion and enforced rigid discipline. The results were clear: the death of private judgment and the triumph of stereotyped opinion.[52]

To halt this decline, argued Ostrogorski, government must discard "the use of permanent parties with power as their end," substituting the union of citizens "formed especially for a particular political issue." Accordingly, "combinations forming and reforming spontaneously," would dominate the government. "Citizens who part company on one question would join forces on another," and the evils political organizations generated would be eradicated.[53] Curiously, the French-educated political scientist, after two enormous volumes, reached conclusions identical with America's earliest attitudes toward party. Recognizing his sympathy with Liberal Republicans and Mugwumps, who kept these notions alive, he praised their wisdom and quoted them at length. Not surprisingly, therefore, more casual and less talented American writers, after little research or forethought and well in advance of Ostrogorski's studies, arrived at similar conclusions. They were, after all, more familiar with the rhetoric.[54]

Despite contrary arguments, the new appreciation of party's place in democratic government spread through the nation. Senators commanded a wide audience, and popular houses published

the straightforward prose of the political scientists. Many newspapers still remained party organs—the "independent" press was
just making its appearance—and their columns repeated often the
defense of party. "We must not forget," Whitelaw Reid told the
readers of the *New York Tribune,* "that governing the United
States is an art . . . and it cannot be learned in a week or two by
smart lawyers, merchants, ministers, and authors, who have had
no experience in the management of men and parties . . . The
country is governed by parties, and probably always will be, and
the management of parties requires a certain tact, adroitness, and
worldly wisdom which are only gained by long experience."[55]

Journals in the Midwest and West also stressed the importance
of unity and discipline. The *Commonwealth* in Topeka declared:
"The most efficient way to advance political principles, is through
efficient compact party organization. Political principles in a
popular form of government are valueless without party organization to carry them out." In Omaha the *Daily Herald* preached
the necessity of caucus solidarity—"No man is bigger than his
party"—and the Bismarck *Daily Tribune* boosted the virtues of
party discipline—"A regiment of well trained and well disciplined
soldiers will defeat an unorganized force of tenfold its number
any time." Geography was no barrier to the message.[56]

The appeal of these assertions went far beyond the attractions
of their logic. For one thing, the recent war experience sensitized
the nation to the value of discipline. In the last decades of the
nineteenth century, politicians were habitually compared to
soldiers, and political programs to strategic battle campaigns. "A
mob of five thousand men cannot stand up against a disciplined
force of two hundred and fifty tried soldiers," one party manager
typically reminded Wisconsin senator William Vilas. "The cause
that the five thousand believe in may be a righteous one, still the
two hundred and fifty will rout them for lack of organization."[57]
Then too, in an era when Darwinian notions of struggle grew
current, the conflicts of Democrats and Republicans for supremacy seemed likely to promote national progress. More-

over, the "age of organization" was a popular designation of these years; parties appeared to be one more manifestation of a general movement to specialization. For sharing the qualities of infantrymen, giraffes, and corporation presidents, politicians and two-party politics swelled in esteem.

Finally, the people had just witnessed the most striking evidence of the crucial relationship between party and democracy. When political organizations shattered before the blows of slavery, democracy failed and war ravaged the country. Men now began to look to antebellum parties and leaders to answer the question of why a civil war had occurred in America. One of the great lessons of the years from 1861 to 1865 for the next generation was the significance of united organizations to the welfare of a democratic nation.[58]

The elements that transformed the Senate were found in the nation as well as in Washington. Skilled leaders helped alter the chamber's practices; yet the place of party in the capital ultimately reflected its importance in the country. The professionalization of political careers, the demands of Washington life, the centralization of state politics, and the efforts of pressure groups combined to bring to power the sort of senator who would promote organization. The intellectual defense of party government appeared in this context. Speeches, books, and newspapers, inspired by personal experience, by the lessons of the war, or by some watered-down version of Darwinism, repeatedly spelled out the message: two-party politics was vital to democracy. These notions legitimized, and thereby reinforced, the changes that came to post-Civil War America.

Americans could not ignore these events. Party obligations and loyalties became a favorite topic of discussion. Earnestly debated by college societies, it carried equal appeal in the plots of popular dramas and novels. And when people looked to the Senate, party was well to the forefront of their minds.

Part Three

The Uses of Power

☆ ☆ ☆ ☆ ☆

☆ IX ☆

THE PEOPLE AND THEIR GOVERNMENT

> The doctrine of a distribution of authority . . . still possesses the
> common mind . . . The constitutional ideal is noble; but the
> politicians are vile. If only the checks could be established be-
> yond the strength of the politicians to arrange—or above all, if
> some barriers could be erected, so tight and strong as to shut the
> politicians out altogether—the constitution would work perfectly.
> Therefore, more checks upon the abuse of power; more con-
> trivances to baffle the politicians, whose machinations pervert
> the constitution and corrupt the government.
>
> Henry Jones Ford, *The Rise and Growth*
> *of American Politics,* 1900

"No: the people don't like the Senate," a Pennsylvania high
school English teacher informed George Hoar in 1897. "It grows
in disfavor daily."[1] The newspapers and magazines of the day
confirmed the truth of his observations. During the last decade of
the century, the Senate became a favorite topic for feature writers
and correspondents, and invariably their opinions were harsh and
critical. Articles commonly opened with the statement: "It should
seem that most Americans who think of politics at all entertain
an uneasy feeling about the United States Senate. The degradation
of the Senate has of late years . . . become so painfully apparent
to the American people."[2] Newspaper editorials, noting that "the
changes of recent years have been such as to lower the collective
ability of the Senate," proclaimed: "The Senate ranks lower in
popular estimation today than it has at any time in the history of
the country." "To be a Senator," the press concluded, "is to be
a suspect."[3]

Senators disputed the justice of these judgments, but they could not doubt their accuracy. "I know that the general estimate placed on the body by newspapers, etc., is wholly unwarranted," argued Stephen White. But he too was forced to confess that the Senate "is the most unpopular branch of the government."[4] And George Hoar himself admitted: "It cannot be doubted that there is a widespread and growing impatience with the condition of things in the Senate. Indeed . . . it has already become distrust."[5]

There was no lack of popular opinion on how best to compensate for the Senate's declining character. Some earnestly insisted upon the propriety of abolishing the institution; others, with more conservative temperaments, recommended shortening the length of terms or limiting the scope of legislative power. Suggestions were frequent and diverse, but by 1900 it was clear that out of the maelstrom of dissatisfaction, an amendment proposing the popular election of senators would eventually be enacted.[6]

From the time of the constitutional convention of 1789, proponents sporadically urged the merits of direct election. Not until the end of the nineteenth century, however, was the idea transformed into a movement. After 1890 the Senate received countless petitions from state legislatures and devoted considerable time to debating the requests. Innumerable articles and handbooks argued its worth, and the Populists made it a prominent plank in their platform.[7] "Some relief will be found necessary," William Allison conceded to George Hoar in 1899;[8] but attempts to frame compromises and delay or prevent the change were in vain. By 1900 most observers of national politics realized that it was only a question of time before the amendment was adopted.

The most widespread explanation for the existence of the Senate at once made it vulnerable to a devastating critique and stimulated the movement for direct election. "The necessity of a senate," declared the authors of the *Federalist* papers, "is not less indicated by the propensity of all single and numerous assemblies to yield to the impulse of sudden and violent passions."⁹ Their contention was the first in a series of declarations defending the notion that the Senate, as one of its essential functions, ought to check and sit in judgment upon the popular will. As the rivalry between small states and larger neighbors—the consideration most responsible for the Senate's constitutional structure—became a textbook concern lacking any pertinence or importance to modern circumstances, the image of the Senate as the bulwark of the government grew even more current. In the post-Civil War decades, both senators and constituents agreed that the institution primarily existed to serve as a sort of national superego, protecting the people from themselves.

Louisiana Democrat Donalson Caffery quoted the *Federalist* with delight to substantiate his conclusion that "our government was so framed as to present a check to the tyranny of popular fury and vacillation . . . The Senate is that check." The proposition was also obvious to William Allison. The Senate was "the conservative element in our government," and its part in the legislative process supplied the vital time for "debate and reflection."¹⁰ The discontented Pennsylvania schoolteacher subscribed to the doctrine, although he was less than satisfied with the chamber's performance. "Poor *sober second thought* indeed," he told Senator Hoar, "when like some I could mention and whom you know all too well sit in second thought on what is our first thought."¹¹ James Bryce also followed the *Federalist* argument, not unhappy with the realities of political life. Confident that the Senate "frequently but not invariably restrained" the popular passions, he returned to England convinced that here, if anywhere, the institution excelled.¹²

Serving as the conscience to the nation, the Senate, even under ideal circumstances, could have anticipated the reward of a less than honored reputation. Interfering with government decisions when the citizenry was most stubborn and emotional and least rational and calculating, the chamber knew the people's fury whenever it blocked the immediate enactment of its will. Members could only trust that when the crisis dissolved and passions cooled, the country would value their performance. The hope was, at best, flimsy. No one was astonished at the prevailing estimate of the Senate.

Widespread hostility to the sober second thoughts of the Upper House appropriately provoked effective efforts to amend election procedures. The chamber's peculiar mode of selection, by state legislators rather than by the people, was designed to insulate it from public pressures; indirect election removed the institution from the citizens' control. Men like William Jennings Bryan, believing that the practice was a remnant from a more conservative past, condemned it as aristocratic, antidemocratic, and an insult to the public intelligence. Popular election, in turn, was predicated upon a trust in the people's ability directly to conduct all the affairs of government.[13] The argument was repeatedly and persuasively presented,[14] and those who disagreed were hard pressed for an answer. To plead the significance of a check on the popular will would not gain widespread approval. "I trust the Senate may be preserved with the duration of this Government," declared William Evarts, "but it will never be preserved by assuming . . . to be the guardians of the people against the people themselves."[15] Politicians especially knew the futility of going to battle against the virtues of the common man.

The Senate was also more susceptible to criticism because the public somehow expected it to occupy an extraordinary place in the government structure. The numerous congressmen, chosen from small districts scattered throughout cities and villages performed obvious and necessary tasks; in close communication with their constituencies, representatives, as their title implied, echoed the voice of the people in Washington. The state's two senators, however, could never be as intimate with the voters as their House colleagues; and lacking their convenient rationale, senators' roles remained open to question. Guardians of the Republic from the evils of momentary and transient excitements—yes. But this carried too many derogatory implications.

Much less ambiguous or controversial was the notion that the Senate would be a forum for great national statesmen. Whether derived from some faint image of the House of Lords or the King's Privy Council, many citizens assumed that the Senate should tower in stature over all other political institutions. Elderly, bearded gentlemen educated in the ways of the world, solons all, would gather in the comfortable chamber, and without temper or passion methodically and prudently settle the questions agitating the country. Like revered fathers, the wise men would calmly instruct the nation as if it were a wayward or puzzled child.

The attraction of some version of this fantasy was great, almost as great as the gap that separated it from reality. Entertaining such presumptions, the public could not help but suffer disenchantment. Woodrow Wilson felt compelled to remind his readers that the Senate could only reflect "the condition of public life in this country." A stream could be no purer than its source. "The Senate is in fact, of course, nothing more than a part, though a considerable part, of the public service; and if the general conditions of that service be such as to starve statesmen and foster demagogues, the Senate itself will be full of the latter kind, simply because there are no others available." Wilson lucidly argued his point and James Bryce accurately repeated it, but nevertheless, popular images persisted.[16] Although the expectations were neither logical nor just, disillusionment still contributed heavily to the institution's unpopularity. The campaign for direct election gained fresh support.

To be sure, the place of the second chamber in a democratic government presented problems of definition, and the public indulged in fanciful hopes. Yet these difficulties did not suddenly confront America at the end of the nineteenth century. For years similar sentiments, by themselves, had not given weight to the idea of election reform. The movement succeeded because an entirely new set of circumstances had intervened. Events peculiar to these decades made it a favorite issue.

The widespread appeal of direct election coincided with the discovery that the power of party turned the wheels of government. The Senate's degradation was inevitably linked to the pernicious quality of party politics, and since the institution occupied a crucial place in government, the evil permeated and perverted national and state practices. Critics confidently assumed that if the power of party could be short-circuited, if some method could be devised to effectively end its extensive authority, then once again the Senate would properly exercise its prerogatives and the country would enjoy responsible government. The means to accomplish this grandiose task were clear: an amendment for the popular election of the Senate.

Nearly every post-Civil War commentator on American government agreed on the Senate's preeminence. Columns in the *Nation* and *Atlantic Monthly* reiterated identical truisms: "The most striking circumstance in connection with the power of the Senate is that it holds a commanding place in the centre of the government." The chamber in past years had "held the President and the House by the throat, and kept them dangled till they should accept its terms."[17] Correspondents argued in the pages of the *North American Review* that next to the Senate, the House had become "an insignificant factor," and Congressman William Moody, attempting to defend the honor of the Lower House, was unable to dissent. "It is idle to deny and useless to exaggerate the importance of the Senate in our political system," he conceded. "It is to-day the most powerful of all conspicuous legislative bodies."[18] To reform the Senate would strike at the very heart of the political structure. Advocates of direct election could be at least satisfied that theirs was a major undertaking.

Exponents of the amendment insisted that it would, above all else, limit the authority of party in government. "If we must have parties," declared Wendell Garrison in the *Atlantic,* "it is highly desirable that they should arise spontaneously on clearly formulated principles and with definite objects." In authentic Mugwump tradition he hoped "that they should cease to exist as soon as possible after these objects have been attained; that they should be easily attacked when the love of power becomes the real motive for existence." To fulfill these expectations, Garrison turned to direct election. "The abrogation of the existing statute regulating the election of Senators," would curtail the evils of partisanship.[19]

The lengthy catalogue of party sins invited and justified efforts to cripple its organization. Popularly elected senators would unhesitantly "baffle the cut and dried schemes of the caucus and the machine." Once party power was curtailed, the enormous expenditure of campaign funds would immediately cease. "Elected without great outlay or preliminary organization . . . the men thus sent up will become independent of party."[20] Leadership would lose its ability to discipline members. "The present system of electing Senators is a discouragement to independent voters . . . The less independent voting the greater the power of the bosses and their machine. Popular choice of United States Senators would tend to shorten the reign of bosses in both local and national politics."[21]

When senators blatantly ignored and thwarted the demands of the people, again the blame rested with party, and the cure with the proposed amendment. Elected by state legislators with a constantly changing membership, a senator simply could not "feel himself under any strict responsibility to such a 'kaleidoscopic constituency.'" Invariably renouncing "any attempt to keep in sensitive touch with the people . . . he feels that he must put his political faith in some power that abides; and hence he turns to the 'organization' and relies upon that to secure him his reelection as the reward for his subservience." Once the fulcrum of party was dislodged, and senators recognized the need to win public approval at the polls, they would heed the people and not the machine. "The expert wire-puller may be ever with us," nevertheless, "qualities of a different order" would become prerequisites for officeholding.[22]

Other indictments of the Senate named the horrors of tyrannical party rule. No refrain was more faithfully repeated during these years than the cry that millionaires dominated the "Rich Man's Club" in Washington. "It is harder for a poor man to enter the United States Senate," claimed one typical aphorism, "than for a rich man to enter Heaven." Here again the fault rested with the parties and would be eliminated only after the adoption of the popular vote.

The accusation, although vastly exaggerated, continued unmodified and all attempts to correct the impression were unavailing. "The statement of your Sunday school superintendent as to the Senate," John Spooner patiently informed a constituent, "is absurd and false. There are some millionaires in the Senate . . . [but] I believe it is safe to say that a majority of the Senate would not be able to live comfortably in Washington without their salaries."[23] Orville Platt argued in similar tones that "in no body of men is influence more justly proportioned to ability and wise judgment than in the Senate. A Senator's wealth . . . cuts little figure in the Senate."[24] The public paid no heed to these valid contentions. The party structure made the Senate a logical resting place for millionaires. Willing to "fill the party chest and do the boss's bidding," they made ideal members. When "party fealty and not competence or honesty or patriotism, [became] the credential for office holding," machine rule was unavoidable. Concomitantly, "the purchasability of Senatorships, and the decline of the federal Senate to what we now see it, in large a medley of 'millionaires' and 'bosses,' " became inevitable.[25]

Proponents of direct election argued that removing the choice of senators from party councils would at the same time halt the corruption spread by the corporations. The self-interest of political organizations was so great that to finance campaigns they willingly trafficked with all potential donors from millionaires to company presidents. Anxious to accumulate funds, they lost all sense of responsibility, inviting illicit alliances: corporations, for their part anxious to influence the legislative process, proved willing partners. Organizations permitted no scruples to separate them from office. The quest for power trampled the public interest. Only when men and not parties contested Senate seats would honest ballots choose candidates free from bondage to business interests. "To directly elect the Senators," concluded David Turpie, "would do these aggregates great harm." Their contributions would no longer guarantee political power.[26]

Since state legislatures selected the senators, party's pernicious influence spread into every county and ward, even pervading the election of local assemblymen. The cause was obvious: "The prize of a seat in the Senate is so great that party cannot afford to neglect any step which may lead to its attainment." And the results were shocking: "No matter what may be the personal character of the two men who may be nominated for the legislature, the choice of the voter is dictated not by personal fitness of the candidate . . . but upon whether he is a member of this or that national party."[27] If party considerations were excluded from elections, "the name of many a candidate for the legislature, now put forward with brazen assurance, would never be heard of, when questions of his qualifications . . . could no longer be droned out by the party drum."[28] The demands of contemporary organizations were so compelling that the best intentioned men abandoned private judgments. To restore integrity, election should be the exclusive right of the people.

As soon as parties lost interest in the legislature, a host of benefits would accrue to the states. Representation would be immediately reformed and rotten boroughs abolished; for "the determination on the part of the party in power to perpetuate, as far as possible, a fortuitous party advantage," maintained these inequities. Furthermore, the general tone of the assembly would be elevated. A member now traveled to the state capital expressly "to do his party service in voting for its candidate for the Senate; and, in consequence of this dominating task, almost every question before the legislature comes to take on a party color." In the absence of political organizations, legislators would be at liberty to perform their rightful tasks with integrity and ability. Proceedings would no longer be delayed by deadlocked Senate elections, and a proper regard for state issues would replace recurring party feuds.[29]

Finally, popular election would promote home rule for outsiders would end their unwelcomed interference. At present, "if party control in the Senate is wavering, and if the result in a given state is in doubt, then the Administration takes a hand in the game." Managers persistently visited every rural borough, overwhelming and intimidating the local politicians. "To make the choice of members of the State legislature depend upon their preferences for . . . Senator," declared the reformers, "is to subordinate in a State election all matters of State politics and State interests to considerations of national politics."[30] If popular elections removed even some of these influences, the amendment was worth enacting. To strike a blow against the precedence of party interests would inevitably improve the quality of American political life.

Senate leaders found little favor with the movement for direct election. William Allison saw no sense in the idea, and James McMillan maintained that whatever evils currently existed could not be altered by a simple change in election methods. The suggested remedy, he contended, bore no relation to the alleged diseases.[31] George Hoar, having discoursed at length on the essential quality of party in a democracy, devoted equal energies to combating the amendment;[32] and other writers also linked a defense of the party system to an attack on the proposed amendment. "In discussing such a question as this," declared one opponent of direct election, "we must remember that this is a political country; that no country is more political; that our governments, state and national, are carried on, and will be carried on by political parties."[33] There was no value in deploring partisanship or in attempting to eradicate political organization.

Not all those who defended the party's role were critical of the reform. The issue quickly became a political question, and senators often acted in response to the desires of their constituents rather than in logical accord with pronounced views. In most instances, however, men who held vital positions of leadership or who vigorously defended the place of party in democracy came down against the amendment. Its implications and assumptions were clear.[34]

Opponents raised the very practical question of how senators would be elected if state legislatures were bypassed. Reformers gave as little time as possible to the issue, preferring to disparage the established method rather than outline a new system. However, the defenders of the party argued that precisely at this juncture the propositions urging popular election broke down. Somehow the majority was to register its decision at a convention rather than in a state legislature. Ostensibly there would be no interference by parties; supposedly, the system would discourage corporations and lobbyists, and limit the expenditures of funds. But American politics, critics of the amendment persistently explained, did not operate in a vacuum. Regardless of the precise wording of any proposition, organizations would dominate the convention exactly to the degree that they controlled the proceedings of the assemblies. At best, the change would not matter in the least, and at worst, would promote more evils than it solved.[35]

The opposition hastened to inform the public that nomination and election were not identical processes. Even if senators were elected by a general ballot, the truly vital work—the nominations —would be performed at party conventions. And conventions possessed few desirable attributes. George Hoar reeled off a list of drawbacks: they were composed of delegates subject to no oath of office, meeting only for a day, and not ultimately responsible to a constituency. "Are not these bodies quite as likely," demanded Hoar, "to be susceptible to mistakes or to corrupt manipulation as a State legislature?"[36] The direct election of senators, asserted William Allison, would simply transfer the choice "from the well-ordered consideration of a responsible legislature to the hurry and chance of a party convention."[37] Others wondered what improvements could possibly emanate from a body whose "members meet as strangers, acting under the lax supervision of their friends in the party, and for the sole purpose of making a nomination to promote someone's interest in working for a much coveted office."[38] The faults of party government would only assume added prominence in political conventions.

Popular balloting would not even raise the quality of senatorial elections. George Vest, for one, could not understand how the public would be adequately prepared to pass on the senatorial credentials of a candidate they never met, put forward by a convention they never attended. Constituents would do better, he told his colleagues, to judge the qualifications of their neighbors and acquaintances running for the state legislature, evaluating their abilities to reach a proper choice.[39] More important, should voters be dissatisfied with the work of the party convention and unhappy with the selection of a particular candidate, their only available option would be to support the opposition. But the rival party, in all likelihood, subscribed to repugnant doctrines; whether to favor an unsound program or to promote an incompetent candidate would become the common dilemma. Citizens would probably stand by their parties; if not, as George Hoar explained, the results would be disastrous. "The correction of mistakes made by political conventions is only to be made at the cost of destroying the character of the country because of the character of the candidate."[40] Direct election would provoke only dangerous innovations. The cure was far more dreadful than the disease.

Opponents presented other objections to the amendment, but none were persuasively or effectively argued. They maintained that state legislatures were not that corrupt. Deadlocked elections occurred only in certain areas; factors other than Senate elections blurred national and state issues. Often, defenders of the *status quo* resorted to stratagems to evoke common prejudices. Popular voting would give weight to mere numbers, disenfranchising rural constituents while enhancing the power of city masses. Surely it was absurd to leave the nation's fate to the whims of newly arrived immigrants.[41]

With somewhat more courage they appealed to the people to exercise self-control, to trust to the restraints imposed by the Senate. With greater delight, however, they set out to protect the sacrosanct character of the Constitution. The wisdom of the Founding Fathers should not be lightly dismissed; amendments were offered at the peril of the country. "Great reasons," Hoar bombastically announced, "moved our fathers to establish this Chamber which they hoped would last in unbroken succession until time shall be no more:" this was, after all, "a question of centuries not of years."[42] George Edmunds declared incredulously that a "new school of politicians has now appeared who profess to believe that the Fathers were mistaken in their theory of the surest foundation of our national republic." How compare the profundity of the Fathers with the machinations of mischievous politicians![43] These rhetorical maneuvers were weak and unconvincing. The most valid and pertinent opposition to direct election insisted that party, no matter what proposals were offered, would continue to pervade the government structure.

The arguments for and against the reform, proceeding from contradictory assumptions, prevented the two sides from uniting on a common ground. To those anxious to effect the change, the evils permeating the government were directly traceable to the place of party in politics. Their targets were many: corruption, oligarchies, millionaires, and irresponsibility; and by circumscribing party authority they hoped to cure them. The commands of the bosses muted the voice of constituents. The boundless ambitions of organizations perverted state politics. As the power of party swelled, the Senate degenerated; and its unprecedented significance made the genius of the past irrelevant. The progress of the nation demanded the end of anarchronistic procedures.

On the other hand, those who judged party government vital to democracy, and not a devilish spirit deserving exorcism, contended that the measure was foolish and unnecessary. Whatever propositions were devised, party would still exercise authority. The inherited system possessed many commendable features, and simple mechanical changes would not correct its minor faults. In this way, the debate on direct election came down to an argument on the value of party in the American democracy.

The popularity of the amendment revealed the public's remarkable distaste and antipathy for party rule. Obviously, direct election could not effect serious alterations in government practices; governors and other prominent officials were already nominated in state conventions without appreciably diminishing party strength. Perceptive observers in 1900 recognized that the frantic hopes stimulated by the movement were destined for disappointment; no procedural change could, in fact, revolutionize the nation's political life.[44] Nevertheless, by the end of the century it was evident that the reform would soon be adopted. No matter that expectations could not be fulfilled. The sentiment mustered to circumscribe party authority was massive, and the strategic importance of the Senate added distinction to the crusade. If only political organizations in the chamber could somehow be limited, the benefits would permeate the country. Direct election could not satisfy these singular expectations; party was not eradicated from the Senate. But the measure prompted an emotional zeal that more than compensated for any rational failings, and it was enacted.

The widespread antagonism to party was testimony to its new prominence. Opposition to particular legislative policies sponsored by one of the organizations was often translated into a general distrust of the political system. As soon as effective discipline dominated the legislative proceedings, the public could pinpoint responsibility; and once able to locate power, it could assign blame. When protectionists were unhappy, a caucus was the villain, and when free traders were displeased, a conference. No group was ever completely satisfied with congressional action, and criticism was far more prevalent than commendation. Unflagging discontent found a convenient scapegoat. Only a short step separated hostility to a specific action from disgust with the entire process. Not surprisingly, party rule bore a poor reputation.

Moreover, as membership assumed added significance, organizations were held responsible for a wide range of conduct. Wherever corruption occurred, the party, not individual failing, was held at fault. Public men no longer sinned privately; any transgression reflected upon their official position. Personal shortcomings represented the deficiencies in the political process. Party now operated in the glare of a spotlight the beam of which illuminated every misstep.

Popular estimates were also buttressed by the willingness of prominent officials to attack the party and its machinery. Rivals disagreeing with a party policy often took the opportunity to denounce the iron quality of discipline, the strength of the chains that choked adherents. The public listened carefully, and the lamentations on the pernicious effects of party legislation documented their own particular notions. Telling the people what they wished to hear, the politicians sustained and promoted their prejudices. Anxious to parade the glory of their own independence, Senators helped lower the stature of the chamber.

Ultimately, however, dissatisfaction with party rule had even deeper roots. The public listened most attentively to the criticisms of discipline and organization, not to their able defense. During these years, for the first time, a sentiment that the government stood distinctly apart from the people gained widespread popularity. The notion spread that an unbridgeable gap divided the interests of the officeholder from his constituents. In point of fact, the nation was growing larger. More and more Americans lived in areas remote from Washington; others, congregating in cities, were not likely to meet or become friendly with their representatives, let alone their senators. Communications could not keep pace with the expansion, and proceedings in the capital seemed more remote than ever. Then too, the nation was undergoing a complex development. Heterogeneous immigrants, giant industries, aggregates of capital, and amalgamations of workers were some of the new and strange components of modern America. A general malaise gripped the country, and every innovation excited hostility. Efforts to exclude newcomers, to break up corporations, to discourage the unions increased. And in politics identical fears provoked the movement to abolish the authority of party organization.[45]

The nation condemned the party for usurping authority and for isolating the government from the people. The complaint that the doors of the Senate were shut to men of common birth was as popular as it was mistaken. The obsession with the number of millionaires in the chamber partook of the same emotion; there was as little opportunity to enter the Senate as there was to accumulate the fortunes of McMillan and Hanna. Horatio Alger stories, after all, were believed by children, not adults. Some even talked of a court at the Capitol; the common citizen was as likely to win election as to inherit a throne. Others complained that the very style of senatorial life had passed beyond the tastes and habits of typical Americans. In earlier days members ate sandwich lunches from paper bags in simple surroundings; now fashionable chefs prepared rich cream sauces for dinners in resplendent marble halls. Ostensibly, senators were an elite apart from their constituents.[46]

To ordinary Americans it seemed that unless they were blessed with some special attribute, such as fantastic wealth for which organizations made extraordinary allowances, they could enter high political office only after devoted and single-minded service on behalf of party. Politics, they sensed, was a specialized vocation. Professionalization, to be sure, affected other callings without prompting great concern; but in politics people deemed the movement intolerable. Government, after all, was their property, and party should not be permitted to monopolize it. When office was reserved exclusively for dedicated partisans, citizens were alienated from power. Thus, they believed that to strike a blow against organization was to reassert the preeminence of individual Americans; and primaries, direct legislation, recall, and popular election of the judiciary received wide attention and approval. Certainly from their perspective, no reform could do more to return authority to the nation, releasing it from the grip of the party, than the direct election of the Senate.[47]

Finally, popular evaluations of party rule became entangled with fundamentally ambivalent attitudes toward the proper role of government in democratic society. Whatever doubts existed about the appropriate scope of federal power were reflected in the judgments of its driving force, the party.

Curiously, the Senate in the last decade of the nineteenth century was criticized with startling regularity for not proceeding with greater speed and efficiency. Every threat of a filibuster, every delay in the passage of legislation, set off a chain of indignant letters and editorials, denouncing the weakness and ineptitude of the institution. The workings of the Senate were compared, unfavorably of course, to the functioning of a business corporation. "The time has certainly come," one executive notified John Sherman in 1891, "when the U.S. Senate ought to do business on business principles . . . The people are tired of fool Senatorial customs, traditions and courtesies, that stand in the way of prompt transaction of business."[48] The Senate has lost popularity, concluded a Kentucky newspaper six years later, "because it has not, in harmony with the utilitarian spirit of the day . . . corrected its methods in legislation so as to expedite the transaction of public business." Many observers contended that, "the Senate of the United States has become fossilized." The "effeminacy of the Senate," became a common lament, and the need for some "good practical, sensible Senators," a customary plea.[49]

Yet despite this emphasis on speed and efficiency, the mechanisms that might have furthered them were subjected to derision. Party discipline, caucus rule, and strong leaders were customarily depicted as the bane of democratic government. Yes, the party should stand for well-defined principles, but any attempt to bring cohesion to the membership met cries of despotism. Yes, the Senate should quickly pass desired legislation, but any maneuver to hold the ranks in line prompted challenges of tyranny. The ambivalence did not escape popular notice; the contradictions were evident. Efficiency but no discipline, unity but no caucus, principles but no leadership.[50]

The ambiguity of popular judgments revealed a nation torn between conflicting expectations. It valued efficiency and harmony, the prerequisites for an effective government. But at the same time, the overwhelming antagonism to party, the one agent that might have encouraged the full exercise of authority, reflected a fundamental distrust of power not bound and circumscribed by checks, balances, and limits. Fearing that government might become effective, that constitutional barriers might collapse under the influence of party, the voters fretfully attacked organization and discipline. Students pleaded for increased party responsibility, but Henry Jones Ford, for one, and A. Lawrence Lowell, for another, recognized that the people welcomed "more checks upon the abuse of power," dreading the effects of party strength. The public desired "more contrivances to baffle the politician, whose machinations pervert the constitution and corrupt the government," not the establishment of a smoothly operating two-party system.[51] The next generation would more easily accept the notion that an active government could promote the general welfare. The vigor of the attacks on party at the end of the nineteenth century, however, made clear that although the potentiality for power now existed, its implications were still too frightening.

Assuredly, there were some valid reasons for judging party's performance in the Senate harshly. The ambivalence shared by many observers toward the value of the system was not without cause for the two organizations did not always fulfill their functions in a way that would inspire trust and confidence. Not that they simply ignored all the leading issues of the day. Senators debated and passed legislation that bore on many pressing questions, such as the currency, the tariff, the trusts, and the railroads. However, they did not manage to deal firmly and consistently with them. And as the most important political institution of the period, the Senate's lapses were crucial.

Contemporaries, along with future Progressives and their sympathizers, commonly blamed every failure on that most convenient of villains, the businessman. Ostensibly, corporations and their agents skillfully prevented legislation from effectively settling vital issues; when measures proved ambiguous and ineffective, it was testimony to lobbyists' skills and company money. The greedy businessman, according to the popular rhetoric, in nefarious alliance with corrupt bosses, monopolized and then perverted power. The people? They were seemingly helpless victims.

The story of these years, however, was not that simple. There can be no question that economic interests paid little heed to significant social questions and were almost invariably ignorant of any consideration save their own advantage; still, that is not to say that they dictated political decisions. The businessmen, narrow in vision, do not warrant exoneration and certainly cannot qualify as heroes in post-Civil War politics. Yet they have served too long as a convenient scapegoat, sparing historians and citizens alike the need to re-examine more basic difficulties in this era.

By the end of the nineteenth century, party caucus and leadership enjoyed a new authority in government affairs. Men entered the Senate and gathered in caucus prepared to follow party dictates and respect its decisions. This transformation, however, did not guarantee the nation that government would be responsive to its interests. On the contrary, the welfare of the party often took precedence over any other consideration. The reason for this preoccupation was not difficult to understand. Senators, from their first entrance into politics, learned to depend upon party machinery; long careers and innumerable campaigns only served to heighten their sensitivity. Even their most basic ideas on government were bound up with party; how else might a free people be governed? By training and attitude, senators identified what was good for the organization with what was good for the nation. Unfortunately, the equation did not necessarily hold true.

The prominence of party helped establish the rule of compromise in the Capitol. Habits of conciliation, of holding the center of the road, of adopting the least controversial solution, became virtues. "Results can be obtained only by a subordination of individual opinion to the expressed will of the whole." "One must remember that there are 88 Senators and there are not 88 ways of doing the same thing; in other words, if a man gets his own way one time out of 88 he is getting his fair share as a Senator." These rationales became the Senate's rallying cries.[52]

Legislation was often ambiguous and subject to varying interpretations because members split the difference down the middle, even if it meant avoiding a clear-cut resolution of the problem. At least party unity would be maintained and caucus leaders favorably impressed. There was no conspiracy to injure the public. Rather, intent on maintaining harmony, party members anxiously adjusted or ignored divisive issues. The politicians in post-Civil War America were trained in pragmatic attitudes, not avid commitments. With absolute justification, Ostrogorski concluded: "The atmosphere of Congress is, as it were, saturated with opportunistic habits of compromise."[53] Senators were reasonable and even cautious men. But in their readiness to keep the peace, they often lost sight of other objectives.

An unwillingness to spark public interest in specific social and economic problems matched senators' desires to compromise inside the Capitol. Hoping to avoid controversy, Democrats and Republicans hesitated to make the country sensitive to the problems that accompanied the growth of modern America. They did not stimulate inquiry into the fate of the farmer or spark debate on the place of labor. It customarily fell to third parties to provoke division—and hence their frequent appearance during these years. The established organizations preferred not to tamper with the system. Improvisation could be dangerous.

Even though party did not lead, it was not often directed. During these decades, political organizations grasped a new authority. Effective and consistent programs might have been enacted when leaders carried bills through the chamber and members abandoned private judgments before party demands. However, most interests in the society, with the notable exception of the businessmen, did not take these changes into account. Party was regularly left to its own devices, more or less free to raise and dispose of issues as it would. Potentialities were not realized.

Traditionally, the people had guided the political process through the ballot box; by casting their votes, they had let their will be known. But in post-Civil War America this traditional resource of democracy lost most of its influence. As state leaders became entrenched in power, they were not so easily turned out of office. Hard work and full campaign chests made a strong alliance. Moreover, when questions facing the electorate were comparatively straightforward, popular votes might conceivably offer some guidance to well-meaning politicians. But by the end of the nineteenth century, the issues facing an industrial society were so numerous and complex that election resembled the Delphic Oracle, yielding only the most veiled clues.

Public awareness of these limitations came slowly. Dissatisfactions with the political process during these years stimulated attempts to restore the significance of the ballot. The movement for primaries and direct elections aimed to bring officeholders into closer contact with constituents, thereby returning government to popular control. Yet these tactics were designed to eliminate the power of party, not to control it; they aimed to eradicate political organizations, not direct them. In short, these programs looked back to the nineteenth century, not ahead to the twentieth. Not surprisingly, they proved ineffective in achieving their goals.

Particular business interests in the nation responded differently to the alterations of these years. Rather than trust to the ballot, they organized their efforts, descended on Washington, and announced their proposals. Such practices were almost unique for the more common reaction was to try and ban the lobbyist, not to dispatch one's own. In time others would duplicate businessmen's tactics, and farmers, laborers, professionals, consumers, ministers, and a host of special groups would appear in Washington. But here, doubts on the proper scope of government authority and fears about power not carefully circumscribed, together with the notion that election reforms would solve the problems, combined to limit action. Thus, business enterprises enjoyed one great advantage at the close of the nineteenth century: they were nearly alone in their efforts. In the end their monopoly did not corrupt the political process. Party was more than equal to their influence and lobbyists devoted most time to publicizing programs and assisting friends already won to the cause. Still, at a time when compromise appeared so attractive, it helped to have one's needs well known. And from a lobbyist's point of view, even the smallest fraction of the loaf was better than nothing at all. Finally, because corporations were heard most clearly and frequently in the capital, the public grew even more disenchanted with party government. Convinced that to speak was to command, they denounced corruption and shied further away from Senate corridors. The ambiguities in their position would not be easily resolved.

The lessons and legacies of the post-Civil War era offer cause for satisfaction as well as disappointment. The nation faced difficult questions that defied simple solution; changes in the economy and society posed problems that were not quickly solved. Nevertheless, there were many positive accomplishments in these decades. The press of industrialization, accompanied by urbanization and immigration, in other countries spelled the decline of political freedom. American institutions, however, proved equal to the challenge. The Senate, rather than flounder and abdicate power, transformed its procedures and traditions. Parties and leaders assumed unprecedented authority, bringing new practices to the chamber.

The innovations did not immediately promote responsible government, capable of dealing effectively with all pressing issues. Disciplined parties were content to keep controversy to a minimum, permitting unity to take precedence over action. Yet during these years, the party created the forum to which particular interests could bring their proposals and it provided a gathering place where senators were forced to think in terms broader than section. It set up committees to order the chamber business, to guide legislation on the floor, to formulate decisions and look after their enactment. With power there came abuses. Politics was not without examples of ugliness, personal greed, and corruption. Nevertheless, by 1900 the Senate organizations were capable of dealing efficiently with the problems of government. The first generation did not take full advantage of these changes. But successors would fare better.

The years that followed Teddy Roosevelt's inauguration brought many alterations to American political life. The Senate's prominence in the government declined; even under weak twentieth-century Presidents, it rarely enjoyed the prerogatives it exercised in the decades following Reconstruction. The office of the presidency revealed a fresh capacity to lead, and the public frequently turned to government and party organization for the protection and promotion of the general welfare. Curiously, however, party retained something of its unpopular reputation. The country recognized that whatever would be accomplished in politics would have to be effected by its organization. But an unsavory quality still enveloped it. Even after the Second World War, a group of political scientists could feel it bold to proclaim that what the country needed most was a responsible two-party system, and Senator William Fulbright did not believe he repeated a truism when declaring: "This is a party government. We have two parties. I think it is proper that the party in power does control it, otherwise you have got absolute chaos."[54] But despite the innumerable times that these very same words were spoken over the previous eighty years, party politics carried a remnant of distrust in the popular mind, and the "independent" and "non-partisan" deemed more honored terms. The rise of totalitarian, one-party governments strengthened the association of two-party politics and democracy. But abstract intellectual commitments did not secure their hold on the people's affections.

Furthermore, the twentieth century witnessed no vast increase of the power of party in the government process. By 1900 the privileges of Democratic and Republican leadership in the Senate were fixed. Party chairman enjoyed the identical control that they do today, the steering committee possessed equal responsibilities, and the caucus had similar duties. The organizations functioned as efficiently when first created as they did seventy years later. Yet it might have been anticipated by the contemporaries of Allison, Aldrich, and Gorman that the party would continue to enlarge its authority, that its discipline would eventually approximate the English model, uniting the various arms of government. These changes have not occurred. At the end of the nineteenth century, party achieved as much control as it may be destined to wield in the American system.

Although Americans grew accustomed to party government, they did not become very comfortable with it. In 1960 as in 1890, fundamental suspicions marked their attitudes. The nation, on some level, still distrusted its government. The systematic exercise of power appeared more dangerous than ineffectual and inconsistent legislation; and no matter what mechanical solutions political scientists devised to promote party prerogatives, they could not overcome the effects of the vague hostility. Post-New Deal generations now seem to share something of a new outlook and they may reverse inherited traditions. But from all appearances, such changes will be gradual—even if they be vital.

Appendixes
Bibliographical Note
Notes
Index

☆ ☆ ☆ ☆ ☆

APPENDIX A

PROCEDURES FOLLOWED IN PRESENTING THE CAREERS OF UNITED STATES SENATORS

SOURCES OF INFORMATION

Senators were prominent men, and their life histories were outlined in numerous sources. The *Dictionary of American Biography, The Biographical Directory of the American Congress,* 1774–1949, and the *National Cyclopedia* invariably included more or less detailed accounts. By the last decades of the nineteenth century, famous men of the various states had their biographies collected into special volumes, and biographical dictionaries, compiled by publishers hoping for profits, were growing common. Moreover, many of the leading Senate figures had their careers set down by careful scholars; occasionally, the family of a deceased senator published his life and letters, and in several instances the men themselves found time to record their reminiscences. Newspapers were also a valuable source for at the time of a senator's election they often included an accurate sketch of his life, and at the time of his death, a detailed obituary. Finally, the senators' personal papers often included some material on their early lives.

With the abundance of sources, then, it was not difficult to put together the details and compile the tables in Chapter IV. The most troublesome pieces of information were the occupations of the senators' fathers and the circumstances in which the senators were raised. The accounts were at times vague and even contradictory, but with the many reports available, accuracy could usually be secured. I have not searched in county court records—the task would have been nearly impossible when dealing with such a large and geographically diverse group. Placing senators into some of the following categories did involve judgment; no simple quantitative breakdown could be used. But the endeavor seemed valuable even if absolutes were beyond reach.

THE SCALE OF SOCIAL ORIGINS

I originally calculated the status of senators' families on a nine-point classification scale devised by P. M. G. Harris for his forthcoming study on American social mobility, sponsored by the Center for the Study of the History of Liberty in America. Harris' scale went from upper class to lower, lower class, but for my purposes a three-point index was sufficient. The Harris scale was sensitive to social as well as economic status, allowing me to distinguish between groupings on the basis of the amount of assistance a father could offer his son starting out on a career. The elite designation was reserved for those whose fathers had wealth and position, whose status made it likely that their children would some day enjoy leadership and power. The chief figures in American business, politics, and the professions were included here. The substantial category included fathers who could offer their children some advantages —for example, assistance in education—but were clearly not members of a national elite. Ordinary town lawyers, doctors, and small merchants typified this group. Finally, families were considered subsistence when they could offer their children no help at all in their careers, that is, fathers who earned barely enough to feed and clothe their offspring. In most instances frontier farmers filled these ranks. I have purposely refrained from discussing "class" distinctions here. Whether a farmer who owned 30 acres of rocky land should be labeled lower class or not is not to my point. My interests here have centered on what advantages he could pass on to his children.

THE GEOGRAPHICAL DIVISION

During the period from 1869–1901, the country was divided into eight geographical areas:

New England: Connecticut, Maine, Massachusetts, New Hampshire, Rhode Island, Vermont.

Middle Atlantic: New Jersey, New York, Pennsylvania.

South Atlantic: Delaware, Florida, Georgia, Maryland, North Carolina, South Carolina, Virginia.

South Central: Alabama, Arkansas, Kentucky, Louisiana, Mississippi, Missouri, Tennessee, Texas.

East North Central: Illinois, Indiana, Michigan, Ohio, West Virginia, Wisconsin.

West North Central: Iowa, Kansas, Minnesota, Nebraska.

Mountain: Colorado, Idaho, Montana, Nevada, North Dakota, South Dakota, Utah, Wyoming.

Pacific: California, Oregon, Washington.

Three states were not yet admitted to the Union: Arizona, New Mexico, and Oklahoma. Because of peculiarities in their political and economic development, the Dakotas, Missouri, and West Virginia were included in different groupings.

THE SCALE OF OCCUPATIONAL SUCCESS

Occupational success readily fitted into a three-point division. Men whose achievements placed them among the top figures in the country were considered national leaders. I did not rely upon any strict income differentiation—that would have weighted the scale to business rather than legal success—but men in business with incomes over $200,000 a year usually filled this category. The figure should be halved for the lawyers. Men of importance in their occupations but who would not have been listed among its leaders—businessmen with over $50,000 a year income—were put into the category of outstanding success. Finally, local merchants and county lawyers were described as average success. They would have to rely to some degree upon the senatorial salary of $5,000 a year to meet their expenses.

THE SCALE OF POLITICAL EXPERIENCE

This category was perhaps the easiest to devise and apply. Senators who had served in key political offices for over six years before coming to the chamber were designated as having considerable experience. Long term congressmen and governors usually filled this category. Those who spent three to six years in key offices, or over six years in secondary posts—state legislature, state cabinet, or state supreme court—or over a decade in a less significant place, as prosecuting attorney for example— were considered to have had average experience. Senators with little experience served less than three years in important posts or less than six years in secondary posts. Men described as having had no experience had not held office before entering the Senate. The careers themselves fit neatly into the categories; men rarely held insignificant posts for very long periods of time.

APPENDIX B

PARTY MEMBERSHIP, SOCIAL ORIGINS, AND POLITICAL CAREERS

Table A–1. Distribution of party strength by regions, 1869–1901
percentage of senators elected

| | Party | | | |
Region	Republicans	Democrats	Others	Number
New England	93	7	—	(30)
Middle Atlantic	67	33	—	(27)
South Atlantic	9	84	7	(44)
South Central	4	96	—	(45)
East North Central	65	33	2	(45)
West North Central	87	3	10	(31)
Mountain	78	11	11	(27)
Pacific	70	30	—	(23)

Table A–2. Party and social origins, 1869–1901
(per cent)

| | Party | |
Origin	Republicans	Democrats
Elite	10	27
Substantial	42	43
Subsistence	48	30
Number	(131)	(108)
Number unknown	(14)	(9)

Table A–3. Occupation and party membership, 1869–1901
(per cent)

| | Party | |
Occupation	Republicans	Democrats
Law	58	81
Business	32	14
Other	10	5
Number	(145)	(117)

Table A–4. Occupational success and party membership
1869–1901 (per cent)

Rating	Party	
	Republicans	*Democrats*
National Leader	20	9
Outstanding	45	32
Average	35	59
Number	(139)	(117)

Table A–5. Political experience and party membership
1869–1901 (per cent)

Experience	Party	
	Republicans	*Democrats*
Considerable	35	28
Average	39	39
Little	21	27
None	5	5
Number	(143)	(117)

BIBLIOGRAPHICAL NOTE

My purpose here is to review the primary and secondary materials most pertinent to a study of the Senate in post-Civil War America. This volume is an outgrowth of my doctoral dissertation, "Party, Power, and the United States Senate, 1869–1901," on deposit in the Harvard University Library. The specialist of these years is occasionally referred to the fuller documentation in the dissertation. But for all intents and purposes, the citations below may be considered complete.

MANUSCRIPTS

Manuscripts were necessarily the single most vital source of information for the story of the Senate and, as is evident from the listing below, many men serving in the chamber between 1869 and 1901 left abundant materials. The collections were often filled with vast, almost discouraging, amounts of useless scraps and scattered all over the country. But the study of federalism makes historians good tourists. To my good fortune, the Senate provided each of its members with a secretary and a typewriter; thus, letter press volumes were carefully maintained and, given the process, extraordinarily legible. Moreover, most of the collections were of manageable size—the era of four secretaries incessantly pounding away at electric typewriters was still in the future—and it was still possible for my wife and me to go through practically every known collection of senators' papers for the late-nineteenth century.

The Republican story was not difficult to reconstruct. The large collections of Aldrich, Allison, Chandler, Dawes, Fish, Morrill, Reid, Sherman, and Spooner proved especially helpful. Three recently opened collections, those of Senators Hoar, Jones, and McMillan, were extraordinarily revealing. Presidential manuscripts often were less rewarding, but the Hayes and Garfield materials were of interest. The Wharton Barker and L. T. Michener Papers were surprisingly useful. The Democrats were more difficult to trace; Southerners often saved their correspondence through 1870 and then discarded the rest, confident it could be of no interest. Nevertheless, scattered in the Bayard, Chilton, Tillman, and Vance collections, and especially in those of Stephen White and Henry Davis, were valuable items for my purposes. Papers of Populist senators were few, but those of Marion Butler were good.

A visit to the mountain states to examine the Dubois, Pettigrew, Stewart, and Warren Papers was very worthwhile. Most information on lobbying and business connections appeared in the senators' letters, but the Huntington correspondence, the Barlow Papers, and the materials at the West Virginia Library also deserve note. The Mahone Papers contained some fascinating stories of nineteenth-century politics.

Since all were important, I include here a full listing of the collections of papers examined in the course of preparing this study.

ABBREVIATIONS

D.U.L.　　Duke University Libraries, Durham, North Carolina.
L.C.　　Library of Congress, Manuscript Division, Washington, D.C.
U.N.C.L.　University of North Carolina Library, Southern Historical Collection, Manuscript Department, Chapel Hill.
W.V.U.L.　West Virginia University Library, West Virginia Collection, Morgantown.

Nelson Aldrich Papers, Library of Congress, Manuscript Division, Washington, D.C.
William Allison Papers, Iowa State Department of History and Archives, Des Moines.
Chester Arthur Papers, L.C.

Wharton Barker Papers, L.C.
Samuel Barlow Papers, Henry E. Huntington Library, San Marino, California.
Thomas Bayard Papers, L.C.
Albert Beveridge Papers, L.C.
James Blaine Papers, L.C.
Francis P. Blair Papers, L.C.
William Buckingham Papers, Connecticut State Library, Hartford.
Marion Butler Papers, University of North Carolina, Southern Historical Collection, Manuscript Department, Chapel Hill.

Donalson Caffery Papers, U.N.C.L.
Johnson Camden Papers, West Virginia University Library, West Virginia Collection, Morgantown.
Andrew Carnegie Papers, L.C.
Thomas Carter Papers, L.C.
Henry Castle Papers, Minnesota Historical Society, St. Paul.

William E. Chandler Papers, L.C.
——— New Hampshire Historical Society, Concord.
Zachariah Chandler Papers, L.C.
Horace Chilton Papers, University of Texas Library, Austin.
Joseph Choate Papers, L.C.
Cassius C. Clay Papers, Duke University Libraries, Durham, North
  Carolina.
Grover Cleveland Papers, L.C.
Richard Coke Papers, University of Texas Library, Austin.
Cornelius Cole Papers, University of California Library, Los Angeles.
Roscoe Conkling Papers, L.C.
Shelby Cullom Papers, Illinois State Historical Library, Springfield.

John Daniel Papers, D.U.L.
——— University of Virginia Library, Charlottesville.
David Davis Papers, Chicago Historical Society, Illinois.
——— Illinois State Historical Society, Springfield.
Henry Davis Papers, W.V.U.L.
Henry Dawes Papers, L.C.
Chauncey Depew Papers, Historical Manuscripts Collection, Yale
  University, New Haven, Connecticut.
Grenville Dodge Papers, Iowa State Department of History and Archives,
  Des Moines.
Fred Dubois Papers, Idaho State College Museum, Pocatello.

Stephen Elkins Papers, W.V.U.L.
William Evarts Papers, L.C.

Charles Fairbanks Papers, Lilly Library, Indiana University, Bloomington.
Charles Faulkner Jr., Papers, W.V.U.L.
——— University of Virginia Library, Charlottesville.
Hamilton Fish Papers, L.C.
Joseph Foraker Papers, L.C.
Joseph Fowler Papers, L.C.

James Garfield Papers, L.C.
Robert Garrett Papers, L.C.
Gibson-Humphrey Papers, U.N.C.L.
Arthur Gorman Papers, Maryland Historical Society, Baltimore.
Adeline Burr Davis Green Papers, D.U.L.
Walter Gresham Papers, L.C.

Benjamin Harrison Papers, L.C.
Joseph Hawley Papers, L.C.
John Hay Papers, L.C.
Rutherford B. Hayes Papers, Rutherford B. Hayes Library, Fremont, Ohio.
Frank Hereford Papers, W.V.U.L.
Nathaniel Hill Papers, State Historical Society of Colorado, Denver.
George Hoar Papers, Massachusetts Historical Society, Boston.
James Hogg Papers, University of Texas Library, Austin.
Timothy Howe Papers, State Historical Society of Wisconsin, Madison.
Huntington-Hopkins Correspondence, Stanford University Library, California.

Jackson-Harding Papers, U.N.C.L.
J. P. Jones Papers, Henry E. Huntington Library, San Marino, California.
———— University of California Library, Los Angeles.

Elisha Keyes Papers, State Historical Society of Wisconsin, Madison.
Samuel Kirkwood Papers, Iowa State Department of History and Archives, Des Moines.

Daniel Lamont Papers, L.C.
Francis Lieber Papers, Henry E. Huntington Library, San Marino, California.
John Logan Papers, L.C.

William Mahone Papers, D.U.L.
Daniel Manning Papers, L.C.
Manton Marble Papers, L.C.
Anson McCook Papers, L.C.
William McKinley Papers, L.C.
James McMillan Papers, Burton Historical Collection, Detroit Public Library, Michigan.
Louis Michener Papers, L.C.
John Morgan Papers, L.C.
Justin Morrill Papers, L.C.
———— Baker Library, Harvard University, Cambridge, Massachusetts.

Thomas Palmer Papers, Burton Historical Collection, Detroit Public Library, Michigan.

Richard Pettigrew Papers, Pettigrew Museum, Sioux Falls, South Dakota.
Orville Platt Papers, Connecticut State Library, Hartford.
Daniel Pratt Papers, Indiana Division, Indiana State Library, Indianapolis.

Alexander Ramsey Papers, Minnesota Historical Society, St. Paul.
Matt Ransom Papers, U.N.C.L.
John Reagan Papers, Archives Division, Texas State Library, Austin.
Whitelaw Reid Papers, L.C.

Carl Schurz Papers, L.C.
John Shaffer Papers, Indiana Division, Indiana State Library, Indianapolis.
John Sherman Papers, L.C.
John Spooner Papers, L.C.
John Stevenson Papers, L.C.
William Stewart Papers, Nevada State Historical Society, Reno.
Charles Sumner Papers, Houghton Library, Harvard University, Cambridge, Massachusetts.

Henry Teller Papers, University of Colorado, Western History Collection, Boulder.
———— Denver Public Library, Colorado.
———— State Historical Society of Colorado, Denver.
Benjamin Tillman Papers, Clemson Agricultural College Library, Clemson, South Carolina.
Lyman Trumbull Papers, L.C.
Tucker Family Papers, U.N.C.L.

Zebulon Vance Papers, North Carolina State Department of Archives and History, Raleigh.
William Vilas Papers, State Historical Society of Wisconsin, Madison.

Benjamin Wade Papers, L.C.
Francis Warren Papers, Archives and Western History Department, University of Wyoming Library, Laramie.
E. B. Washburne Papers, L.C.
Henry Watterson Papers, L.C.
David Wells Papers, L.C.
George Wetmore Papers, L.C.
Stephen Mallory White Papers, Borel Collection, Stanford University Libraries, California.
William Whitney Papers, L.C.

Waitman Willey Papers, W.V.U.L.
James H. Wilson Papers, L.C.
Edward Wolcott Papers, Western History Department, Denver Public Library, Colorado.

PRINTED MATERIALS: GOVERNMENT DOCUMENTS

The debates and voting records of the Senate during these years are fully recorded in the *Congressional Globe* (1869–1872) and *Congressional Record* (1873–1901). Roll calls in Executive Session are found in the *Senate Executive Journal;* Senate rules are listed in the annual *Senate Manual.* The *Congressional Record* is well indexed, making it an easy to use as well as invaluable tool for the researcher.

Of particular interest were two Senate investigations: Pacific Railway Commission, "Report," 50th Cong., 1st sess., *Senate Executive Document*, No. 51; "Investigation of Attempts at Bribery," 53rd Cong., 2nd sess., *Senate Report,* No. 436; No. 457, Pt. I and II, No. 606.

PRINTED MATERIALS: LETTERS, AUTOBIOGRAPHIES, MEMOIRS

Many senators set down their reminiscences, or their families diligently collected an assortment of their speeches and letters. The results ranged enormously in value, but on the whole they formed a disappointing series. They were neither frank nor thorough nor especially enlightening. Some of the better ones included, Blanche Butler Ames, *Chronicles from the Nineteenth Century: Family Letters of Blanche Butler and Adelbert Ames,* 2 vols. (privately printed, 1957); *Arguments and Speeches of William Maxwell Evarts,* ed. Sherman Evarts, 3 vols. (New York, 1919); Edward Mayes, *Lucius Q. C. Lamar: His Life, Times, and Speeches, 1825–1893* (Nashville, 1896); John Sherman, *Recollections of Forty Years in the House, Senate, and Cabinet,* 2 vols. (Chicago, 1895). *Reminiscences of Senator William M. Stewart, of Nevada,* ed. George R. Brown (New York, 1908); David Turpie, *Sketches of My Own Time* (Indianapolis, 1903); Thomas Dawson, *Life and Character of Edward Oliver Wolcott,* 2 vols. (New York, 1911). I found the well-known works by James Blaine, Champ Clark, Alfred Conkling (on Roscoe), Shelby Cullom, Chauncey Depew, Joseph Foraker, John B. Gordon, George Hoar, Thomas Platt, and Carl Schurz more helpful for biographical information than for anything else.

Historians have also edited collections. Particularly helpful were Allan Nevins' edition of the *Letters of Grover Cleveland, 1850–1908* (Boston, 1933), and C. R. Williams' edition of the *Diary and Letters of Rutherford Birchard Hayes*, 5 vols. (Columbus, 1922–1926).

For understanding the process of lobbying in Washington, the collection of Collis Huntington letters was of great value:

Letters from Mark Hopkins, Leland Stanford, Charles Crocker, Charles F. Crocker, and David Colton to Collis P. Huntington, August 27, 1869–December 30, 1879 (New York, 1891).

Letters from Collis Huntington to Mark Hopkins, Leland Stanford, Charles Crocker, E. B. Crocker, Charles F. Crocker, and David Colton, August 20, 1867–August 5, 1869 (New York, 1892).

Letters from Collis Huntington to Mark Hopkins, Leland Stanford, Charles Crocker, E. B. Crocker, August 5, 1869–March 26, 1873 (New York, 1892).

Letters from Collis Huntington to Mark Hopkins, Leland Stanford, Charles Crocker, and D. D. Colton, April 2, 1873–March 31, 1876 (New York, 1894).

Ellen Colton V. Leland Stanford et. al., in the Superior Court of California, Sonora County, 1883.

These volumes are at the Stanford University Libraries, Stanford, California and the Henry E. Huntington Library, San Marino, California.

PRINTED MATERIALS: CONTEMPORARY ANALYSES OF SENATE ACTIVITIES

The popular studies on American politics in this era devoted particular attention to the Senate, and invariably their comments were challenging and provocative, if not always accurate. The well-known works by Henry Adams (including his perceptive novel, *Democracy*), James Bryce, Henry Jones Ford, A. Lawrence Lowell, Moisei Ostrogorski, and Woodrow Wilson were very helpful. The pages of the *Arena,* the *Atlantic Monthly,* the *Forum,* the *Nation,* and the *North American Review,* were filled with articles on the workings of the Senate, quite apart from more specific reviews of its day-to-day activities.

Newspapers were especially important on several accounts. Washington affairs occupied a much more prominent place in the press in the late-nineteenth century than they had previously—committee assignments often making the front page of the *New York Times, Washington Post,* or *National Republican.* Moreover, the details of a battle for a committee place were covered with the intensity devoted to presidential excursions in the twentieth century. The Hill was in every way the center of political attention.

Moreover, the story of Senate elections in the legislature received full coverage in the state newspapers, and the accounts clarified electoral procedures and politics. In every capital, one newspaper at least carried full details of the Senate election. The *Baltimore Sun, Lousiville Courier Journal, Montana Helena Herald, St. Louis Globe Democrat, Salt Lake Tribune, Seattle Post Intelligencer,* and the *Wheeling Register* were typical of the papers consulted for the January event.

The details of a factional fight recounted in the press were usually accurate, and the published reports of ostensibly secret caucus meetings almost always agreed with the story as told in the manuscripts. However, in other instances the press was all too ready to present as fact what was unsubstantiated rumor at best, and its judgments of politicians' motives often bore little resemblance to reality. The newspapers were an invaluable source, but they had to be used with extraordinary caution.

BIOGRAPHICAL GUIDES

The uses of nineteenth-century biographical guides are discussed in Appendix A, above. The format remained constant, only the names of the particular states changed. The *Biographical Encyclopedia of Connecticut and Rhode Island* (1881) became the *Historical and Biographical Cyclopedia of Delaware* (1882) or the *Encyclopedia of Contemporary Biography of West Virginia* (1894). The *Bar and Bench of West Virginia* (1904) had its duplicate in the *Bar and Bench in Missouri* (1898), and Virginia was by no means the only state to celebrate its *Men of Mark* (1906).

BIOGRAPHIES

Almost every leading political figure of these decades has been the subject of a biography. These works are well known and may be found in any of the standard guides to historical literature. Of particular help to me were, Harry Barnard, *Rutherford B. Hayes and His America* (Indianapolis, 1954); Nelson Blake, *William Mahone of Virginia: Soldier and Political Insurgent* (Richmond, 1935); Richard Current, *Pine Logs and Politics: A Life of Philetus Sawyer* (Madison, 1950); Elmer Ellis, *Henry Moore Teller: Defender of the West* (Caldwell, Idaho, 1941); Dorothy C. Fowler, *John Coit Spooner: Defender of Presidents* (New York, 1961). John R. Lambert, *Arthur Pue Gorman* (Baton Rouge,

1953); Oscar D. Lambert, *Stephen Benton Elkins: American Foursquare* (Pittsburg, 1955); Horace Merrill, *Bourbon Leader: Grover Cleveland and the Democratic Party* (Boston, 1957) and *William Freeman Vilas: Doctrinaire Democrat* (Madison, 1954); Allan Nevins, *Hamilton Fish: The Inner History of the Grant Administration* (New York, 1936); Leon Richardson, *William E. Chandler: Republican* (New York, 1940); Leland L. Sage, *William Boyd Allison: A Study in Practical Politics* (Iowa City, 1956); Harry S. J. Sievers' first two volumes on *Benjamin Harrison: Hoosier Warrior* (Chicago, 1952) and *Hoosier Statesman* (New York, 1959); Nathaniel Stephenson, *Nelson W. Aldrich: A Leader in American Politics* (New York, 1930); Charles C. Tansill, *The Congressional Career of Thomas F. Bayard* (Washington, D.C., 1946); Edwin Bruce Thompson, *Matthew Hale Carpenter: Webster of the West* (Madison, 1954); C. Vann Woodward, *Tom Watson: Agrarian Rebel* (New York, 1938).

STATE POLITICS

Studies of state politics in post-Civil War America varied widely in quality; and the field is a neglected one too. One series of volumes was devoted to Reconstruction in particular states, while another examined the Populist experience. But the nature of state politics under less exceptional circumstances was largely unexplored. Some of the more suggestive works included; Allen J. Going, *Bourbon Democracy in Alabama, 1874–1890* (University, Ala., 1951); Albert D. Kirwan, *Revolt of the Rednecks: Mississippi Politics, 1876–1925* (Lexington, Ky., 1951); Charles Knapp, *New Jersey Politics during the Period of the Civil War and Reconstruction* (Geneva, N.Y., 1924); Howard Lamar, *Dakota Territory, 1861–1889: A Study of Frontier Politics* (New Haven, 1956); George Mowry, *The California Progressives* (Berkeley and Los Angeles, 1951); Daniel Robison, *Bob Taylor and the Agrarian Revolt in Tennessee* (Chapel Hill, 1935). V. O. Key's *Southern Politics* (New York, 1949) fills a good part of the gap later, and he often begins his story in the late nineteenth century.

In general, the student must rely on the standard multi-volumed state histories and scattered articles in state journals. To be sure, many of the biographies listed above serve as a good introduction to state events, even if the perspective is limited to the individual involved. Washington has been the focus for most historians as well as for most politicians after the Civil War.

POLITICAL INSTITUTIONS AND
PARTY BEHAVIOR

Recent works by political scientists provided interesting points of comparison. Donald Matthews, *U.S. Senators and Their World* (Chapel Hill, 1960) and especially David Truman, *The Congressional Party: A Case Study* (New York, 1959) were exceptionally useful volumes. Ralph Huitt's "Democratic Party Leadership in the Senate," *American Political Science Review*, 45:333–344 (1961), "The Morse Committee Assignment Controversy," *American Political Science Review*, 41:313–329 (1957), and "The Outsider in the Senate: An Alternative Role," *American Political Science Review*, 45:566–575 (1961) were also very helpful. So too were Alexander Heard, *The Costs of Democracy* (Chapel Hill, 1960) and Hugh Bone, *Party Committees and National Politics* (Seattle, 1958). Despite its many obvious lacks, William S. White's *Citadel: The Story of the United States Senate* (New York, 1950), still had some significant things to add; as did Joseph Clark, *The Senate Establishment* (New York, 1963).

Some earlier works on Congress contained good detail. Lauros G. McConachie, *Congressional Committees: A Study of the Origin and Development of Our National and Local Legislative Methods* (New York, 1898), Ralph V. Harlow, *The History of Legislative Methods in the Period before 1825* (New Haven, 1917), as well as Paul Hasbrouck, *Party Government in the House of Representatives* (New York, 1927) were valuable. The standard history of the Senate, George Haynes', *The Senate of the United States*, 2 vols. (Boston, 1938), had much significant data, although it isolated the material from any broader considerations. George Galloway's *History of the House of Representatives* (New York, 1961), was far from definitive, but offered good background.

GENERAL WORKS ON POST-CIVIL WAR
POLITICS

Matthew Josephson, *The Politicos, 1865–1896* (New York, 1938) is still referred to as the standard work on these years, although his scholarship is very much less than satisfactory. In the Josephson tradition, there is Horace Merrill, *Bourbon Democracy of the Middle West, 1865–1896* (Baton Rouge, 1953). Ray Ginger's chapters on politics in *Age of Excess: The United States from 1877 to 1914* (New York, 1965), repeat these arguments, and so does a fatuous study by Robert and Leona Rienow, *Of Snuff, Sin and the Senate* (Chicago, 1965). Slowly a body of work is building up that will undoubtedly culminate in a reinterpretation of these years. For the directions it will take see Lee Benson, *Merchants, Farmers, and Railroads: Railroad Regulation and New York Politics, 1850–1887* (Cambridge, Mass., 1955); Vincent DeSantis, *Republicans Face the Southern Question: The New Departure Years, 1877–1897* (Baltimore, 1959); Ari Hoogenboom, *Outlawing the Spoils: A History of the Civil Service Reform Movement, 1865–1883* (Urbana, 1961); Richard Hofstadter, *The Age of Reform* (New York, 1955); Morton Keller, *The Life Insurance Enterprise, 1885–1910* (Cambridge, Mass., 1963); Edward Kirkland, *Industry Comes of Age: Business, Labor, and Public Policy, 1860–1897* (New York, 1962); Robert Sharkey, *Money Class, and Power: An Economic Study of Civil War and Reconstruction,* Johns Hopkins University Studies in Historical and Political Science, ser. LXXVII (Baltimore, 1959). However, the quality of the essays in *The Gilded Age: A Reappraisal,* edited by H. Wayne Morgan (Syracuse, 1963), reveals that unfortunately there remains much to be done.

NOTES

CHAPTER I: The Limits of Party

1. Quoted in Henry Adams, *The Education of Henry Adams* (New York: Modern Library Edition, 1931), chap. xvii, esp. pp. 260–262; Allan Nevins, *Hamilton Fish* (New York, 1936), pp. 107–108; Timothy Howe to Grace Howe, March 10, 1869, Howe Papers, State Historical Society of Wisconsin, Madison.

2. *New York Tribune*, July 9, 1872.

3. Newspaper scrapbook collection of Henry Dawes, January–March 1870, Dawes Papers, L.C. Joseph Medill to Justin Morrill, February 1, 1869, Morrill Papers, Baker Library, Harvard University, Cambridge, Massachusetts.

4. Hamilton Fish to J. A. Kasson, March 4, 1878, Fish Papers, L.C.; Royal Cortissoz, *The Life of Whitelaw Reid* (New York, 1921), I, 255. Cf. David Davis to James Harvey, July 1880, David Davis Papers, Illinois State Historical Library, Springfield; Jacob Schiff to John Sherman, November 5, 1892, Sherman Papers, L.C.

5. Jacob D. Cox to David Wells, July 22, 1871, and Charles Nordhoff to David Wells, January 4, 1879, Wells Papers, L.C. William B. Hesseltine, *Lincoln and the War Governors* (New York, 1948), p. 2; C. Vann Woodward, *Origins of the New South, 1877–1913,* ed. W. H. Stephenson and E. M. Coulter, *A History of the South.* (Baton Rouge, 1951), pp. 2–5.

6. J. Franklin Jameson, "The Origin of the Standing Committee System in American Legislative Bodies," *American Historical Association, Annual Report for the Year, 1893,* pp. 393–399. For the role of party in committee assignments see Lauros G. McConachie, *Congressional Committees* (New York, 1898), esp. chap. viii. Cf. also Ralph V. Harlow, *The History of Legislative Methods in the Period before 1825* (New Haven, 1917). George Haynes, *The Senate of the United States* (Boston, 1938), I. 284–305, reviews this material well but is typical in isolating his facts from any broad considerations. George L. Robinson, "The Development of the Senate Committee System," unpub. diss. New York University, 1955; cf. also Ray Swanstrom, "The United States Senate, 1787–1801," unpub. diss. University of California, Berkeley, 1958.

7. *Congressional Globe,* 35th Cong., 1st sess., p. 40 (December 16, 1857).

8. Party influence in legislative proceedings prior to the Civil War has received scant attention; most investigations have been confined to the question of party origins prior to 1809. See Noble Cunningham, *The Jeffersonian Republicans: The Formation of Party Organization, 1789–*

1801 (Chapel Hill, 1958); cf. also William N. Chambers, *Political Parties in the New Nation: The American Experience, 1776–1809* (New York, 1963) and Joseph Charles, *The Origins of the American Party System* (Williamsburg, 1956). The greatest difficulty with these studies is their tendency to exaggerate the, importance of party in Congress. Compare especially, Cunningham, pp. 71, 84, and Chambers, pp. 88, 93. See also dissertation, p. 6.

9. George F. Milton, *The Eve of Conflict: Stephen A. Douglas and the Needless War* (Boston, 1934), p. 433; cf. also Robert Sharkey, *Money, Class, and Power*, Johns Hopkins University Studies in Historical and Political Sciences, ser. LXXVII (Baltimore, 1959), *passim;* Timothy Howe to Grace Howe, February 21, 1866 and June 2, 1866, Howe Papers.

10. *Congressional Globe*, 41st Cong., 2nd sess, p. 3277 (May 6, 1870). Lyman Trumbull to William Jayne, August 5, 1870, Trumbull Papers, Illinois State Historical Library, Springfield. Cf. also *National Republican* (Washington, D.C.), March 4, 1873, March 9, 1875.

11. T. Harry Williams, *Lincoln and the Radicals* (Madison, 1942), *passim;* cf. also Harry J. Carman and Reinhard H. Luthin, *Lincoln and the Patronage* (New York, 1943) and William F. Zornow, *Lincoln and the Party Divided* (Norman, Okla., 1954). For congressional legislative activities during the war see Sharkey, *Money, Class and Power,* esp. pp. 29–49, 76–79, 131–132.

12. Hamilton Fish to George Bancroft, January 25, 1870, and Hamilton Fish to Sickles, June 23, 1870, Fish Papers.

13. W. B. Parker, "Henry Anthony," in *Dictionary of American Biography,* ed. Allen Johnson *et al.* (New York, 1928), I, 316–317. Anthony chaired the Committee on Printing, with its household duties, and also served on the committee of Naval Affairs and Mines.

14. The Committee on Committees membership was listed in the press at the start of each congressional session. News of Washington affairs was much more prominent in the papers of the late-nineteenth century than today and so this information can invariably be found in the *New York Times* (1851–   ), the *New York Tribune* (1841–   ), the *New York Herald* (1835–1924), the *National Republican* (1860–1888), and the *Washington Post* (1877–   ). The list appeared two to three days after the session's commencement. For the lack of debate on the Committee's decisions, see the *National Republican,* March 8, 1877. The Republican Committee on Committees, for example, at the second session of the Forty-first Congress was chaired by Henry Wilson of Massachusetts, no friend of Grant, and John Sherman, no closer to the general, headed it at the start of the Forty-second Congress. The *National Republican,* December 7, 1869, and the *New York Herald,* March 8, 1871.

15. *Congressional Record,* 44th Cong., 1st sess. (January 10, 1876, January 12, 1876), *passim.* Cf. also Haynes, *Senate of the United States,* I, 249–259; H. H. Gilfrey, "The President of the Senate *pro tempore,*"

62nd Cong., 1st sess., *Senate Executive Document*, No. 104. The Vice President of the United States, as President of the Senate, was of even less importance; Haynes, I, 209–239.

16. Fifteen men served on the Committee on Committees during the Forty-first Congress and only two held the post more than once. The chairmen of Finance (Sherman) and Appropriations (Fessenden and then Morrill of Maine) never were appointed; nor were Senators Conkling, Sumner, Carpenter, or Schurz.

17. Party action in the caucus was officially secret and no one kept minutes of the proceedings. In 1913, Carl Loefler, secretary of the Senate for the Republicans, began to keep a record, noting in his initial entry that he was the first to do so. His records are today located in the Capitol. The Democrats, it seems, did not keep records until 1933. However, information on caucus actions was available. Newspapers, in the best tradition, published accurate reports, and senators supplied full accounts in letters and diaries. Finally, in the midst of debate on the chamber floor, through temper or rivalry, caucus activities were often discussed.

18. *Congressional Globe*, 40th Cong., 1st sess., pp. 492–495 (July 5, 1867).

19. *Ibid.; New York Tribune*, March 9, 10, 11, 1869.

20. *Congressional Globe*, 40th Cong., 1st sess., p. 495 (July 5, 1867).

21. *Ibid.*, pp. 492–495.

22. *Congressional Record*, 43rd Cong., 1st sess., p. 2488 (March 24, 1874). Cf. also James Bryce, *The American Commonwealth*, 3rd ed. (New York, 1895), I, 203–205.

23. Committee assignments, by name of committee, were published in the *Congressional Record* at the start of each session. My wife performed the difficult task of arranging a complete chronological record of the committee assignments, session by session, for each of the three hundred senators. See McConachie, *Congressional Committees*, pp. 268–269, for the Morrill incident.

24. *New York Times*, March 10, 1871; Amos Pickard to Cornelius Cole, October 16, 1871, and Schuyler Colfax to Cornelius Cole, November 13, 1871, Cole Papers, University of California Library, Los Angeles.

25. Thomas G. and Marva R. Belden, *So Fell the Angels* (Boston, 1956), *passim*, esp. pp. 222–229; for Sprague's harangues see *Congressional Globe*, 41st Cong., 1st sess., pp. 64–66 (March 15, 1869), pp. 243–245 (March 24, 1869), pp. 260–262 (March 30, 1869), and pp. 614–617 (April 8, 1869). See also Hamilton Fish to Nicholas Fish, August 18, 1879, Fish Papers, and Kate Sprague to Pomeroy, October 15, 1881, Arthur Papers, L.C.

26. Henry Anthony to Hamilton Fish, May 13, 1869, Fish Papers; Henry Anthony to Justin Morrill, October 18, 1869, Morrill Papers, L.C. (Unless otherwise stated, correspondence from the Morrill Papers is in

the Library of Congress collection). See also the *National Republican,* March 10, 1873.

27. Hamilton Fish to J. C. Hamilton, June 23, 1870, Fish Papers.

28. A general account of the affair may be found in Nevins, *Fish,* chap. xix, although my argument differs substantially. Nevins stressed Stalwart revenge but even those removed from any contact with Grant were convinced that Sumner deserved to be removed. See Justin Morrill to Charles Sumner, September 5, 1870, Sumner Papers, Houghton Library, Harvard University, Cambridge, Massachusetts; Timothy Howe to Charles Sumner, July 21, 1870, *ibid.;* Timothy Howe to Charles Sumner, August 23, 1870, and Charles Sumner to Timothy Howe, August 28, 1870, Howe Papers. Cf. also dissertation, p. 18.

29. Hamilton Fish to Timothy Howe, August 6, 1870, Howe Papers. Justin Morrill to Hamilton Fish, July 18, 1870, Morrill Papers; Justin Morrill to Hamilton Fish, September 5, 1870, Fish Papers. The caucus action was fully reported in the *National Republican;* see its columns from March 7 through March 13, 1870, especially March 10.

30. Timothy Howe to Elisha Keyes, March 17, 1871, Keyes Papers, State Historical Society of Wisconsin, Madison; Timothy Howe to Theodore Tilton, March 22, 1871, reprinted in *The Golden Age,* April 1, 1871. Howe always maintained that he and the committee did not follow the lead of Grant. Timothy Howe to Hamilton Fish, December 22, 1877, Fish Papers. Sumner admitted he had ceased all social intercourse with the President and his Secretary of State (see his untitled pamphlet, Sumner Papers.) Cf. also dissertation, p. 20.

31. *Congressional Globe,* 42nd Cong., 1st sess., pp. 43ff. (March 10, 1871).

32. *Ibid.,* pp. 45ff.; *National Republican,* March 10, 1871; William Buckingham to his son, March 10, 1871, Buckingham Papers, Connecticut State Library, Hartford. Morrill and Sherman, unwilling to throw the first stone, quickly joined the crowd.

33. Matthew Josephson's *The Politicos* (New York, 1938) sums up the standard interpretation on this and so many other issues that he deserves special attention. His sympathy here, of course, rests with Sumner; Morton is inaccurately described as the Senate whip and his comments on the need for party organization exaggerated out of all context (p. 147). This incident is vital to Josephson's argument that party dominated the Senate during the decade of the 1870's, a view I believe mistaken.

34. T. S. Allen to Elisha Keyes, July 20, 1873, Keyes Papers.

35. Earle D. Ross, *The Liberal Republican Movement* (New York, 1919). More interpretive is Ari Hoogenboom, *Outlawing the Spoils* (Urbana, 1961). Lyman Trumbull to William Jayne, January 10, 1872, Trumbull Papers, L.C. Francis Lieber to Charles Sumner, July 14, 1871

and July 18, 1871, Lieber Papers, Huntington Library, San Marino, California.

36. *Congressional Globe*, 42nd Cong., 2nd sess., pp. 394ff. (May 28, 1872).

37. Joseph Fowler to Charles Sumner, January 20, 1872, Sumner Papers; *New York Tribune*, April 17, June 22, 1872. Joseph Fowler to Lyman Trumbull, February 1, 1872, Trumbull Papers. This argument is taken over by Josephson, *Politicos*, pp. 107, 138–139.

38. *New York Herald*, March 8, 1871; *National Republican*, December 7, 1871.

39. Grant knew early who his enemies were; see Homer Porter (the President's private secretary) to Hamilton Fish, December 16, 1871, Fish Papers. Among the Republicans without patronage who joined the Liberal Republican movement were Reuben Fenton in New York, Willard Warner in Alabama, Alexander McDonald in Arkansas, Thomas Tipton in Nebraska, and Carl Schurz in Missouri. See dissertation, p. 24. John Sherman, on the other hand, had no patronage but did not bolt; see John Sherman to Cecilia Sherman, November 24, 1876, Sherman Papers. The relationship between national and state politics will be explored below in Chapter VI.

40. *National Republican*, December 3–6, 1872; the quotations are found in an editorial of December 7, 1872. Josephson, *Politicos*, p. 164, quotes a Liberal Republican to substantiate the argument that the party was all powerful and arbitrary.

41. J. P. Jones to Georgina Jones, April 12, 1881, Jones Papers, Huntington Library, San Marino, California; Hamilton Fish to Charles Marseilles, October 12, 1891, Fish Papers. For less friendly comments see John Sherman to James Garfield, January 23, 1881, Garfield Papers, L.C.; August Belmont to Thomas Bayard, March 27, 1881, Bayard Papers, L.C.

42. Biographical data can be gathered from Donald B. Chidsey, *The Gentleman from New York, Roscoe Conkling* (New Haven, 1935), and Alfred R. Conkling, *Life and Letters of Roscoe Conkling* (New York, 1889). Material on state politics is also found in D. S. Alexander, *A Political History of New York, 1774–1882* (New York, 1906–1909) vol. III, *passim*. How Grant and Conkling came together is not altogether clear but see Chidsey, *Gentleman from New York*, pp. 143–147, and Whitelaw Reid to James Garfield, September 11, 1870, Reid Papers, L.C. Cf. also dissertation, pp. 26–27. There is no doubt, however, that by 1869 Grant and Conkling were friends as well as allies. See the small miscellaneous collection of Conkling Papers in the Library of Congress; U. S. Grant to Roscoe Conkling, August 12, 1869, August 22, 1870, and November 18, 1870.

43. Angus Cameron to Elisha Keyes, December 1, 1877, Keyes

Papers; cf. also Hamilton Fish to Charles Marseilles, October 12, 1891, Fish Papers.

44. Wilmer C. Harris', *The Public Life of Zachariah Chandler* (Lansing, Mich., 1917), is mediocre. As Conkling voted on political questions, so voted Southern Republicans.

45. J. P. Jones to Georgina Jones, January 26, 1877, and Georgina Jones to J. P. Jones, April 20, 1881, Jones Papers. The two men also carried on various business enterprises together; see Roscoe Conkling to J. P. Jones, March 26, 1879, Jones Papers.

46. Timothy Howe to Grace Howe, February 10, 1871, typescript; Roscoe Conkling to Timothy Howe, May 2, 1879, Howe Papers.

47. In March, 1873, for example, William Stewart chaired the five-man committee and Conkling served on it along with three other supporters; *New York Times,* March 7, 1873.

48. John Logan headed the 1875 committee and the Illinois Senator was friendly to Conkling; men like Timothy Howe, Frederick Frelinghuysen, Aaron Sargent, and Spencer himself gave Conkling a majority. For the 1877 incident see the *National Republican,* December 6, 1877.

49. Oliver Morton to his wife, April 5, 1871, John Brayton Papers, Indiana Division, Indiana State Library, Indianapolis. W. D. Foulke, *Life of Oliver P. Morton* (Indianapolis, 1899), II, 178. Cf. also Nevins, *Fish,* pp. 495–496, and dissertation, p. 30.

50. Angus Cameron to Elisha Keyes, December 1, 1887, Keyes Papers; *New York Herald,* March 13, 1873. Autobiographical Memoir of Henry Dawes, "Incidents in Congressional Life," Dawes Papers.

51. For example, see Conkling's votes on the Bland-Allison Act, *Congressional Record,* 45th Cong., 2nd sess., pp. 1097, 1112 (February 15, 1878), and the Sinking Fund Bill, *ibid.,* 45th Cong., 2nd sess., pp. 2383–2384 (April 9, 1878). Chapter III considers legislative proceedings and party cohesion in detail.

52. *National Republican,* December 21, 26, 1874; *New York Times,* March 10, 1875.

53. December 15, 1878.

54. *New York Times,* December 9, 1874; *National Republican,* December 4–7, 1878.

55. The facts of this conflict are well known; see Hoogenboom, *Outlawing the Spoils,* chap. ix. Cf. also Harry Barnard, *Rutherford B. Hayes and His America* (Indianapolis, 1954), chap. lxvii.

56. *Diary and Letters of Rutherford Birchard Hayes,* ed. C. R. Williams (Columbus, 1922–1926), III, 514. Most writers have been content to cite "senatorial courtesy." Obviously courtesy was not determinative as the confrontation with Garfield would soon reveal.

57. John Sherman to William Allison, January 31, 1879, Allison Papers, Iowa State Department of History and Archives, Des Moines; cf.

also, *Washington Post,* February 3, 1879, and Timothy Howe to Grace Howe, December 20, 1877, typescript, Howe Papers. For the final votes, see *Senate Executive Journal,* 45th Cong., 3rd sess., p. 502 (Feb. 3, 1879).

58. Josephson (*Politicos*) again conveniently sums up the standard interpretation. The Stalwarts were interested in patronage, while the Half-breeds "were known at least to devote part of their time to the framing of laws, to the study of prosaic budget reports and tariff schedules" (p. 179). But even in Josephson's own terms this division will not hold for supposedly the Stalwarts were well allied with business interests and surely then they would not neglect budgets and tariffs (p. 191). See John Sherman to James Garfield, January 23, 1881, and James Blaine to James Garfield, January 13, 1881, Garfield Papers. Cf. Rutherford Hayes to William Phelps, December 4, 1879, Hayes Papers, Rutherford B. Hayes Library, Fremont, Ohio. See also dissertation, pp. 34–35.

59. William Allison to James Blaine, August 7, 1874, November 26, December 3, 1877, Allison Papers. Josephson's technique was simple; when anything of which he disapproved was said, the speaker was labeled Stalwart (*Politicos,* p. 101). John Sherman to James Garfield, January 23, 1881, and James Blaine to James Garfield, January 13, 1881, Garfield Papers. Cf. also Rutherford B. Hayes to William Phelps, December 4, 1879, Hayes Papers. Cf. dissertation, pp. 34–35.

60. Garfield, *Diary,* December 19, 1880, February 16, 1881, Garfield Papers. J. P. Jones to Georgina Jones, February 15, 1881, February 20, 1881, Jones Papers; Whitelaw Reid to James Garfield, June 26 and December 24, 1880, Reid Papers.

61. On the Readjustors see C. C. Pearson, *Readjustor Movement in Virginia* (New Haven, 1917) and Nelson M. Blake, *William Mahone of Virginia* (Richmond, 1935). William Mahone to William Burwell, November 17, 1880, and George Gorham to William Mahone, November 21, 1880, Mahone Papers, D.U.L.

62. James Brady to William Mahone, January 13, 1881; George Gorham to William Mahone, February 18, 1881, Mahone Papers. For the difficulties with Garfield *et al.,* see George Gorham to William Mahone, February 8, 1881, Mahone Papers; Garfield, *Diary,* December 29, 1880, Garfield Papers. John Sherman to A. C. Fahnestock, April 17, 1885, Sherman Papers. That Mahone enjoyed the patronage is clear; George Gorham to William Mahone, January 1, 1880, and William Mahone to Thomas James, May 23, 1881, Mahone Papers. Cf. also dissertation, p. 36.

63. Garfield, *Diary,* March 20, 1881, Garfield Papers.

64. Garfield's motivations here were less than clear. Blaine's biographers insist on his crucial role in this matter (cf. D. S. Muzzey, *James G. Blaine* [New York, 1934], pp. 189ff.), but Garfield privately and

publicly maintained that he had the notion all along (*Diary,* March 23, 1881). For the support Garfield received see James Blaine to Whitelaw Reid, March 31, 1881, Reid Papers; James Garfield to Thomas Nichol, May 29, 1881, Garfield Papers; John Sherman to James Garfield, January 23, 1881, and Garfield, *Diary,* April 3, May 8, 1881, Garfield Papers.

65. John Hay to Whitelaw Reid, April 4, 1881, Reid Papers.

66. J. P. Jones to Georgina Jones, May 18, 1881, Jones Papers.

67. Garfield, *Diary,* April 2, 1881, April 30, 1881, Garfield Papers; cf. also Joseph Hawley to General W. A. Aiken, May 13, 1881, William Buckingham Papers, and Joseph Hawley to James Garfield, May 11, 1881, Garfield Papers.

68. Matthew Butler to John Daniel, May 16, 1881, Daniel Papers, D.U.L.; cf. also August Belmont to Thomas Bayard, March 27, 1881, and Francis Kernan to Thomas Bayard, May 9, 1881, Bayard Papers. This attitude was no secret from the Republicans; cf. J. P. Jones to Georgina Jones, May 6, 1881, Jones Papers.

69. Garfield, *Diary,* April 2, 1881, Garfield Papers.

70. Henry Anthony to Hamilton Fish, May 28, 1881, and Hamilton Fish to Henry Anthony, May 21, 1881, Fish Papers; John Hay to Whitelaw Reid, May 26, 1881, Reid Papers; Garfield, *Diary,* May 16, 1881, Garfield Papers.

71. J. P. Jones to Georgina Jones, July 15, 1881, Jones Papers; Whitelaw Reid to James Garfield, April 11, 1881, Reid Papers.

72. Orville Platt to Nelson Aldrich, March 12, 1883, and Anson McCook to Nelson Aldrich, November 28, 1883, Aldrich Papers, L.C. Cf. also *New York Times,* December 12, 15, 1883; *New York World,* January 12, 1884.

73. August Belmont to Thomas Bayard, March 15, 1875, Bayard Papers; cf. also John Gordon to Matt Ransom, October 7, 1878, and Matt Ransom to Thomas Bayard, June 21, 1876, and Thomas Bayard to Matt Ransom, June 1, 1877, Ransom Papers, U.N.C.L.; Wade Hampton to Zebulon Vance, September 24, 1878, Vance Papers, North Carolina State Department of Archives and History, Raleigh.

74. Allan Thurman to Thomas Bayard, September 21, 1872, Bayard Papers; Thomas Bayard to John Randolph Tucker, July 19, 1884, Tucker Papers, U.N.C.L.

75. Thomas Randolph to Whitelaw Reid, March 13, 1876, Reid Papers.

76. *National Republican,* March 17 and 18, 1879, December 5, 1879. See too William Wallace to Matt Ransom, December 9, 1879, and George Pendleton to Matt Ransom, September 27, 1881, Ransom Papers.

77. Horace S. Merrill, *Bourbon Democracy of the Middle West, 1865–1896* (Baton Rouge, 1953) and *Bourbon Leader: Grover Cleveland and the Democratic Party* (Boston, 1957). The argument here is supported

by a comparison of Democratic votes on three key issues: the Bland-Allison Act, the Sinking Fund Bill (see note 51, above), as well as the Tariff of 1883, *Congressional Record,* 47th Cong., 2nd sess., p. 2992 (February 20, 1883). See also Lee Benson, *Merchants, Farmers, and Railroads* (Cambridge, Mass., 1955), and cf. dissertation, p. 43.

78. *Biographical Album of Prominent Pennsylvanians,* 1st ser. (Philadelphia, 1898), pp. 133–137; cf. also Albert V. House, "The Democratic Convention of 1880," *Pennsylvania History,* 27:188–216 (1960). See also J. Clement Carroll to Thomas Bayard, April 13, 1875, and J. McKibbin to Thomas Bayard, April 9, 1879, Bayard Papers.

79. Thurman headed Judiciary, while Eaton of Connecticut, very much in opposition, stood at the top of Foreign Relations. Gordon chaired Commerce and Ransom headed Railroads, but Beck of Kentucky, who rarely agreed with them, served as secretary of the Caucus and sat on Finance and Appropriations as well.

80. Eli Saulsbury to George S. Houston, December 18, 1879, George Houston Papers, D.U.L.

81. John Tyler Morgan to Virginia Clay, January 2, 1885, C. C. Clay Papers, D.U.L. See also the *Vicksburg Daily Commercial,* January 4, 1881.

82. For Senate rules see McConachie, *Congressional Committees,* chap. ix, and Haynes, *Senate of the United States,* I, chaps. vii and viii. Cf. also Thomas McKee, *A Manual of Congressional Practice* (Washington, D.C., 1887). The rules debate in 1885 was the last major review of Senate procedures until 1946. The discussions were long and helpful; see the *Congressional Record,* 48th Cong., 1st sess., December 13, 1883 through January 11, 1884.

83. *Congressional Record,* 47th Cong., 1st sess., pp. 675–676 (January 27, 1882), and pp. 870–874 (February 3, 1882).

84. *Ibid.;* cf. also *Congressional Record,* 47th Cong., 1st sess., February 6, 1882 through February 8, 1882, esp. pp. 913, 939, 984; April 26, 1882 through April 28, 1882, esp. pp. 3305–3308, 3345, 3400–3401.

85. *Congressional Record,* 47th Cong., 1st sess., p. 873 (February 3, 1882).

86. *Ibid.,* 48th Cong., 1st sess., pp. 172–173 (December 19, 1883).

87. *Ibid.,* pp. 144ff. (December 13, 1883), pp. 177–78 (December 19, 1883), and p. 310 (January 9, 1884).

88. Woodrow Wilson, *Congressional Government* (Boston, 1885), pp. 212–213.

89. *Ibid.,* pp. 205–206, 92, 99, and 315.

90. Cf. Walter Bagehot, *Physics and Politics* (Boston: Beacon Edition, 1956); Wilson, *Congressional Government,* pp. 59–61, 94–96, 117–118.

91. Wilson, *Congressional Government,* pp. 326, 329–330.

CHAPTER II: The Dynamics of Leadership

1. Moisei Ostrogorski, *Democracy and the Organization of Political Parties* (New York, 1902), II, 542.

2. Dawes Memoir, "Talks about Congress Continued," pp. 10–11, Dawes Papers; the *Washington Post*, March 7, 1897.

3. Alonzo Stewart to William Allison, November 8, 1895, Allison Papers. David Truman, in *The Congressional Party* (New York, 1959), recognized that "much of the formal machinery of party leadership in both houses either emerged or was considerably strengthened . . . between 1870 and 1913" (p. 98). He emphasized the increase in the size of the membership but noted that although the changes "must certainly have facilitated the management of larger numbers . . . they did not occur wholly in response to such increases."

4. James McMillan to George M. Morgan, February 24, 1896, March 19, 1896, McMillan Papers, Burton Historical Collection, Detroit Public Library.

5. James McMillan to Hugh McMillan, January 27, 1897, and James McMillan to William McMillan, February 6, 1897, May 13, 1898, McMillan Papers. Cf. also Joseph Hawley to Nelson Aldrich, July 28, 1892, Aldrich Papers.

6. Charles Manderson to William Allison, May 4, 1897, Allison Papers; James McMillan to William Washburn, January 29, 1895, McMillan Papers; John Spooner to William Allison, May 12, 1898, Spooner Papers. L. C. McMillan's friends presented him with a birthday cup in 1898, see Spooner Papers, May 1898. The donors formed the School of Philosophy Club. On its legislative importance see James McMillan to James McMillan Jr., February 12, 1901, McMillan Papers.

7. Charles Moore, "James McMillan," *Michigan Historical Collections* 39:173–187 (1915).

8. William Allison to James McMillan, March 24, 1891, and James McMillan to William Allison, August 27, 1894, McMillan Papers.

9. Charles Brayton to Nelson Aldrich, January 25, 1900, Aldrich Papers.

10. For a detailed account of Spooner's life see Dorothy C. Fowler, *John Coit Spooner* (New York, 1961). John Spooner to William Washburn, April 9, 1892, Spooner Papers. James McMillan to Anson McCook, February 8, 1896, and James McMillan to William Washburn, January 23, 1896, McMillan Papers.

11. Claude Bowers, *Beveridge and the Progressive Era* (Boston, 1932), p. 138. See also Leland L. Sage, *William Boyd Allison* (Iowa City, 1956). Dawes Memoir, "Talks about Congress Continued," Dawes Papers.

12. See Nathaniel Stephenson, *Nelson W. Aldrich* (New York, 1930), for an acceptable if not imaginative biography of Aldrich.

13. Thomas Platt to William Allison, July 26, 1899, Allison Papers.

14. Louis A. Coolidge, *An Old Fashioned Senator, Orville H. Platt* (New York, 1910), supplies some information.

15. Anthony Higgins to James H. Wilson, March 5, 1900, Wilson Papers, L. C.; George Edmunds to William Allison, April 30, 1898, Allison Papers; Mark Hanna to William McKinley, February 14, 1901, McKinley Papers, L. C.; Edward Wolcott to William Allison, March 2, 1900, Allison Papers.

16. David Phillips, in his 1906 articles (*The Treason of the Senate* [New York, reprint, 1953]), argued that campaign contributions by Aldrich to his colleagues corrupted them. Receiving the funds from corporate interests, he dispensed them with business welfare in mind. Phillips, with minor variations, has set the tone of later interpretations. See George Mowry, *Theodore Roosevelt and the Progressive Movement* (Madison, 1946), p. 48. Josephson (*Politicos,* pp. 389, 444–447) added a page on the secret powers of the caucus. In one of the most misleading sentences of his volume, he tried to connect the two points by noting that there were twenty-five multimillionaires in the Senate by 1900 "or enough to control all legislation through the mechanism of the committee system and party organization" (p. 444). Josephson is correct; twenty-five men could control party organization. But the unwary reader might conclude that twenty-five millionaires dominated the chamber. In point of fact, this was not true. Aldrich's biographer, Nathaniel Stephenson, simply argued that the personality of the Senator and the rights of seniority gave him power (Stephenson, *Aldrich,* pp. 132–137, 266–273).

17. Steering Committee membership was less frequently printed in the newspapers than that of the Committee on Committees; the personal papers of the senators, however, invariably turned up some record of the slates. Edmunds and Sherman only infrequently chaired the Steering Committee. Cf. George Edmunds to Nelson Aldrich, February 5, 1887, Aldrich Papers; George Edmunds to John Sherman, March 29, 1888, August 3, 1888, Sherman Papers.

18. Eugene Hale to William E. Chandler, 1896 (n.d; probably between April and June), Chandler Papers, L. C. Allison himself, Aldrich, Hale, and Cullom served on the committee from 1897 on. Spooner and Hanna joined them later and also continued there session after session.

19. In the 1897 slate, Hale and Aldrich represented New England, Shelby Cullom and Cushman Davis as well as Allison, the Midwest, William Sewell, the Mid-Atlantic, and Thomas Carter, the West. A similar geographical division can be found in the 1900 group; William Allison to John Spooner, February 23, 1900, Spooner Papers. Cf. also William Allison to Nelson Aldrich, January 4, 1904, Aldrich Papers.

20. The chairmen of Commerce (Frye), Foreign Relations (Davis), Cuba (Platt), Naval Affairs (Hale), and Rules (Spooner) were also on the Steering Committee. William Frye to William Allison, 1900 (n.d.), Allison Papers.

21. *Washington Post, New York Times,* December 5, 6, 1895. The dissidents composed a list of nine men and Sherman chose Mitchell of Oregon, Teller of Colorado, Pettigrew of South Dakota, Pritchard of North Carolina, and William Chandler of New Hampshire.

22. *Washington Post,* March 7, April 24, 1897; William Allison to John Spooner, March 31, 1897, Spooner Papers.

23. See a speech by Charles Manderson, Nebraska senator (1883–1895), delivered in Omaha, November 10, 1909, copy in the Aldrich Papers. "When the Steering Committee came to be organized," Manderson noted, "the majority of the steering committee was of that little school of philosophy."

24. John Tyler Morgan, remarks in *Congressional Record,* 48th Cong., 1st sess., p. 232 (January 7, 1883).

25. William Allison to John Spooner, November 7, 1899, Spooner Papers. Cf. H. L. Austin to John Spooner, April 2, 1897, Spooner Papers and the remarks of Robert La Follette, *Congressional Record,* 60th Cong., 1st sess., p. 7191 (May 29, 1908).

26. Eugene Hale to Orville Platt, November 11, 1903, Platt Papers, Connecticut State Library, Hartford. The forms were always identical; see Orville Platt to John Spooner, December 5, 1901, Spooner Papers. The turnover on this committee stayed high and the chairman, together with Allison, dominated its meetings.

27. John Spooner to Eldon DeWitt, December 16, 1899, Spooner Papers. For the current actions of the Committee on Committees, see Donald Matthews, *U.S. Senators and Their World* (Chapel Hill, 1960), pp. 124ff.

28. Francis Warren to A. J. Parshall, December 18, 1899, Warren Papers, Archives and Western History Department, University of Wyoming Library, Laramie.

29. Memorandum in the Orville Platt Papers by his secretary, Kathleen Lawler, November 2, 1904.

30. There is no history of seniority in the Senate but see George Goodwin, "The Seniority System in Congress," *American Political Science Review,* 52:412–436 (1959). Cf. also Haynes, *Senate of the United States,* I, 294–305 and Matthews, *U.S. Senators,* pp. 148–152. When Sumner was deposed, no one talked about a violation of the seniority system as such, although the unusual character of the move was emphasized. When the Democrats took control of Congress in 1879 it was not certain that they would follow the dictates of seniority until, as the *National Republican* noted on March 17, "after some discussion an

understanding was reached that seniority of service on a committee should entitle the Senator to its chairmanship."

31. Commerce made appropriations for rivers, harbors, and other internal improvements and looked after the general welfare of the nation's commerce. The Judiciary Committee exercised jurisdiction over the judicial organization of the country but was also called upon by various committees to settle questions of law at issue in legislation. For a contemporary comparison see Matthews, *U.S. Senators*, pp. 152–158.

32. James McMillan to John H. Mitchell (Committee on Committees chairman), December 7, 1895; James McMillan to William Washburn, January 23, 1896, and to Thomas Bell, April 26, 1896, McMillan Papers.

33. James McMillan to William McMillan, February 11, February 15, 1901, and William McMillan to James McMillan, February 13, 1901, McMillan Papers.

34. John Spooner to C. W. Porter, March 12, 1888, and to Theodore Heiss, April 6, 1890, Spooner Papers.

35. John Spooner to Mark Barnum, July 24, 1888, Spooner Papers.

36. William Stewart to William Herrin, April 11, 1888, Stewart Papers, Nevada State Historical Society, Reno.

37. Charles Fairbanks to Shelby Cullom, January 25, 1897, and Shelby Cullom to Charles Fairbanks, January 29, 1897, Fairbanks Papers, Lilly Library, University of Indiana, Bloomington.

38. William Chandler to Eugene Hale, December 9, 1891, Chandler Papers.

39. William Stewart to Shelby Cullom, December 7, 1891, Stewart Papers. Cf. also Richard Pettigrew to J. C. Williams, January 15, 1896, Pettigrew Papers, The Pettigrew Museum, Sioux Falls, South Dakota, and Henry Cabot Lodge to Nelson Aldrich, December 8, 1905, Aldrich Papers. Cf. Matthews, *U.S. Senators*, p. 148.

40. Orville Platt to William Chandler, July 6, 1895, Chandler Papers, New Hampshire Historical Society, Concord. (Except where otherwise stated, the Chandler Papers refer to the Library of Congress collection.) Orville Platt to William Chandler, November 26, 1895, Chandler Papers. Fred Dubois to John H. Mitchell, December 8, 1895, Dubois Papers, Idaho State College Museum, Pocatello.

41. Dubois' account is in an uncompleted autobiography in his Papers. Richard Pettigrew to Robert Dollard, November 12, 1894, Pettigrew Papers. Orville Platt to John H. Flag, June 24, 1895, quoted in Coolidge, *Orville H. Platt*, p. 540, and John H. Flag to Orville Platt, June 17, 1895, Platt Papers.

42. Louis T. Michener to Albert Beveridge, January 25, 1899, Beveridge Papers, L.C.

43. Albert Beveridge to Charles G. Dawes, January 28, 1899, and Charles G. Dawes to Albert Beveridge, February 2, 1899, Beveridge Papers.

44. Albert Beveridge to William Allison, March 20, 1899, Beveridge Papers.

45. Albert Beveridge to G. W. Perkins, March 13, 1899, Beveridge Papers.

46. Albert Beveridge to William Allison, March 20, 1899, Beveridge Papers.

47. Albert Beveridge to Garret Hobart, March 20, 1899, and to G. W. Perkins, March 13, 1899, Beveridge Papers; M. E. Ingalls to Nelson Aldrich, December 11, 1898, Aldrich Papers. Cf. also Bowers, *Beveridge,* p. 116. Beveridge blamed Fairbanks for his initial failures; Albert Beveridge to Orville Platt, November 10, 1904, Platt Papers.

48. Albert Beveridge to William Allison, September 20, 1899, Beveridge Papers; cf. his letters to Orville Platt, November–December, 1904, Platt Papers.

49. Mark Hanna to Nelson Aldrich, December 8, 1899, Aldrich Papers. Francis Warren to Mark Hanna, February 19, 1896, Warren Papers. Francis Warren to Willis Van Devanter, April 1, 1896, and to Ira Fredendall, November 28, 1898, Warren Papers.

50. John Spooner to Julius Burrows, January 18, 1899, copy in the Aldrich Papers. See also *Washington Post,* April 20, May 3, May 6, 1897.

51. Francis Warren to Clarence Bennett, February 20, 1891, Warren Papers; James McMillan to H. B. Ledyard, February 23, 1895, McMillan Papers; John Spooner to Lyman Abbott, January 3, 1901, Spooner Papers.

52. James McMillan to Charles Farwell, September 1, 1890, and to William Sewell, September 11, 1890, McMillan Papers. John Kean of New Jersey performed the duties of secretary of the caucus.

53. Francis Warren to William Allison, April 30, 1896, Warren Papers; William Allison to Nelson Aldrich, February 27, 1900, Aldrich Papers; James McMillan to William Allison, March 17, 1900, McMillan Papers.

54. Albert Beveridge to J. C. Shaffer, February 7, 1902, Beveridge Papers. For current practices cf. Hugh Bone, "An Introduction to Senate Policy Committees," *American Political Science Review,* 50:339–359 (1956).

55. R. J. Bright to William Allison, August 19, 1897, Allison Papers; John Spooner to Morton Herrick, February 6, 1900 and to M. P. Rindlaub, February 7, 1900, Spooner Papers. Cf. also James McMillan to William E. Chandler, January 14, 1900, McMillan Papers. The mechanics were now worked out by a caucus committee.

56. John Sherman had earlier reached a similar decision, finding the post too confining. John Sherman to Rutherford B. Hayes, November 18, 1887, Hayes Papers.

57. Remarks of James George (Democrat from Mississippi), *Congressional Record,* 51st Cong., 1st sess., p. 2147 (March 12, 1900), and

New Hampshire's Jacob Gallinger, *Congressional Record,* 63rd Cong., 2nd sess., p. 3733 (February 13, 1915).

58. Albert Beveridge to William Allison, November 3, 1902, Allison Papers; Albert Beveridge to Nelson Aldrich, November 3, 1902, Aldrich Papers. William Allison to Albert Beveridge, November 4, 1902, Beveridge Papers.

59. Remarks of Oklahoma's Robert Owen, *Congressional Record,* 63rd Cong., 2nd sess., p. 3733 (February 13, 1915).

60. Party leadership in the Senate today is best described in Truman, *Congressional Party,* chap. iv. Cf. also Matthews, *U.S. Senators,* chap. vi, and William S. White, *The Citadel* (New York, 1956). For the leverage of committee assignments and possible responses to it, see Ralph Huitt, "The Outsider in the Senate: An Alternative Role," *American Political Science Review,* 55: 566–575 (1961), and "The Morse Committee Assignment Controversy," *American Political Science Review,* 51:313–329 (1957).

61. *Congressional Record,* 51st Cong., 1st sess., p. 7059 (July 9, 1890).

62. *Ibid.,* 53rd Cong., 2nd sess., p. 7802 (July 23, 1894). Democrats as well as Republicans appreciated the importance of controlling the Senate; cf. Arthur Gorman to William Whitney, December 7, 1892, Whitney Papers, L.C.; E. C. Wall to William Vilas, January 6, 1892, Vilas Papers, State Historical Society of Wisconsin, Madison.

63. John R. Lambert, *Arthur Pue Gorman* (Baton Rouge, 1953).

64. *Notebooks and Diaries of Horace Chilton,* no. 6, 1897, typescript copy in the Chilton Papers, University of Texas Library, Austin. Quotations are from pages 47–58.

65. Gorman, defeated for the Senate in 1899, returned in 1903 and immediately won re-election as caucus chairman, despite the break in service. Supplement to the *Maryland Journal,* Gorman Papers, Maryland Historical Society, Baltimore.

66. Gorman, *Journals,* December 16, 1903, Gorman Papers. Because of the preponderance of Southerners among the Democrats, geographic distribution was more limited. On the permanence of the appointments, see the *Washington Post,* March 6, 9, 1893, March 10, April 30, 1897. On the importance of the Steering Committee, see the draft of a speech to the Democratic caucus by Ben Tillman, March 15, 1913, Tillman Papers, Clemson Agriculture College Library, South Carolina. Even today Democratic structure is more unified than their rivals'. See Truman, *Congressional Party,* p. 101 and Ralph Huitt, "Democratic Party Leadership in the Senate," *American Political Science Review,* 55:333–344 (1961).

67. Francis M. Cockrell II, *The Senator from Missouri* (New York,

1962), *passim.* See also the *St. Louis Globe Democrat,* January 9, 1881, January 20, 1887, January 19, 1899.

68. "Joseph Clay Stiles Blackburn," *Dictionary of American Biography,* II, 316–317.

69. *Representative Men of Ohio,* 1896–1897, ed. J. K. Mercer and C. W. Vallandigham (Columbus, 1896), pp. 28–36. Cf. also "Calvin Stewart Brice," *Dictionary of American Biography,* III, 31–32. Material on Walthall can be found in Albert D. Kirwan, *Revolt of the Rednecks* (Lexington, Ky., 1951), pp. 48, 88. Lambert, *Gorman,* chap. viii, and Thomas Bayard to Walter Gresham, May 29, 1894, Gresham Papers, L.C.

70. Edith Dobie, *The Political Career of Stephen Mallory White* (Stanford, 1927), *passim.* Charles Richards to Stephen White, February 2, 1893, White Papers, Borel Collection, Stanford University Library, California.

71. Stephen White to Charles Richards, February 10, 1893, White Papers. Like Beveridge, White received advice about the workings of the Senate from several quarters; cf. Charles A. Forman to Stephen White, February 1, 1893, and Stephen White to Charles Forman, February 10, 1893, White Papers. Friends also wrote on his behalf to Senate members; S. W. Fordyce to Matt Ransom, February 21, 1893, Ransom Papers.

72. Stephen White to Arthur Gorman, February 8, 1893, White Papers. Their relationship even improved with time. Cf. Stephen White to Arthur Gorman, March 20, 1897, White Papers; *New York Tribune,* August 18, 1894. Cf. also Tillman caucus speech, Tillman Papers.

73. *Congressional Record,* 53rd Cong., 1st sess., pp. 128–131 (April 12, 1893). Call had introduced a similar bill in 1882 (*Ibid.,* 47th Cong., 1st sess., p. 1947 [March 16, 1882]) but it attracted much less attention.

74. *Congressional Record,* 54th Cong., 1st sess., pp. 132–133 (December 5, 1895). On the vital place of Appropriations cf. George Vest, *ibid.,* 51st Cong., 1st sess., p. 1063 (February 5, 1890) and Francis Warren to N. J. O'Brien, February 14, 1891, Warren Papers.

75. *Congressional Record,* 54th Cong., 1st sess., pp. 1288–1290 (February 4, 1896). Gallinger's comments were made the following day, pp. 1326, 1330.

76. See the remarks of Allison, *ibid.,* pp. 1389–1392 (February 6, 1896), and Hale, p. 1332 (February 5, 1896); 55th Cong., 3rd sess., p. 1212 (January 28, 1899) for the bill's passage. For those favoring the measure, see a petition dated December 8, 1898, in the Chandler Papers. For its effects see Francis Warren to Helen Warren, December 12, 1899, Warren Papers.

77. Compare Democratic votes on the confirmation of William Hornblower (a Cleveland appointee), *Senate Executive Journal* 53rd Cong., 3rd sess., p. 352 (January 17, 1894) with the repeal of the Sherman Silver Purchase Act (*Congressional Record,* 53rd Cong., 1st sess.,

p. 2958 (October 30, 1893) and the schedules of the Wilson-Gorman Tariff (*ibid.*, 53rd Cong., 2nd sess., p. 7115 (July 3, 1894). See also dissertation, p. 88.

78. Tillman's caucus speech, Tillman Papers, makes clear the comparative weakness of Democratic Senate leadership.

79. Gorman, *Journal*, December 12, December 15, 1903, Gorman Papers; Lambert, *Gorman*, pp. 292–308. Gorman noted that it was the first time in its history that the party took such a step.

80. Tillman's caucus speech, Tillman Papers. Eventually he substituted a milder version, also found in his papers, but the changes were only in tone, not in substance. Cf. Francis B. Simkins, *Pitchfork Ben Tillman, South Carolinian* (Baton Rouge, 1944), pp. 508ff. See dissertation, pp. 89–90.

81. See the debate between Joseph Bailey, Texas Democrat, and Thomas Patterson, Colorado Democrat, *Congressional Record,* 59th Cong., 1st sess., pp. 2210–2212, 2216 (February 7, 1906).

82. William Stewart to S. C. Wright, April 7, 1892, Stewart Papers; George Washburn (member of the National Populist Executive Committee) to Marion Butler, December 15, 1896, Butler Papers, U.N.C.L. The J. P. Jones speech was reprinted in the *Virginia* (Nevada) *Chronicle,* September 6, 1894, Jones Papers. Cf. also James H. Ferriss to Marion Butler, February 11, 1897, Butler Papers; manuscript of William Stewart speech, December 1892, Stewart Papers.

83. Manuscript copy of a speech delivered by Marion Butler, dated 1897, filed in the Butler Papers; cf. also Marion Butler to Thomas Watson, September 8, 1896, Butler Papers.

84. *Washington Post,* December 3–7, December 31, 1895 and March 12, April 19–29, 1897. *Congressional Record,* 54th Cong., 1st sess., pp. 422–426 (December 30, 1895).

85. William E. Chandler to William Allison, March 26, 1897, Allison Papers; Francis Warren to Dewey, Gould, and Company, February 6, 1896, Warren Papers. Cf. also James McMillan to E. T. Hance, December 7, 1895, McMillan Papers.

86. *Congressional Record,* 54th Cong., 1st sess., pp. 423–426 (December 30, 1895).

87. Draft of an article by William Stewart for the *North American Review,* dated October 1900, written about September 15, 1900, Stewart Papers. Italics added.

CHAPTER III: The Legislative Process

1. A. Lawrence Lowell, "The Influence of Party upon Legislation in England and America," American Historical Association, *Annual Report for the Year 1901,* I, 321.

2. *Ibid.*, pp. 539–541.

3. The best accounts of the currency problems before 1870 are Sharkey, *Money, Class, and Power,* and Irwin Unger, *The Greenback Era* (Princeton, 1964). General studies include D. R. Dewey, *Financial History of the United States,* 12th ed. (New York, 1934), A. B. Hepburn, *A History of Currency in the United States* (New York, 1915), Alexander D. Noyes, *Forty Years of American Finance, 1865–1907* (New York, 1909).

4. *Congressional Globe,* 41st Cong., 1st sess., March 25, 1869–March 30, 1869. See also 41st Cong., 2nd sess., January 24, 1870–February 2, 1870. John Sherman, *Recollections of Forty Years* (Chicago and New York, 1895), I, 451–458.

5. *Congressional Globe,* 41st Cong., 2nd sess., pp. 1587–1594 (February 28, 1870), pp. 1779–1798 (March 9, 1870), pp. 1838–1843 (March 10, 1870). The bill passed on March 11, 1870 (p. 1884) but did not become law until a lengthy conflict with the House was settled.

6. *Congressional Record,* 43rd Cong., 1st sess., March 22, 1874–April 6, 1874.

7. The final vote was taken on April 6, 1874 (*ibid.*, p. 2835). Sherman, *Recollections,* I, 490–495. See Unger, *Greenback Era,* pp. 213–235.

8. *New York Times,* December 5, 7, 1874; Unger, *Greenback Era,* pp. 252–255.

9. *New York Times,* December 14, 16, 20, 23, 1874; *Congressional Record,* 43rd Cong., 2nd sess., December 22, 1874. In the Sherman Papers is an undated memorandum with the list of committee members and it is reprinted in his *Recollections,* p. 509. "It was well understood," he wrote there, "that the bill was the result of a Republican conference" (p. 511).

10. The debate opened on December 10, 1877 (*Congressional Record,* 45th Cong., 2nd sess.) and continued until the end of January. The final vote was on January 25, 1878 (p. 561); 24 Democrats and 17 Republicans favored the bill, 10 Democrats and 17 Republicans opposed it.

11. The bill was taken up on January 28, 1878, *Congressional Record,* 45th Cong., 2nd sess. For Eaton's remark see *ibid.*, February 5, 1878; Justin Morrill to Benedict, October 22, 1875, Morrill Papers.

12. Sage, *Allison,* p. 153; Sherman, *Recollections,* II, 620–635. Voting was concluded February 15, 1878 (p. 1112) and Hayes' veto overridden February 28, 1878 (p. 1141). Twenty-three Republicans and 26 Democrats supported Allison; 13 Republicans and 9 Democrats voted against the bill.

13. The Senate passed a similar bill in 1880 but the House failed to agree. It was reintroduced January 10, 1882 (*Congressional Record,* 47th Cong., 1st sess.) and debate continued until the end of March. For Bayard's remarks see *ibid.*, p. 305 (January 10, 1882), and Thomas

Bayard to Edward Atkinson, December 24, 1881, Bayard Papers. The measure passed March 28, 1882 by a vote of 38–15–23 (p. 2342); 97 per cent of the Republicans supported it and 63 per cent of the Democrats opposed it. Those who favored the commission likely favored a protective tariff.

14. The tariff bill was discussed and amended in January and February 1883; for a brief survey see F. W. Taussig, *The Tariff History of the United States* (New York, 1892), pp. 230–250. Henry Davis to Stephen Elkins, December 15, 1882, Davis Papers, W.V.U.L.; Henry Davis to Stephen Lee, January 27, 1883, Davis Papers. *Congressional Record,* 47th Cong., 2nd sess., p. 2215 (February 14, 1883). Seven Democrats joined him to raise the coal duty from 50 to 75 cents.

15. For sugar, *ibid.,* p. 1845 (January 30, 1883); lumber was originally to be admitted duty free but Southern votes restored protection (*ibid.,* p. 1147 [January 22, 1883] and p. 2564 [February 13, 1883]). Party lines also dissolved when Sherman tried to win a higher duty for pig iron. Cf. also Ida Tarbell, *The Tariff in Our Times* (New York, 1911), pp. 116–117; her judgments here, unlike most instances, were valid.

16. John I. Mitchell to Wharton Barker, February 14, 1883, Barker Papers, L.C. Mitchell thought the bill "practically . . . a Democratic measure."

17. David Davis to Adeline Burr, February 14, 1883, Adeline Burr Davis Green Papers, D.U.L. Benjamin Harrison to Wharton Barker, February 16, 1883, Barker Papers.

18. The bill first passed the Senate on February 20, 1883, *Congressional Record,* 47th Cong., 2nd sess., p. 2922. The conference report was approved March 2, 1883, see *ibid.,* p. 3586.

19. John I. Mitchell to Wharton Barker, January 31, 1883, December 6, 1883, Barker Papers.

20. Justin Morrill to Wharton Barker, March 10, 1883, Barker Papers.

21. James Swank to Justin Morrill, September 27, 1883, Morrill Papers; H. Jones to John Sherman, August 1, 1883, and John Sherman to H. Jones, August 8, 1883, Sherman Papers. John I. Mitchell to Wharton Barker, December 6, 1883, Barker Papers.

22. *Congressional Record,* 44th Cong., 2nd sess. Gordon introduced his bill on January 12, 1877 and it was reported a week later from the committee by Joseph West. Debate continued until February 27, 1877 when the bill was put over. Cf. C. Vann Woodward, *Reunion and Reaction* (New York: Anchor Edition, 1956), 131–138. For lack of party lines in transportation discussions, cf. *Congressional Record,* 43rd Cong., 1st sess., April 8–April 13, 1874, on a general incorporation railroad law for the territories.

23. Debate recommenced March 12, 1878, *Congressional Record,* 45th Cong., 2nd sess. Key votes were taken on April 9, 1878. A lenient Blaine

amendment was defeated, 23–35–18 (p. 2383) and the bill passed, 40–26–6 (p. 2384). Among the strongest friends of the roads were 18 Republicans and 5 Democrats. On the final vote, party divisions were even more evident. Eighty-two per cent of the Democrats and 56 per cent of the Republicans supported it.

24. *Congressional Record,* 48th Cong., 2nd sess., December 18, 1884, and esp. p. 805 (January 17, 1885). The bill was raised again March 17, 1885 and debated sporadically for the next few months. Considered once more in January 1887, it finally passed January 14, 1887 (see roll calls, pp. 664, 666).

25. *Congressional Globe,* 41st Cong., 3rd sess., pp. 1167–1184 (February 13, 1871). Alexander Ramsey, *Diary,* March 14, 15, 1871, Ramsey Papers, Minnesota Historical Society, St. Paul; cf. also *Congressional Globe,* 41st Cong., 1st sess., pp. 620, 653–663 (April 8–April 9, 1870). On the Pinchback case, see *Congressional Record,* 44th Cong., 1st sess., March 16, 1875, esp. p. 91. Cf. also *ibid.,* p. 1557 (March 8, 1876).

26. *Congressional Globe,* 42nd Cong., 2nd sess., pp. 3727–3736 (May 21, 1872). Thirteen Democrats and 9 Republicans voted for moderate provisions (p. 3735).

27. *Congressional Globe,* 41st Cong., 3rd sess., pp. 73–82 (December 13, 1870). *Congressional Record,* 46th Cong., 1st sess., p. 807 (April 24, 1879).

28. *Ibid.,* 43rd Cong., 1st sess., pp. 4167 and 4176 (May 22, 1874).

29. Woodward, *Reunion and Reaction, passim,* esp. chaps i, ii, ix. Henry Dawes to Electa Dawes, January 21, 1877, Dawes Papers.

30. *Congressional Globe,* 42nd Cong., 3rd sess., p. 2184 (March 3, 1873). *Congressional Record,* 47th Cong., 2nd sess., pp. 204ff. (December 12, 1882); 48th Cong., 1st sess., p. 2724 (April 7, 1884).

31. Cf. the 1876 Appropriation Bill, *ibid.,* 44th Cong., 1st sess.; the roll calls of July 13 (pp. 4543, 4546, 4548) offer pertinent examples. When it was moved to decrease a Michigan appropriation, Republicans split, 12 in favor, 9 against, and so did the Democrats, 7 in favor, 12 against. Similarly, when a motion was made to cut back a Cleveland appropriation, 13 Republicans agreed, 10 did not, 5 Democrats agreed, 14 did not. The bill passed on August 3, 1876 (p. 5122) with 4 Democrats and 7 Republicans opposed. Cf. dissertation, p. 109.

32. *Ibid.,* 47th Cong., 1st sess.; see the voting records of July 11, 1882 (p. 5896) on an appropriation for a Mississippi river; 24 Democrats favored it, 6 opposed while 6 Republicans favored it and 16 opposed. The bill passed with more evenly divided nonpartisan support (July 12, 1882, p. 5950) with 8 Democrats and 17 Republicans voting against it. On August 2, 1882 (p. 6770), the Senate overrode Arthur's veto. Sixteen Republicans stayed with the President, 18 left him; 30 Democrats opposed him, 5 agreed.

33.

Legislation	Congressional Record			
	Congress	Session		
(1)	47th,	1st,	2342	(March 28, 1882)
(2)	47th,	2nd,	2696	(February 15, 1883)
(3)	47th,	2nd,	2662	(February 14, 1883)
(4)	47th,	2nd,	2992	(February 20, 1883)
(5)	47th,	2nd,	3583	(March 2, 1883)
(6)	41st,	1st,	370	(March 30, 1869)
(7)	41st,	2nd,	1884	(March 11, 1870)
(8)	43rd,	1st,	2489	(March 26, 1874)
(9)	43rd,	2nd,	208	(December 22, 1874)
(10)	45th,	2nd,	561	(January 25, 1878)
(11)	45th,	2nd,	1112	(February 15, 1878)
(12)	44th,	1st,	4543	(July 13, 1876)
(13)	44th,	1st,	5122	(August 3, 1876)
(14)	47th,	1st,	5896	(July 11, 1882)
(15)	47th,	1st,	5950	(July 11, 1882)
(16)	47th,	1st,	6770	(August 2, 1882)
(17)	42nd,	2nd,	2599	(April 19, 1872)
(18)	43rd,	1st,	3042	(April 13, 1874)
(19)	45th,	2nd,	2383	(April 9, 1878)
(20)	45th,	2nd,	2384	(April 9, 1878)
(21)	49th,	2nd,	664	(January 14, 1887)
(22)	49th,	2nd,	666	(January 14, 1887)
(23)	41st,	3rd,	1184	(February 13, 1871)
(24)	42nd,	2nd,	3378	(May 21, 1872)
(25)	43rd,	1st,	4176	(May 22, 1874)
(26)	45th,	1st,	797	(November 22, 1877)
(27)	46th,	1st,	807	(April 24, 1879)
(28)	44th,	2nd,	913	(January 24, 1877)
(29)	41st,	1st,	333	(March 29, 1869)
(30)	41st,	1st,	395	(March 31, 1869)
(31)	42nd,	3rd,	2184	(March 3, 1873)
(32)	48th,	1st,	2724	(April 7, 1884)

34.

Legislation	Congressional Record			
	Congress	Session		
(1)	50th,	2nd,	1105	(January 22, 1889)
(2)	51st,	1st,	9909	(September 9, 1890)
(3)	51st,	1st,	9943	(September 10, 1890)
(4)	51st,	1st,	10740	(September 30, 1890)
(5)	53rd,	2nd,	5759	(June 5, 1894)
(6)	53rd,	2nd,	5501	(May 31, 1894)
(7)	53rd,	2nd,	7136	(July 3, 1894)

(34. *Continued*)

Legislation	Congressional Record		
	Congress	Session	
(8)	55th,	1st,	1679 (June 11, 1897)
(9)	55th,	1st,	1921 (June 22, 1897)
(10)	55th,	1st,	2240 (July 2, 1897)
(11)	55th,	1st,	2447 (July 7, 1897)
(12)	51st,	1st,	6173 (June 17, 1890)
(13)	51st,	1st,	7109 (July 10, 1890)
(14)	53rd,	1st,	2958 (October 10, 1893)
(15)	53rd,	2nd,	2981 (March 14, 1894)
(16)	56th,	1st,	1835 (February 15, 1900)
(17)	51st,	2nd,	3421 (February 27, 1891)
(18)	55th,	3rd,	2302 (February 24, 1899)
(19)	51st,	1st,	2611 (March 25, 1890)
(20)	51st,	1st,	3153 (April 8, 1890)
(21)	51st,	2nd,	18 (December 2, 1890)
(22)	51st,	2nd,	912 (January 5, 1891)
(23)	51st,	2nd,	1740 (January 22, 1891)
(24)	55th,	1st,	Exec. Sess., 104 (May 6, 1897)
(25)	55th,	2nd,	4040 (April 18, 1898)
(26)	55th,	2nd,	5541 (June 4, 1898)
(27)	55th,	2nd,	6172 (June 16, 1898)
(28)	55th,	3rd,	1847 (February 14, 1899)
(29)	55th,	3rd,	Exec. Sess., 1284 (Feb. 7, 1899)

35. Orville Platt to Wharton Barker, December 22, 1886, Barker Papers.

36. John Spooner to C. W. Porter, March 12, 1888, Spooner Papers; James Swank to Justin Morrill, April 20, 1888, Morrill Papers; John Sherman to Benjamin Harrison, August 4, September 12, 1888, Sherman Papers. On the 1888 presidential election and Republican strategy, see Frank Hiscock to Whitelaw Reid, July 21, 23, 1888, Reid Papers; Frank Hiscock to Benjamin Harrison, July 12, 1888, Harrison Papers, L.C.

37. John Spooner to Elisha Keyes, July 24, 1888, Spooner Papers.

38. William Allison to Benjamin Harrison, July 3, 1888, and William Chandler to Benjamin Harrison, July 18, 1888, Harrison Papers. Frank Hiscock to Whitelaw Reid, July 26, 1888, Reid Papers.

39. William Chandler, *Diary*, entry of July 25, 1888, Chandler Papers, Concord. John Spooner to Horace Rublee, July 27, 1888, Spooner Papers. Cf. also John Sherman to John A. Bingham, July 27, 1888, Sherman Papers, and Henry Dawes to Electa Dawes, July 26, 1888, Dawes Papers.

40. William Allison to Benjamin Harrison, August 4, October 7, 1888, and John Sherman to Benjamin Harrison, August 17, 1888, Harrison

Papers. John Spooner to Horace Rublee, July 31, August 7, 1888, Spooner Papers. Henry Dawes to Electa Dawes, September 23, 1888, Dawes Papers; J. P. Jones to Georgina Jones, September 8, 1888, Jones Papers. See also dissertation, p. 115.

41. *Congressional Record,* 50th Cong., 1st sess., p. 9360 (October 4, 1888); Congress adjourned October 20, 1888 without taking action. The bill came up again in December; see *ibid.,* 50th Cong., 2nd sess., p. 142 (December 11, 1888), for Gorman's remarks.

42. William Allison to Justin Morrill, June 23, 1890, Morrill Papers. Aldrich made no secret of his tactics, *Congressional Record,* 51st Cong., 1st sess., p. 7851 (July 24, 1890). Obedience was evident in debate. The bill was reported July 18, 1890 and unlimited discussion continued until September 3, 1890. A five-minute limit was placed on each speech and the bill passed September 10, 1890. See James McMillan to Charles Farwell, September 1, 1890, McMillan Papers. Cf. also George Edmunds to John Sherman, September 8, 1890, Sherman Papers.

43. *Congressional Record,* 51st Cong., 1st sess., p. 8419 (August 11, 1890), p. 8442 (August 12, 1890), and p. 7885 (July 30, 1890). Cf. also Gorman's remarks, *ibid.,* p. 7850 (July 29, 1890).

44. *Ibid.,* p. 9659 (September 4, 1890). The bill passed September 10, 1890 (p. 9943) with only one Republican dissenting. The conference report usually followed the Senate and was quickly agreed to on September 30, 1890.

45. John Spooner to James Johnson, June 18, 1890, and to Frank Avery, August 17, 1890, Spooner Papers.

46. The tariff came to the Senate on February 2, 1894 but was not passed until July 3, 1894. The conference raised new problems not settled until August 13, 1894. Eppa Hunton to John Daniel, March 1, 1894, Daniel Papers. See the remarks of George Vest, "Investigation of Attempts at Bribery," 53rd Cong., 2nd sess., *Senate Report,* No. 606, pp. 514–515. Cf. also Arthur Gorman to William Vilas, April 24, 1894, Vilas Papers, and the comments of James K. Jones and Isham Harris, *Congressional Record,* 53rd Cong., 2nd sess., pp. 7804–7805 (July 23, 1894). See Festus Summers, *William L. Wilson and Tariff Reform* (New Brunswick, N.J., 1953), chap. xii.

47. Stephen White to John Reynolds, June 25, 1894, White Papers; *Congressional Record,* 53rd Cong., 2nd sess., pp. 7745–7746 (July 20, 1894).

48. *Ibid.,* p. 7802 (July 23, 1894).

49. *Ibid.,* pp. 4020, 4154, 2620, 4260 (April 24, 27, March 6, April 30, 1894).

50. *Congressional Record,* 53rd Cong., 2nd sess., p. 4263 (April 30, 1894).

51. *Ibid.*, pp. 3884–3885 (April 20, 1894) and p. 4219 (April 28, 1894). Cf. also the remarks of George Hoar, *ibid.*, p. 4476 (May 8, 1894) and John Sherman, *ibid.*, p. 5506 (May 31, 1894).

52. *Ibid.*, Appendix p. 691 (April 3, April 4, 1894). William Allison to Edward Atkinson, 1894 (n.d.), Allison Papers.

53. James McMillan to William McPherson, May 26, 1894, and to E. K. Warren, July 5, 1894, McMillan Papers; George Edmunds to Justin Morrill, May 1, 1894, and Justin Morrill to Walseman, August 4, 1894, Morrill Papers.

54. Stephen Elkins to Henry Davis, December 19, 1893, February 10, 1894, Elkins Papers, W.V.U.L. William Sewell to Henry Davis, November 3, 1893, Davis Papers. Stephen Elkins to Johnson Camden (senator from West Virginia), March 21, April 17, 1894, Camden Papers, W.V.U.L.

55. Johnson Camden to William P. Thompson, May 30, 1894, Camden Papers.

56. "Attempts at Bribery," no. 606, *passim.* Cf. also *Congressional Record*, 53rd Cong., 2nd sess., pp. 7802–7805 (July 23, 1894). It was passed on June 5, 1894 (p. 5759) with solid Democratic support. Josephson, *Politicos*, pp. 103, 105, ignored these complexities.

57. Summers, *Wilson and Tariff Reform*, pp. 204–205; S. C. Neale to Stephen Elkins, July 20, 1894, Elkins Papers.

58. The bill came to the Senate April 1, 1897 and was reported favorably May 4, 1897. On the Republican caucus see Francis Warren to B. B. Brooks, July 1, 1897, Warren Papers; William Chandler to Edward Wolcott, June 21, 1897, Chandler Papers. Cf. also John Spooner to Edward Scofield, May 28, 1897, Spooner Papers. The decisions did not escape comment; *Congressional Record*, 55th Cong., 1st sess., pp. 1904–1906 (June 22, 1897). Cf. also Shelby Cullom to William Allison, June 24, 1897, Allison Papers and Stephen White to Mssrs. Weill and Alexander, May 22, 1897, White Papers.

59. James McMillan to Colonel A. T. Bliss, June 8, 1897, and to J. J. Woodman, June 8, 1897, McMillan Papers; cf. also George Hoar to Professor Alden, June 11, 1897, Hoar Papers, Massachusetts Historical Society, Boston.

60. *Congressional Record*, 55th Cong., 1st sess., p. 1623 (June 10, 1897).

61. *Ibid.*, pp. 1670–1671 (June 11, 1897).

62. James McMillan to A. T. Bliss, June 8, 1897, and to William McMillan, June 8, 1897, McMillan Papers; cf. also William Chandler to Edward Wolcott, June 27, 1897, Chandler Papers.

63. On such matters as matting (inexpensive floor coverings), independents combined with Democrats to remove the tariff (*Congressional Record*, 55th Cong., 1st sess., p. 2174 [July 1, 1897]) and supported

Teller's efforts to reduce it on cyanamide (*ibid.*, p. 2446 [July 7, 1897]). However, on most important issues, such as wool, the independents split (*ibid.*, p. 1921 [June 22, 1897]), and Republicans had their way. The bill passed July 7, 1897 (p. 2447) with solid Republican ranks and only one Democrat failed to oppose it. Two independents voted for it, 3 against it, and 7 abstained. William Stewart to T. L. Thomas, August 3, 1897, Stewart Papers. Cf. also J. P. Jones to Georgina Jones, May 1, 1897, Jones Papers. See dissertation, p. 125.

64. *Congressional Record*, 55th Cong., 1st sess., p. 2909 (July 24, 1897).

65. *Congressional Record*, 51st Cong., 1st sess., p.1765 (February 27, 1890), for the start of debate. For the passage of the bill see p. 3153 (April 8, 1890).

66. Vincent P. DeSantis, *Republicans Face the Southern Question* (Baltimore, 1959), pp. 198ff.

67. James McMillan to William McMillan, July 10, 1890, McMillan Papers; cf. also John Spooner to Henry Payne, July 23, 1890, Spooner Papers. See Fowler, *Spooner*, pp. 36–37.

68. Joseph Hawley to N. T. Adams, August 26, 1890, Hawley Papers, L.C.

69. James McMillan to William McMillan, July 10, 1890, McMillan Papers; cf. also Orville Platt to William Chandler, July 22, 1890, Chandler Papers.

70. John Spooner to Henry Fink, August 17, 1890, Spooner Papers.

71. James McMillan to William McMillan, August 21, 1890, McMillan Papers.

72. Joseph Hawley to N. T. Adams, August 26, 1890, Hawley Papers.

73. John Spooner to Henry Payne, August 23, 1890 and to Benjamin Harrison, September 13, 1890, Harrison Papers. See dissertation, p. 127.

74. *Congressional Record*, 51st Cong., 2nd sess., p. 126 (December 5, 1890). William Stewart to J. T. Leonard, February 19, 1891, Stewart Papers.

75. John Spooner to David Williams, January 11, 1891, Spooner Papers.

76. *Congressional Record*, 51st Cong., 2nd sess., p. 1740 (January 22, 1891). Wolcott was joined by Republicans Cameron, J. P. Jones, Teller, Stanford, Stewart, and Washburn.

77. *Congressional Record*, 51st Cong., 1st sess., p. 8847 (August 20, 1890).

78. *Ibid.*, 51st Cong., 2nd sess., p. 885 (December 30, 1890). See also p. 1653 (January 22, 1891).

79. For surveys cf. Dewey, *Financial History*, chap. xix, Hepburn, *History of Currency*, chaps. xvi, xx, and Sherman, *Recollections*, II, 1061–1069. The course of this legislation was confusing because five bills were

considered. Cf. *Congressional Record,* 51st Cong., 1st sess., p. 6121 (June 16, 1890).

80. Richard Pettigrew to S. J. Conklin, May 10, 1890, Pettigrew Papers. Fred Welborn, "Influence of Silver Republican Senators, 1889–1891," *Mississippi Valley Historical Review,* 14:462–480 (1928).

81. Orville Platt to James McMillan, March 22, 1890, McMillan Papers; *Congressional Record,* 51st Cong., 1st sess., pp. 6167, 6171 (June 17, 1890). For the strength of free silver forces see the roll calls of June 17, 1890 (pp. 6169, 6173, 6183).

82. *Ibid.,* p. 7020 (July 8, 1890), p. 7059 (July 9, 1890). Francis Newlands to Benjamin Harrison, June 5, 1890, Harrison Papers. The final vote was taken on July 10, 1890 and passed by a strict party division. Cf. also Sherman, *Recollections,* II, 1069–1074.

83. J. P. Nichols, "Silver Repeal in the Senate," *American Historical Review,* 41:26–53 (1935); Grover Cleveland to John Carlisle, January 22, 1893, reprinted in the *Letters of Grover Cleveland,* ed. Allan Nevins (Boston, 1933), p. 314. William Vilas to Grover Cleveland, May 1, 1893, Cleveland Papers, L.C. Grover Cleveland to William Vilas, August 13, 1893, Vilas Papers.

84. Grover Cleveland to Henry Thurber, August 20, 1893, *Letters,* p. 331. Cf. also Zebulon Vance to Florence Vance, August 29, 1893, September 3, 1893, Vance Papers.

85. *New York Times,* October 17, 1893; Nichols, "Silver Repeal," pp. 41–42. James McMillan to James McMillan, Jr., September 14, 1893, McMillan Papers.

86. *Congressional Record,* 53rd Cong., 1st sess., p. 2585 (October 11, 1893), p. 2106 (October 4, 1893).

87. *Ibid.,* p. 1049 (August 30, 1893) and p. 2596 (October 17, 1893).

88. *Ibid.,* p. 2904 (October 28, 1893); Nichols, "Silver Repeal," pp. 43, 50–51.

89. James McMillan to W. H. Withington, September 13, 1893, McMillan Papers.

90. James McMillan to C. W. Watkins, October 16, 1893, and to William McMillan, October 21, 1893, McMillan Papers. Nichols, "Silver Repeal," p. 52. Thirty-one Republicans joined with 20 Democrats to do Cleveland's bidding; 12 Republicans and 23 Democrats stood against him. The bill passed October 30, 1893 (*Congressional Record,* 51st Cong., 1st sess., p. 2958).

91. Grover Cleveland to William Vilas, August 13, 1893, Vilas Papers.

92. Richard Coke to James Hogg, December 7, 1893, Hogg Papers, University of Texas Library, Austin.

93. Populist Party Platform, July 4, 1892; J. P. Jones to Georgina Jones, February 22, 1895, December 6, 1895, Jones Papers.

94. James McMillan to William Washburn, January 23, 1896, and to

Anson McCook, February 8, 1896, McMillan Papers; Stephen White to Thomas Thompson, February 23, 1896, White Papers.

95. Fred Dubois to William Balderston, March 3, 1896, and to Henry Teller, February 14, 1896, Dubois Papers; J. P. Jones to Georgina Jones, January 11, January 17, 1896, Jones Papers.

96. Francis Warren to H. Glafoke, March 16, 1896 and to E. A. Slack, January 17, 1896, and to H. G. Hay, June 6, 1897, Warren Papers; James McMillan to William Washburn, January 23, 1896, McMillan Papers. Cf. also William Chandler, Diary, entries of April 19 and April 23, 1897, Chandler Papers, Concord.

97. Nelson Aldrich to William Allison, May 9, May 26, 1899, and Edward Wolcott to William Allison, March 2, 1900, Allison Papers. Debate on the bill began January 14, 1900.

98. *Congressional Record*, 56th Cong., 1st sess., pp. 777, 903 (January 11, 17, 1900). Cf. also debates of January 14 and 25, 1900.

99. *Ibid.*, p. 1835 (February 15, 1900).

100. Stephen White to Warren Olney, September 3, 1897, White Papers.

101. Charles Fairbanks to John Conner, March 17, 1900, Fairbanks Papers; George Hoar to William Lovering, February 3, 1899, Hoar Papers. But note how Hoar, unlike someone like George Boutwell, will not leave the party over the issue; see Hoar to Boutwell, March 21, 1904, Hoar Papers.

102. Francis Warren to N. J. O'Brien, February 14, 1891, and to A. J. Parshall, December 18, 1899, and to Elwood Mead, February 1, 1898, Warren Papers. Here too, bills passed the Senate without roll calls.

103. *Congressional Record*, 55th Cong., 1st sess., March–July 1897 for procedures followed in Rivers and Harbors and Appropriations bills. In almost every instance the committee bill was followed and no vote was taken. In the 1870's, interruptions and amendments were more common. Cf. also the Rivers and Harbors bill of 1899 (February), *ibid.*, 55th Cong., 3rd sess., for further examples.

CHAPTER IV: Ascent to Power

1. Eighty-five per cent of the 117 senators first elected in the 1870's were born between 1815 and 1834. Eighty-two per cent of 72 senators first elected in the 1880's were born between 1820 and 1844. Eighty-two per cent of the 83 senators elected in the 1890's were born between 1835 and 1859. Thus in the tables below, the clearest comparisons are often between the decade of the 1870's and the 1890's. Data here are included on every senator to serve at least one Congress, that is two years, between 1869 and 1901. Senators serving in Washington in 1869 but elected during the war years were not included, nor were Southern Republicans elected from states undergoing Reconstruction.

2. In the tables below East north central is often kept separate from East and West categories for of her 45 senators, 27 were born in the states they represented and 18 migrated. In the eastern states, 86 per cent of the 146 senators were born in the states they served in Washington.

3. Cf. Stephan Thernstrom, *Poverty and Progress: Social Mobility in a Nineteenth Century City,* (Cambridge, Mass., 1964), pp. 87, 256, n. 7.

4. Cf. *ibid.,* pp. 22, 113, 136.

5. Sixty-nine per cent of the 45 lawyers in western states held their first political office before the age of thirty. In the East only 54 per cent of the 99 lawyers held office before thirty.

6. Herbert Croly, *The Promise of American Life* (New York: Capricorn Edition, 1954), pp. 134–135.

7. The careers of Republican Senators Aldrich, Allison, Cullom, Hale, Hanna, McMillan, Orville Platt, and Spooner, and Democratic Senators Blackburn, Brice, Cockrell, Gorman, Isham Harris, James K. Jones, Walthall, and White form the basis for these statements. Eleven of these sixteen were lawyers, seven carried on ordinary occupations, four were outstanding, and five, leaders. Six served long terms in Congress, seven were diligent party workers. Seven had considerable experience politically, others had average experience.

8. P. M. G. Harris, completing his study of social mobility of the careers of prominent Americans (those included in the *Dictionary of American Biography*), sponsored by the Center for the Study of the History of Liberty in America, kindly reviewed with me some of his preliminary findings. For purposes of comparison, the senators listed in the *DAB.*—approximately two thirds of those who served in the Senate through the end of the nineteenth Century— were tabulated separately. Since my scale of social origins was derived from the one devised by Harris (see Appendix A), comparisons could be made. Of senators born before 1825, 27 per cent came from families that could be clearly identified as Elite. Of those born between 1780 and 1819, usually serving in the Senate between 1825 and 1865, 14 per cent were from Elite families. In the post-Civil War decades, the figure remains constant at 15 per cent. Within the pre-Civil War years, looking at the data year by year, there is evident a downward secular trend beginning about 1825 and continuing to the 1860's when it levels off, with men from Elite origins losing their prominence in the institution. As for the lower part of the scale, again the post-1825 period reveals a higher degree of members from humble origins than earlier, and the post-Civil War decades show no evidence of any tightening. There are, as I note below, several short-term changes of significance within these periods, and Harris' data reveal much of the same fluctuations. There are few reliable studies of political recruitment, but see Sidney Aronson, *Status and Kinship in the*

Higher Civil Service (Cambridge, Mass., 1964); Matthews, *U.S. Senators,* offers contemporary comparisons.

9. See Appendix B for comparisons of party membership and social origins, political careers, occupational choices and success.

CHAPTER V: The Political Profession

1. John B. Ellis, *The Sights and Secrets of the National Capital* (New York, 1869).

2. Waitman T. Willey, *Diary,* December 3, 4, 1869, Willey Papers, W.V.U.L.; Elizabeth F. Ellet, *The Court Cirles of the Republic* (Hartford, 1869), pp. 581–583.

3. Cornelius Cole to William Cole, April 20, 1896, Cole Papers; Henry Dawes, Autobiographical Memoir, chapter entitled "Etiquette," Dawes Papers (hereafter cited as "Etiquette.")

4. Cornelius Cole to Olive Cole, January 12, 1872, Cole Papers; George Hoar to Ruth Hoar, November 8, 1877, Hoar Papers. Randall Gibson to his sister, February 4, 1882, Gibson-Humphreys Papers, U.N.C.L. Cf. also J. P. Jones to Georgina Jones, May 26, 1881, Jones Papers.

5. Zebulon Vance to Mrs. Florence Martin, March 8, 1880, Vance Papers.

6. Blanche Butler to Adelbert Ames, May 7, 1870, Blanche Butler Ames, *Chronicles from the Nineteenth Century* (Privately printed, 1957), I, 124.

7. Olive Cole to Cornelius Cole, June 28, 1870, Cole Papers; George Hoar to Rockwood Hoar, January 20, 1877, Hoar Papers.

8. J. P. Jones to Georgina Jones, April 2, 1881, Jones Papers.

9. Zebulon Vance to Mrs. Florence Martin, April 9, 1880, Vance Papers.

10. See the excellent political novel of Henry Adams, *Democracy,* first published in 1880 when Adams lived in Washington; Henry Dawes, "Etiquette," Dawes Papers.

11. Precise information on the status and occupation of senators' fathers-in-law was difficult to obtain and may have been available only when the father-in-law was of some prominence. Of 132 senators, a quarter had married into elite families; nearly all of the others entered substantial households. But the gaps are so great that these conclusions must be regarded as tentative.

12. Mary P. Nimmo, *Etiquette of Society at the National Capital* (Washington, D.C., 1892), pp. 29–44. John Hay to Whitelaw Reid, January 28, 1895, Reid Papers. Cf. also Randolph Keim, *Society in Washington* (Harrisburg, Pa., 1887), pp. 27–36, 85.

13. Mrs. Nathaniel P. Hill to Mrs. Edward Wolcott, February 6, 1880,

Wolcott Family Papers, Western History Department, Denver Public Library, Colorado.

14. Henry Dawes, "Etiquette," Dawes Papers; John Hay to Whitelaw Reid, May 2, 1895, Reid Papers.

15. James McMillan to Thomas Bell, January 17, 1891, McMillan Papers. Cf. also Henry Dawes to Electa Dawes, May 25, 1879, Dawes Papers.

16. *Congressional Record,* 51st Cong., 1st sess., pp. 1062–1063 (February 5, 1890).

17. Frank Richmond to Albert Beveridge, January 26, 1899, Beveridge Papers.

18. Benjamin Harrison to M. Peltz, May 12, 1881, Harrison Papers.

19. *New York Times,* December 8, 1895.

20. Benjamin Tillman to H. M. Chaplin, January 7, 1896, Tillman Papers.

21. George Hoar to Ruth Hoar, October 16, 1877, Hoar Papers. Cf. also, Francis Warren to H. Donzelman, December 6, 1890, to A. J. Parshall, February 13, 1892, Warren Papers.

22. John Spooner to Henry Sanford, July 24, 1888, Spooner Papers.

23. Albert Beveridge to Orville Platt, July 4, July 13, July 27, August 1, 1903; Orville Platt to Albert Beveridge, August 3, 1903, Platt Papers.

24. Nathaniel Hill to Frank Hall, April 10, 1879, Hill Papers, State Historical Society of Colorado, Denver; Benjamin Tillman to Sallie Tillman, December 3, 1895, Tillman Papers.

25. John Spooner to Edward Clark, July 9, 1899, and to Charles Amidon, February 23, 1899, Spooner Papers.

26. Timothy Howe to Grace Howe, July 4, 1868, typescript in the Howe Papers.

27. Nathaniel Hill to Frank Hall, April 10, 1879, Hill Papers; Albert Beveridge to J. C. Shaffer, October 21, 1899, Shaffer Papers, Indiana Division, Indiana State Library, Indianapolis.

28. Richard Coke to John H. Reagan, March 12, 1894, copy in the Hogg Papers. Cf. also J. P. Jones to Georgina Jones, April 15, 1880, February 5, 1897, Jones Papers. Waitman Willey, *Diary,* March 3, 1871, Willey Papers.

29. Francis Warren to S. E. Tuttle, February 26, 1892, Warren Papers.

30. Matt Ransom to Pattie Ransom, February 5, 1873, Ransom Papers; J. P. Jones to Georgina Jones, December 19, 1899, March 4, 1903, Jones Papers.

31. George Hoar to Ruth Hoar, July 13, 1897, Hoar Papers.

32. Henry Dawes to Electa Dawes, August 24, 1890, June 20, 1884, Dawes Papers; J. P. Jones to Georgina Jones, February 14, 1899, Jones Papers.

33. Daniel Pratt to John Wheeler, January 25, 1870, Pratt Papers,

Indiana Division, Indiana State Library, Indianapolis. Matt Carpenter to Elisha Keyes, February 7, 1873, April 3, 1873, Keyes Papers.

34. Francis Warren to W. C. Irvine, February 24, 1891, to Helen Warren, August 18, 1891, and to Henry Hay, January 28, 1896, Warren Papers.

35. John Sherman to Whitelaw Reid, January 22, 1887, Reid Papers; John Spooner to H. O. Fairchild, January 27, 1888, and to W. R. Finch, February 18, 1888, Spooner Papers. Cf. also William Stewart to John Conness, March 14, 1893, Stewart Papers.

36. Francis Warren to A. A. Johnson, April 27, 1896, Warren Papers.

37. Donelson Caffery to Bethia Caffery, July 15, 1899, Caffery Papers, U.N.C.L. Cf. also, Benjamin Tillman to Sallie Tillman, December 3, December 4, 1895, Tillman Papers.

38. Timothy Howe to Grace Howe, December 15, 1871, Howe Papers.

39. J. P. Jones to Georgina Jones, April 8, 1880, October 7, 1881, Jones Papers.

40. John Spooner to J. L. Linderman, March 24, 1890, Spooner Papers. Cf. also his letters there to Henry Tarrant, June 18, 1890, and to G. O. Jones, July 27, 1890.

41. William Stewart to S. D. R. Stewart, January 29, 1889 and to M. Power, February 7, 1889, Stewart Papers. I have condensed the letter from its original version.

42. William Vilas to Messrs. Crosby and Gordon, March 25, 1892, Vilas Papers; Zebulon Vance to Florence Martin Vance, November 3, 1885, Vance Papers; George Hoar to Ruth Hoar, November 17, 1877, Hoar Papers.

43. J. Scott Harrison to Benjamin Harrison, June 21, 1871, Harrison Papers.

44. Frank Munsey to Albert Beveridge, December 13, 1898; L. T. Michener to Albert Beveridge, November 18, November 25, 1898, Beveridge Papers.

45. Francis Warren to A. A. Johnson, April 27, 1896, Warren Papers. Cf. also C. R. Miller, "Has the Senate Degenerated?" Forum, 23:281 (1897).

46. Stephen White to John T. Gaffey, April 14, 1896, Gaffey-Stearns Papers, Huntington Library, San Marino, California. Stephen White to R. M. Clarkson, May 22, 1897, to John Hamilton, November 22, 1897, to Raleigh Barcar, November 30, 1897, and to J. C. Sims, April 19, 1897, White Papers.

47. James Fair to Johnson Camden, December 2, 1885, November 6, 1886, Camden Papers; James Fair to Matt Ransom, January 18, 1887, Ransom Papers. Johnson Camden to James Fair, December 5, 1885, and James Fair to Johnson Camden, June 14, 1887, November 6, 1887, Camden Papers.

48. J. P. Jones to Georgina Jones, February 2, 1881, Jones Papers. Henry Davis to the editor of the *Register*, November 16, 1882, Davis Papers; cf. also William Stewart, Autobiographical Sketch, January, 1896 (page 474 in his letterpress), Stewart Papers.

49. Albert Beveridge to William Allison, September 20, 1899, Beveridge Papers; George Hoar to Ruth Hoar, November 17, 1877, Hoar Papers.

50. Benjamin Harrison to Fred Knefler, March 5, 1885, Harrison Papers.

51. Benjamin Harrison to C. C. Henry, June 28, 1886, Harrison Papers; cf. also George Hoar to Ruth Hoar, August 2, 1876, Hoar Papers.

52. Stephen White to S. R. Mallory, January 28, 1893, White Papers; James McMillan to James McMillan, Jr., January 5, 1892, McMillan Papers.

53. Francis Warren to W. G. Shapcott, December 5, 1890, to S. B. Tuttle, December 1, 1890, and to E. M. Warren, December 5, 1891, Warren Papers.

54. Charles Fairbanks to W. D. Fairbanks, December 13, 1897, Fairbanks Papers.

55. Johnson Camden to Marshall Depue, November 25, 1880, Camden Papers. The letter was written to a member of the House of Delegates and Camden was trying to win his vote. The development of the region, not some private nefarious scheme, was the appeal Camden used here.

56. David B. Henderson to William Allison, September 24, October 5, October 12, 1881, Allison Papers; cf. also Sage, *Allison*, pp. 159–160.

57. John Spooner to S. H. Clough, February 14, 1897, Spooner Papers; Donalson Caffery to his children, July 15, 1899, Caffery Papers.

58. Georgina Jones to J. P. Jones, March 24, June 22, 1878; J. P. Jones to Georgina Jones, February 23, April 15, 1880, September 3, 1884, May 5, 1894, February 27, 1900, Jones Papers. The sums accumulated by John Logan were often exaggerated also; see John Logan to Mary Logan, March 8, 1877, June 8, 1881; Mary Logan to John Logan, August 19, 1877, Logan Papers, L.C. Cf. also Orville Platt to William E. Chandler, October 21, 1897.

59. Joseph Hawley to Whitelaw Reid, June 25, 1885, Reid Papers; Justin Morrill to G. G. Benedict, March 11, 1877, quoted in W. J. Parker, *Life and Public Services of Justin Smith Morrill* (Boston, 1924), pp. 226–227.

60. John Spooner to W. D. Washburn, April 9, 1892, Spooner Papers. William Stewart to J. R. Williamson, January 29, 1889, Stewart Papers; William Thompson to Johnson Camden, November 28, 1888, Camden Papers. Fred Dubois to J. G. Johnson, September 4, 1896, Dubois Papers. See also dissertation, p. 200.

61. Johnson Camden to C. J. Faulkner Jr., June 29, 1887, Faulkner Papers, W.V.U.L. Johnson Camden to W. E. Lively, November 30, 1892,

John T. McGraw to Johnson Camden, March 28, 1892, E. B. Stahlman to Johnson Camden, May 5, 1892, Camden Papers.

62. William Thompson to Johnson Camden, November 24, 1888, Camden Papers.

63. Henry Dawes to Electa Dawes, July 21, 1886, Dawes Papers; Zebulon Vance to Florence Martin Vance, November 28, 1882, Vance Papers.

64. Francis Warren to Amos Barber, April 19, 1892, Warren Papers; James Berry, "An Autobiography," (Privately printed, Bentonville, Ark. n.d.), p. 19.

65. Stephen White to D. A. Ostrom, January 12, 1890, White Papers. See Simkins, *Pitchfork, Ben Tillman*, pp. 262–265.

66. James Blaine to Justin Morrill, November 15, 1865, Morrill Papers; John Daniel, Speech of May 30, 1889, copy in the Daniel Papers.

67. Henry Dawes, Autobiographical Memoir, "Talks About Congress," IV, Dawes Papers.

68. J. P. Jones to Georgina Jones, October 3, 1881, Jones Papers.

69. John Spooner to S. H. Clough, December 22, 1888, and to Edwin Reynolds, January 8, 1901, Spooner Papers.

70. Edward Pierce to Charles Sumner, January 20, 1869, Sumner Papers; James Clarkson to William Allison, December 10, 1896, Allison Papers.

71. William Allison to Frank Campbell, February 6, 1889, Allison Papers; John Spooner to S. H. Clough, December 22, 1888, Spooner Papers. Cf. also Warner Bateman to John Sherman, December 4, 1888, Sherman Papers.

72. James Clarkson to William Allison, December 10, 1896, Jonathan Dolliver to William Allison, December 28, 1888, Allison Papers. Also, leading party members hesitated to weaken the force in the Senate; cf. Joseph Hawley to Benjamin Harrison, December 27, 1888, Harrison Papers.

73. James Clarkson to William Allison, December 10, 1896, Allison Papers.

74. John Spooner to J. M. Rusk, November 20, 1888, Spooner Papers; David Davis to Nellie Rockwell, January 26, 1877, and to B. H. Bristow, May 16, 1877, April 5, 1878, Davis Papers. Chicago Historical Society. Stephen White to C. C. Wright, March 4, 1896, White Papers.

75. George Hoar to John Daniel, September 7, 1898, Daniel Papers; Justin Morrill to George Hoar, September 21, 1897, and George Hoar to William McKinley, September 14, 1898, Hoar Papers. Cf. also Timothy Howe to Hamilton Fish, September 3, 1870, Fish Papers.

76. Edward Mayes, *Lucius Q. C. Lamar* (Nashville, 1896), pp. 204–205; Richard Pettigrew to W. P. Mahony, February 4, 1896, Pettigrew Papers.

77. L. Q. C. Lamar to Virginia Clay, December 28, 1877, C. C. Clay

Papers; Henry Cooper to Thomas Bayard, September 22, 1877, Bayard Papers.

78. Samuel Pasco (senator from Florida) to John Spooner, May 1, 1899, John Spooner to Samuel Pasco, May 12, 1899, Spooner Papers.

79. Albert Beveridge to Remey, January 5, 1901, Beveridge Papers. Cf. Richard Hofstadter, "The Spoilsmen: An Age of Cynicism," *American Political Tradition* (New York: Vintage Edition, 1954), for another view.

CHAPTER VI: The Structure of State Politics

1. Jerome Chaffee to John Logan, June 23, 1888, Logan Papers.

2. The literature on politics and politicians before the Civil War is voluminous but there are few works on the nature of state politics. For suggestions see Cunningham, *Jeffersonian Republicans;* Lee Benson, *The Concept of Jacksonian Democracy: New York as a Test Case* (Princeton, 1961).

3. *Baltimore Sun,* January 5, 1886; Charles Brayton to Nelson Aldrich, January 12, 1885, Aldrich Papers.

4. George Haynes, *The Election of Senators* (New York, 1912), pp. 180–185. *Louisville Courier Journal,* May 12, 1890; Stephen White to William Harris, May 4, 1890, White Papers. John Spooner to William Chandler, November 2, 1896, Chandler Papers. Cf. also dissertation, p. 211.

5. Charles Brayton to Nelson Aldrich, January 25, 1900, Aldrich Papers; Anthony Higgins to James Wilson, September 15, 1900, Wilson Papers; D. S. Alexander, *Four Famous New Yorkers* (New York, 1923), p. 325.

6. John Braeman, "Rise of Albert J. Beveridge to the Senate," *Indiana Magazine of History,* 53:355–382 (1957).

7. Justin Morrill to Crosby Miller, June 27, 1884, and Redfield Proctor to Justin Morrill, August 30, 1878, Morrill Papers.

8. James Wilson to Grenville Dodge, November 8, 1871, Dodge Papers, Iowa State Department of History and Archives, Des Moines; Grenville Dodge to William Allison, December 21, 1875, Allison Papers. John Sherman to William McKinley, January 7, 1897 and Mark Hanna to William McKinley, January 13, 1897, McKinley Papers.

9. Roscoe Conkling to Simon Cameron, July 17, 1875, Cameron Papers, L.C.

10. Chauncey Depew to Benjamin Harrison, March 4, 1890, Harrison Papers.

11. W. W. Phelps to Whitelaw Reid, November 10, 1890, and August 15, 1889, Reid Papers.

12. Richard Current, *Pine Logs and Politics: A Life of Philetus Sawyer* (Madison, 1950), pp. 178–179, 188–193, 239; E. Bruce Thompson, *Matthew Hale Carpenter* (Madison, 1954), pp. 227ff.; Fowler, *Spooner,*

pp. 48, 73ff. John Spooner to George Hoar, April 19, 1895, Spooner Papers.

13. Hamilton Fish to John Cadwalader, October 20, 1875, Fish Papers; cf. also H. M. Dilla, *The Politics of Michigan, 1865-1878* (New York, 1912) and Harris, *Chandler*, pp. 105-131.

14. Moore, "James McMillan," pp. 173-187.

15. James McMillan to C. W. Bennett, October 22, 1888, to Henry Boutwell, October 22, 1888, and to J. H. Berry, October 30, 1888, McMillan Papers.

16. Memorandum, "Contributions to the State Central Committee for the Campaign of 1888," McMillan Papers; James McMillan to E. N. Orr, October 30, 1888, and to E. S. Tice, November 14, 1888, McMillan Papers.

17. Hugh McMillan to W. I. Babcock, November 15, 1888, McMillan Papers.

18. E. W. Allen to Hugh McMillan, November 1, 1888, McMillan Papers.

19. H. C. Tillman to James McMillan, April 17, 1889, McMillan Papers.

20. James Lyford, *Life of Edward H. Rollins* (Boston, 1906), pp. 74-75, 191, 207; Richardson, *Chandler,* p. 30; Edward Rollins to William Chandler, February 2, February 18, 1870, William Chandler to Austin Pike, December 16, 1872, Chandler Papers, Concord.

21. William Chandler to Benjamin Harrison, July 6, 1889, Chandler Papers, Concord; William Chandler to Benjamin Harrison, July 8, 1889, Harrison Papers. Jacob Gallinger to Charles Marseilles, September 22, 1895, Gallinger Papers, New Hampshire Historical Society, Concord.

22. William Chandler to Nelson Aldrich, September 22, 1900, Chandler Papers; William Chandler to William McKinley, September 1, October 25, 1900, McKinley Papers. Leon Richardson, *William E. Chandler: Republican.* (New York, 1940), pp. 419ff.

23. Eugene Hale to William Chandler, September 7, 1900, William Frye to William Chandler, September 8, 1900, Redfield Proctor to William Chandler, September 10, 1900, Chandler Papers, Concord.

24. William Chandler to Nelson Aldrich, September 8, 1900, Chandler Papers; Nelson Aldrich to William Chandler, September 25, 1900, Chandler Papers, Concord; William Chandler to Nelson Aldrich, October 4, 1900, Chandler Papers.

25. A. K. McKlure, *Oldtime Notes of Pennsylvania* (Philadelphia, 1905), pp. 520-529; House, "Democratic Convention."

26. Elmer Ellis, *Henry Moore Teller* (Caldwell, Idaho, 1941), pp. 62-120, 152-160.

27. William Stewart to J. P. Jones, June 28, 1886; J. P. Jones to Georgina Jones, October 14, 1898, Jones Papers.

28. J. P. Jones to Georgina Jones, September 16, 1888, 1886 (n.d.), November 3, 1882, and May 12, 1896, Jones Papers.

29. Cf. also Kenneth R. Toole, "Genesis of the Clark-Daly Feud,"

Montana Magazine of History, 1:21–33 (1951); William Clark to William Whitney, November 15, 1892, and Marcus Daly to Arthur Gorman, January 18, 1893, Whitney Papers. And dissertation, p. 222.

30. Lambert, *Gorman;* James A. Bear Jr., "Thomas Staples Martin," unpub. thesis, University of Virginia, 1952.

31. George R. Bentley, "Political Activity of the Freedmen's Bureau in Florida," *Florida Historical Quarterly,* 28:28–37 (1949); Ella Lon, *Reconstruction in Louisiana after 1868* (New York, 1918).

32. Adelbert Ames to Blanche Butler Ames, June 20, 1871, *Chronicles,* pp. 288–290; October 14, 1871, pp. 332–333; June 27, 1873, pp. 466–467; August 23, 1873, pp. 536–537. Willard Warner to Whitelaw Reid, January 8, 1870, January 19, 1871, August 7, 1871, Reid Papers. Cf. also dissertation, pp. 223–224.

33. Most studies of Reconstruction end with chapters on redemption. Cf. Farrar Newberry, *A Life of Mr. Garland of Arkansas* (Arkadelphia, Ark., 1908) and Manly W. Wellman, *Giant in Gray: A Biography of Wade Hampton* (New York, 1949). Cf. also Woodward, *Origins,* pp. 1–22.

34. E. D. Hale to Matt Ransom, February 2, 1894, T. Ransom to Matt Ransom, February 6, 1894, Ransom Papers; Josephus Daniels, *Tar Heel Editor* (Chapel Hill, 1939), pp. 450–453. Allen J. Going, *Bourbon Democracy in Alabama, 1874–1890* (University, Ala., 1951). Thomas Martin to John Daniel, December 8, 15, 1885, Daniel Papers; J. S. Barbour to Robert Garrett, October 30, 1883, Garrett Papers, L. C. Kirwan, *Revolt of the Rednecks,* pp. 3–122.

35. John T. Morgan to Claude Shoster, October 19, 1886, Morgan Papers, L. C.

36. See Robert Cotner, *James Stephen Hogg* (Austin, 1959); C. Vann Woodward, *Tom Watson: Agrarian Rebel* (New York, 1938) and Simkins, *Pitchfork Ben Tillman.*

37. W. T. Jackson, "The Governorship of Wyoming, 1885–1889," *Pacific Historical Review,* 13:1–11 (1944); M. D. Beal, *A History of Southeastern Idaho* (Caldwell, Idaho, 1941), pp. 302–304. Howard Lamar's *Dakota Territory, 1861–1889* (New Haven, 1956). Richard Pettigrew to A. J. Simmons, October 1, 1890, Pettigrew Papers; M. H. McCord to John Sherman, December 15, 1892, Sherman Papers.

38. Warren Tryon, "Agriculture and Politics in South Dakota," *South Dakota Historical Society, Collections,* 13:284–310 (1926). Fred Dubois to James K. Jones, September 4, 1896, and to Wharton Barker, September 5, 1896, Dubois Papers.

39. W. P. Harrington, "Populist Party in Kansas," *Kansas State Historical Society, Collections,* 16:403–450; (1923–1925); David McFarland Jr., "The Ingalls Amendment to the Sherman Anti-Trust Act," *Kansas Historical Quarterly,* 11:173–198 (1942); *Topeka Weekly Cap-*

ital, January 15, 22, 29, 1891; *Topeka State Journal,* January 20, 21, 22, 1893.

40. Claudius Johnson, "George Turner," *Pacific Northwest Quarterly,* 34:257–262 (1943). On Kyle and Hanna see Richard Pettigrew to C. A. Jewett, December 14, 1896, to H. L. Loucks, February 22, 1897, January 29, 1898, and to U. S. G. Cherry, March 2, 1897, Pettigrew Papers; A. J. Plowman to Marion Butler, March 5, 1897, Butler Papers.

41. Kathryn T. Abbey, "Florida Versus the Principles of Populism, 1896–1911," *Journal of Southern History,* 4:462–475 (1938); Jeter Pritchard to William Chandler, November 12, 1896, Chandler Papers. James Bonner, "The Alliance Legislature of 1890," *Essays Presented to John H. T. McPherson* (Athens, Ga., 1940).

42. Cf. also, S. A. Delap, "Populist Party in North Carolina," Trinity College Historical Society, *Papers,* XIV (1922); Marion Butler, "A Square Fight for Principle," Speech of January 22, 1896, Butler Papers; L. L. Witherspoon to Marion Butler, January 11, 1897, Butler Papers.

43. Haynes, *Election of Senators,* pp. 36–51, 59–63; W. A. Cleland to John Whitehead, March 6, 1897, Spooner Papers; John Spooner to Frank Bigelow, March 1, 1898, Spooner Papers; Joseph Dolph to William Allison, January 24, 1896, Allison Papers. Francis Warren to Willis Van Devanter, January 4, 1893, and L. C. Baker to Francis Warren, January 22, 1893, Warren Papers.

44. On Wanamaker see James Swank to William Allison, October 21, 1899, Allison Papers; on Delaware, Mark Hanna to William McKinley, November 12, 1900, McKinley Papers; *Wilmington* (Delaware) *Every Evening,* January 7, 15, 17, 1895. For Montana, William Clark to William Whitney, November 15, 1892, Arthur Gorman to William Whitney, January 19, 1893, Marcus Daly to William Whitney, January 18, 1893, Whitney Papers; Marcus Daly to Arthur Gorman, February 7, 1899, Gorman Papers.

45. W. Bates (McMillan's private secretary) to H. C. Tillman, April 8, 1890, McMillan Papers; James McMillan to William McMillan, May 30, 1894, December 31, 1895, to E. O. Durfee, February 26, 1896, and to William McMillan, April 4, 1896, April 2, 1900, McMillan Papers. Cf. Lowell, "Party," pp. 347–349 and Josephson, *Politicos,* pp. 93–98.

46. John Spooner to O. H. Fethers, April 26, 1888, Spooner Papers. W. W. Johnston to Henry Castle, February 11, 1892, Castle Papers; Richard Pettigrew to A. T. Free, May 24, 1890, Pettigrew Papers.

47. Grenville Dodge to William Allison, December 23, 1875, Allison Papers.

48. Mark Hanna to John Sherman, December 4, 1891, and C. H. Grosvenor to John Sherman, December 5, 1891, Sherman Papers. Cf. also *Wilmington Every Evening,* January 1, 1895.

49. John Sherman to Benjamin Harrison, November 8, 1891, Harrison Papers; *Baltimore Sun*, January 10, 1896.

50. Richard Pettigrew to George Shoup, September 29, 1890, Pettigrew Papers.

51. Stephen White to George Robertson, August 8, 1892, White Papers.

52. John Sherman to H. C. Jones, December 13, 1881, to Warner Bateman, December 20, 1880, and to Thomas Beer, January 12, 1881, Sherman Papers.

53. *Baltimore Sun*, January 10, January 14, 1896; *New York Tribune*, September 25, 1898; C. F. Perkins to William Allison, March 4, 1893, Allison Papers.

54. William Smith to Rutherford Hayes, January 16, 1879, Hayes Papers.

55. Garfield, *Diary*, May 25, May 28, May 31, 1881, Garfield Papers. See also the entry of December 2, 1880 for a similar attitude toward Sherman's candidacy in Ohio.

56. James Blaine to Stephen Elkins, May 18, 1881, typescript, Elkins Papers; Blaine foolishly denied any involvement although it was far from secret; the *Washington Post*, May 25, 26, 1881.

57. J. P. Jones to Georgina Jones, July 15, 1881, Jones Papers.

58. Stephen White to Theodore Roosevelt, January 30, 1894, White Papers.

59. James McMillan to F. C. Chamberlain, January 26, 1898, to F. W. Wait, January 20, 1898, McMillan Papers; John Spooner to J. W. Kendrick, April 23, 1897, Spooner Papers. Only rarely did senators complain about patronage divisions; in most instances offices were divided with little fuss.

60. Grover Cleveland to Edward Shepard, April 4, 1894, Nevins, *Letters*, p. 349.

61. Marion Butler to George Washburn, February 5, 1897, Butler Papers. Mark Hanna to William McKinley, November 12, 1900, November 6, 1899, McKinley Papers. On J. K. Jones, cf. Fred Dubois to James K. Jones, September 4, 1896, A. T. Ryan to Fred Dubois, January 11, 1897, and James K. Jones to Fred Dubois, January 25, 1897, Dubois Papers. For the similarity of practices today cf. Hugh Bone, *Party Committees and National Politics* (Seattle, 1958), pp. 3–35, 197–218.

62. "Compilation of Senate Election Cases, 1789–1913," 62nd Cong., 3rd sess., *Senate Executive Document*, No. 1036; Haynes, *Senate*, I, 81–95, 121–199.

63. For the limited role the Committee has continued to play see Hugh Bone, "Some Notes on the Congressional Campaign Committees," *Western Political Quarterly*, 9:134 (1956); Truman, *Congressional Party*, p. 102.

64. James McMillan to William Allison, August 16, 1892, McMillan Papers; W. A. Clark to Arthur Gorman, October 9, 1899, Gorman Papers. John Spooner to Almerin Gillett, November 18, 1890, Spooner Papers.

65. Stephen Elkins to John Spooner, November 8, 1900, Spooner Papers; Charles Fairbanks to Herman Crow, November 21, 1898, Fairbanks Papers; Fred Dubois to Richard Pettigrew, November 11, 1896, and to Henry Teller, November 19, 1896, Dubois Papers.

66. Timothy Howe to Grace Howe, February 28, 1878, typescript, Howe Papers; John Spooner to Henry Scudder, December 20, 1896, Spooner Papers. Cf. John Sherman to George Hoar, December 15, 1892, Hoar Papers.

67. "Report," 50th Cong., 1st sess., Pacific Railway Commission, *Senate Executive Document,* No. 51, p. 1051; cf. also the remarks of Collis Huntington, p. 3741.

68. "Attempts at Bribery," No. 606, pp. 351–353, 366, 411.

69. *Ibid.,* pp. 404–405.

70. Morton Keller, *The Life Insurance Enterprise, 1885–1910* (Cambridge, Mass., 1963), pp. 194–242.

71. Collis Huntington to Charles Crocker, February 3, 1871, *Letters,* no. 620, and to Mark Hopkins, December 2, 1875, *Letters,* no. 63. See Chapter VII, n. 10 and the bibliography for citation of the Huntington material.

72. "Attempts at Bribery," No. 606, pp. 351–353. Merrill, *Bourbon Democracy,* pp. 162, 251.

73. William Chandler to Whitelaw Reid, October 4, 1900, Reid Papers.

74. John Gear to Grenville Dodge, March 3, 1896, Dodge Papers; Stephen White to Patrick Collins, August 24, 1890, White Papers.

75. A. W. Beard to Henry Dawes, September 14, 1886, and John Brayton to Henry Dawes, September 17, 1886, Dawes Papers.

76. Cf. Alexander Heard, *The Costs of Democracy* (Chapel Hill, 1960), pp. 16–35, 371–399, for a current analysis that minimizes the political leverage exercised by campaign contributions.

77. James Swank to William Allison, September 26, 1888, Allison Papers.

78. Ostrogorski, *Democracy,* II, 177–185, 193; the Ostrogorski argument is taken over by Josephson and repeated in Richard Hofstadter, *American Political Tradition* (New York, 1948).

79. Ostrogorski, *Democracy,* II, 183, 196–197.

80. Croly, *Promise of American Life,* pp. 118, 123. E. C. Wall to William Vilas, December 24, 1891, November 30, 1892, Vilas Papers; Richard Pettigrew to R. S. Pearson, June 28, 1892, Pettigrew Papers.

81. Richard Hofstadter, *Age of Reform* (New York, 1955), pp. 267–

269. George Mowry, *The California Progressives* (Berkeley, 1951), pp. 138–139.

82. Even Horace Merrill in his *Bourbon Democracy*, an account surely in the Josephson tradition, states at the outset: Farmers "failed to recognize, however, that if the Democracy was to work *for* them, instead of for the Bourbons, it needed to be worked *by* them—worked with consistency and vigilance." However, their "political apathy" proved fatal. "They did not exercise necessary vigilance and sustained action." (p. 4)

CHAPTER VII: The Business of Influence

1. Bryce, *American Commonwealth*, II, 541–542; Wallace D. Farnham, " 'The Weakened Spring of Government,' " *American Historical Review*, 68:662–680 (1963).

2. Grenville Dodge to William Chandler, April 10, 1869, Dodge Papers.

3. William P. Smith to William Chandler, April 6, 1869; J. C. Reif to William Chandler, March 18, 1874, and Grenville Dodge to William Chandler, March 30, 1874. H. C. Fahnestock to William Chandler, September 28, 1870, Chandler Papers.

4. Jay Cooke to William Chandler, March 25, 1870, June 22, 1870, Henry Cooke to William Chandler, June 7, 1870, H. C. Fahnestock to William Chandler, August 1, 1870, Chandler Papers.

5. Oliver Morton to William Chandler, April 15, 1873, Tom Scott to William Chandler, December 12, 1873, Grenville Dodge to William Chandler, April 11, 1874; Chandler Papers.

6. William Chandler to Grenville Dodge, May 21, 1869, Grenville Dodge to William Chandler, March 30, 1870, Dodge Papers.

7. William Chandler to Grenville Dodge, July 24, 1871, May 2, 1871, March 29, 1873, Dodge Papers. Chandler had good cause for complaint; cf. Oliver Ames to William Chandler, November 28, 1870, Chandler Papers.

8. Ben Butler to William Chandler, September 7, 1869, Chandler Papers, Concord.

9. See the estimate made by the minority, Pacific Railway Commission, "Report," although it is probably exaggerated.

10. The letters of Huntington and his partners are in several different sources. There are four volumes of published correspondence brought together by Huntington's son, Archer. These are referred to here as the *Letters*. Huntington material also was published in a law suit with a lobbyist's widow, and references to that document are cited as *Colton Case*. Finally, many original letters are found in the Huntington-Hopkins Correspondence, Stanford University Libraries, Stanford, California. These will be noted as the Hopkins Papers. See the bibliography for full

citations. Collis Huntington to Charles Crocker, December 21, 1870, *Letters*, no. 592. Cf. also Richard Franchot to Collis Huntington, January 11, 1872, Hopkins Papers.

11. Collis Huntington to David Colton, November 22, 1877, *Colton Case*, no. 384, p. 1806; Collis Huntington to David Colton, November 15, 1877, *Colton Case*, no. 381, pp. 1803–1804. When Huntington complained about the "strikers," he was referring to lobbyists, not congressmen.

12. Collis Huntington to Mark Hopkins, October 8, 1875, Hopkins Papers.

13. Charles Crocker to Collis Huntington, February 12, 1878, *Letters*. Cf. also dissertation, pp. 255–256.

14. Samuel Barlow to William Grant, January 4, 1879, Barlow Papers, Henry E. Huntington Library, San Marino, California. Josephson, *Politicos*, pp. 105–106, assumes that every mention of lobbying is an admission of crime and his adjectives reflect his judgments. Scott "wrests" his lands from the government; Congress does not grant them.

15. Richard Franchot to Collis Huntington, January 11, 1872, and Collis Huntington to Mark Hopkins, May 3, 1872, March 16, 1876, Hopkins Papers.

16. Collis Huntington to David Colton, September 27, 1875, *Letters*, no. 18. Collis Huntington to David Colton, February 14, 1876, *Colton Case*, no. 117, pp. 1707–1708, and October 31, 1877, *ibid.*, no. 375, p. 1801. Collis Huntington to Mark Hopkins, March 30, 1876, Hopkins Papers; Collis Huntington to David Colton, February 26, 1876, *Letters*, no. 124.

17. Collis Huntington to Mark Hopkins, June 7, 1870, *Letters*, no. 536, and December 23, 1869, *ibid.*, no. 405.

18. Collis Huntington to David Colton, January 29, 1876, *Letters*, no. 110, and to Mark Hopkins, February 12, 1876, *ibid.*, no. 116.

19. Collis Huntington to David Colton, October 6, 1875, *Letters*, no. 30.

20. Collis Huntington to Charles Crocker, March 21, 1868, *Letters*, no. 129, and to Leland Stanford, May 26, 1869, *ibid.*, no. 342.

21. Collis Huntington to Leland Stanford, August 2, 1870, *Letters*, and to Mark Hopkins, April 28, 1869, *ibid.*, no. 333. Collis Huntington to Charles Crocker, August 1, 1868, *ibid.*, no. 226. Collis Huntington to Mark Hopkins, March 19, 1872, Hopkins Papers.

22. Collis Huntington to Mark Hopkins, December 17, 1868, *Letters*, no. 304.

23. Collis Huntington to Charles Crocker, August 15, 1868, *Letters*, no. 226.

24. *Morning Call*, December 27, 1883, in Timothy Hopkins Scrapbooks, Hopkins Railroad Library, Stanford University, California, p. 97. Cf. also Pacific Railway Commission, "Report," p. 36.

25. Collis Huntington to Mark Hopkins, February 19, 1876, *Letters,* no. 118; Collis Huntington to David Colton, January 29, 1876, *ibid.,* no. 110.

26. Pacific Railway Commission, "Report," pp. 3705, 3735, 3755.

27. *Ibid.,* pp. 3699–3700; Collis Huntington to Mark Hopkins, March 3, 1876, and John Conness to Collis Huntington, November 9, 1870, Hopkins Papers.

28. Collis Huntington to David Colton, November 10, 1875, *Letters,* no. 47.

29. Collis Huntington to Mark Hopkins, December 22, 1865, Hopkins Papers and December 21, 1867, *Letters,* no. 26.

30. Collis Huntington to Charles Crocker, October 29, 1867, *Letters,* no. 50; Collis Huntington to Mark Hopkins, October 9, 1873, *Letters,* no. 35 and April 6, 1875, *ibid.,* no. 512. Cf. George Spencer to Grenville Dodge, October 23, October 30, 1871, Dodge Papers.

31. John Gordon to Samuel Barlow, July 10, 1876, Barlow Papers.

32. John Gordon to Samuel Barlow, December 13, 1878, Barlow Papers.

33. Collis Huntington to Mark Hopkins, April 21, 1869, *Letters,* no. 330.

34. Collis Huntington to Mark Hopkins, March 7, 1870, *Letters,* no. 454; Collis Huntington to Leland Stanford, February 4, 1875, *ibid.,* no. 471.

35. William Kellogg to William Chandler, July 12, 1871. Chandler Papers; Collis Huntington to David Colton, May 3, 1875, *Colton Case,* p. 1622.

36. Lewis Bogy to Samuel Barlow, March 30, 1875 and Thomas Bayard to Samuel Barlow, March 13, 1872, Barlow Papers.

37. Collis Huntington to Mark Hopkins, November 19, 1875, Hopkins Papers; Collis Huntington to David Colton, December 13, 1875, *Letters,* no. 76, and December 23, 1875, *Colton Case,* pp. 1691–1692.

38. Collis Huntington to Mark Hopkins, April 17, 1876, February 8, 1877, Hopkins Papers; cf. Collis Huntington to David Colton, April 3, 1877, *Colton Case,* no. 276, pp. 1765–1766.

39. Collis Huntington to S. T. Gage, August 16, 1886, Hopkins Papers.

40. Zachary Taylor to Samuel Barlow, February 26, March 9, 1879, Barlow Papers.

41. Richard Franchot to Collis Huntington, March 2, 1873, and Collis Huntington to Mark Hopkins, March 4, 1875, Hopkins Papers. Collis Huntington to David Colton, June 20, 1878, *Colton Case,* no. 469, p. 1834.

42. Francis Warren to Dewey, Gould and Company, January 17, 1896, June 16, 1897, Warren Papers.

43. John Searles to Nelson Aldrich, December 6, 1888, Aldrich Papers; cf. also James Swank to Andrew Carnegie, May 29, 1897, Carnegie Papers, L. C.

44. "Attempts at Bribery," No. 457, pt. II, pp. 8–9; No. 606, 311–319, 519.

45. *Ibid.*, No. 606, p. 422.

46. *Ibid.*, No. 606, p. 422.

47. *Ibid.*, No. 606, pp. 291–292.

48. *Ibid.*, No. 457, pt. II, p. 14; No. 606, pp. 247–248, 519. For a sense of how poorly Josephson used his evidence, compare his statements on the sugar investigation with the hearing material. The contemporary press was even less trustworthy. They thought it proper to print as fact statements of which reporters admitted: "I heard something of that kind. I do not know the source of the information . . . It is one of those things that passes around from mouth to mouth and came to my ears." (*Ibid.*, No. 457, pt. I, p. 28). Cf. dissertation, p. 270.

49. "Attempts at Bribery," No. 606, p. 256; Horace Chilton's Memoir, 1891–1892, Book I, p. 134, Chilton Papers.

50. George Spencer to William Chandler, January 17, 1882, Chandler Papers, Concord.

51. *Congressional Record,* 55th Cong., 1st sess., p. 1963 (June 24, 1897).

52. John Hayes (lobbyist for American woolen interests) to Matt Ransom, May 18, 1878, Ransom Papers; James Swank to Andrew Carnegie, May 29, 1897, Carnegie Papers.

53. James Swank to John Sherman, January 11, 1888, Sherman Papers; cf. also James Swank to Justin Morrill, April 20, 1888, Morrill Papers.

54. George Hoar to Edward Atkinson, January 20, 1899, Hoar Papers; Charles Moore to William Bates (Senator McMillan's secretaries), September 27, 1890, McMillan Papers.

55. James Swank to John Sherman, February 16, 1888, Sherman Papers.

56. "Attempts at Bribery," No. 436, pp. 38, 43–53.

57. Pacific Railway Commission, "Report," p. 121.

58. "Attempts at Bribery," No. 606, p. 422, remarks of Theodore Havermeyer.

59. Nelson Aldrich to Taft (National Association of Wool Manufacturers), November 21, 1883, Aldrich Papers.

60. "Attempts at Bribery," No. 606, pp. 256, 424.

61. *Congressional Record,* 47th Cong., 1st sess., p. 306 (January 10, 1882).

62. Charles Pepper, *Life and Times of Henry Gassaway Davis* (New York, 1920), pp. 10–51.

63. Oscar D. Lambert, *Stephen Benton Elkins* (Pittsburg, 1955), pp. 53–54; Stephen Elkins to Henry Davis, August 15, 1894, Davis Papers.

64. Henry Davis to W. L. Scott, October 19, 1881, to William Keyser, May 14, 1881, Davis Papers.

65. Henry Davis to William Windom, April 10, 1881, Davis Papers; George Harrison to Stephen Elkins, March 4, 1882, Davis Papers.

66. Summers, *Camden,* pp. 370–411. Johnson Camden to James Fair, August 21, 1888, James Fair to Johnson Camden, May 1, 1889, Johnson Camden to George Vest, April 13, 1883, Camden Papers.

67. Zebulon Vance to Arthur Gorman, June 10, 1887, Gorman Papers; Arthur Gorman to Zebulon Vance, June 28, 1887, Vance Papers. John Morgan to Arthur Gorman, December 10, 1894, Gorman Papers; Henry Davis to Matt Ransom, December 2, 1884, Ransom Papers.

68. James McMillan to Hugh McMillan, February 21, 1891, McMillan Papers.

69. James McMillan to Charles Manderson, October 13, 1891, William Washburn to James McMillan, September 27, 1894, McMillan Papers. Chauncey Depew to James McMillan, April 10, 1893, McMillan Papers. The Michigan Senator had several dealings with Aldrich (James McMillan to William McMillan, January 14, 1899, McMillan Papers); and Allison and Aldrich also did business together (William Allison to Nelson Aldrich, August 20, 1898, Aldrich Papers).

70. B. F. T. Lemiken to Eugene Davis (Jones' secretary), January 11, 1892, Jones Papers; John Sherman to Daniel Pratt, July 2, 1874, Pratt Papers.

71. Francis Warren to Dewey, Gould and Company, February 25, 1897, Warren Papers.

72. James McMillan to William McMillan, February 11, 1901, McMillan Papers.

73. Johnson Camden to Henry Flagler, January 17, 1883, Camden Papers.

74. William Grant to Samuel Barlow, February 17, 1879, Barlow Papers.

75. John Gordon to Samuel Barlow, May 17, June 13, September 10, 1877, Barlow Papers. William Bush to Thomas Bayard, February 17, 1879, Bayard Papers.

76. *Congressional Record,* 49th Cong., 1st sess., p. 5494 (June 10, 1886), and pp. 5997–5998 (June 22, 1886).

77. *Ibid.,* pp. 5999, 6039, 6041–6045 (June 23, 1886).

78. *Ibid.,* 49th Cong., 2nd sess., p. 178 (December 15, 1886), p.

1139 (January 28, 1887). The bill went over from the first session to the second but failed again to pass.

79. *Congressional Record,* 47th Cong., 2nd sess., p. 2608 (February 14, 1883). *New York Herald,* 1884, clipping in the Thomas Bayard Scrapbooks, Bayard Papers; Thomas Bayard to Henry Villard, July 20, 1883, Bayard Papers.

80. *Congressional Record,* 49th Cong., 2nd sess., p. 1128 (January 28, 1887).

81. *Ibid.,* pp. 1138–1139 (January 28, 1887).

82. Memorandum by Henry Castle on conflict of interest, January 1896, pp. 3–4, Castle Papers.

83. This is exactly the sort of analysis Josephson is fond of making; because Sherman owned land in Ohio, he was against currency expansion (see *Politicos,* p. 191).

84. *Congressional Record,* 49th Cong., 2nd sess., p. 1129 (January 28, 1887).

85. W. U. Hensel, *Life and Services of Cleveland and Thurman* (1888), p. 333.

86. William Stewart to S. P. Davis, April 18, 1888, Stewart Papers.

87. John Spooner to Thomas Bardon, March 28, 1890, Spooner Papers. *Nebraska State Journal,* January 3, 1895. James McMillan to W. C. Van Horne, June 28, 1890 and W. C. Van Horne to James McMillan, July 14, 1890, McMillan Papers.

88. John Sherman to J. S. Wofford, March 27, 1886, Sherman Papers. Orville Platt to A. W. Gay, September 19, 1904, Platt Papers; George Hoar to George Mercer, December 8, 1899, Hoar Papers.

89. "Attempts at Bribery," No. 457, pt. II, pp. 29–40; No. 606, pp. 497–498. Quay's comments are often quoted out of context, not mentioning that he sold the stock, and at a loss. Harold Faulkner, *Politics, Reform and Expansion* (New York, 1959), 160; Josephson, *Politicos,* p. 549.

90. John Spooner to Daniel Lamont, January 15, 1900 and to J. W. Losey, January 20, 1888, Spooner Papers; Francis Warren to Thomas Fisher, September 6, 1892, Warren Papers.

91. C. E. Perkins to William Allison, March 19, 1887, Allison Papers.

92. Richard Pettigrew to William Sewell, February 9, 1894, to S. L. Tate, January 26, 1892, Pettigrew Papers; William Stewart to H. M. Yerington, September 16, 1888, Stewart Papers. Jacob Gallinger to Cushman Davis, March 31, 1895, Davis Papers, Minnesota Historical Society, St. Paul.

93. *Congressional Record,* 49th Cong., 1st sess., p. 6048 (June 23, 1886).

CHAPTER VIII: In Defense of Party Government

1. Austin Ranney, *The Doctrine of Responsible Party Government* Illinois Studies in the Social Sciences, XXXIV, (Urbana, 1954), p. 5.

2. Cf. Cunningham, *Jeffersonian Republicans,* pp. 75–76, 94, 140, 142, for typical statements of the first views on party.

3. Carl Schurz to H. White, November 12, 1872, Schurz Papers, L. C.

4. Lyman Trumbull to William Bryant, May 10, 1872, quoted in Horace White, *Lyman Trumbull* (Boston, 1913), pp. 386–387. Cf. also J. D. Cox to Charles Sumner, August 3, August 4, 1872, Sumner Papers.

5. Carl Schurz to Charles Sumner, September 30, 1871, Sumner Papers; cf. also *New York Tribune,* June 22, 1872.

6. Foulke, *Morton,* II, 249, 488.

7. *Congressional Record,* 53rd Cong., 2nd sess., p. 1692 (January 3, 1894).

8. John Reagan to his constituents, February 22, 1896, Reagan Papers, Archives Division, Texas State Library, Austin; reprinted in the *Dallas News,* February 23, 1896.

9. *Bismarck Daily Tribune,* February 4, 1893. Cf. also remarks of Randall Gibson, *Congressional Record,* 51st Cong., 2nd sess., Appendix, p. 12 (December 19, 1890) and Rutherford Hayes to Carl Schurz, July 9, 1887, typescript, Hayes Papers.

10. *Congressional Record,* 49th Cong., 1st sess., p. 2786 (March 26, 1886).

11. *Ibid.,* 51st Cong., 2nd sess., pp. 1359, 1363 (January 15, 1891); *Arguments and Speeches of William Maxwell Evarts,* ed. Sherman Evarts (New York, 1919), III, 215–216.

12. Dorman Eaton to George Hoar, April 22, 1895, Hoar Papers.

13. George Hoar to Dorman Eaton, April 25, 1895, Hoar Papers. Cf. also George Hoar to Homer Sprague, December 4, 1900, and Horace Smith to George Hoar, July 4, 1895, Hoar Papers. Cf. *Congressional Record,* 47th Cong., 2nd sess., p. 224 (April 6, 1881), for his earlier views.

14. *Congressional Record,* 48th Cong., 2nd sess., p. 826 (January 19, 1885).

15. Evarts, *Arguments and Speeches,* III, 215–216.

16. *Congressional Record,* 49th Cong., 1st sess., p. 2530 (March 18, 1886).

17. Henry Davis to the *West Virginia Register,* November 11, 1879, Davis Papers.

18. William Chandler to Elihu Washburne, August 26, 1872, Washburne Papers, L. C., and the remarks of John McPherson, Democratic senator from New Jersey, *Congressional Record,* 47th Cong., Special Session, p. 210 (April 5, 1881). Paul Buck, *Road to Reunion* (New York: Vintage Edition, 1959), pp. 75–118, 273–293.

19. Evarts, *Arguments and Speeches,* III, 215–216.

20. *Congressional Record,* 49th Cong., 1st sess., p. 2786 (March 26, 1886). The Mormons realized in the 1890's that two party politics was a prerequisite for democratic government and the Church appropriately divided its forces between Democrats and Republicans. Cf. *Salt Lake Tribune,* January 10, 1896.

21. *Congressional Record,* 51st Cong., 1st sess. (December 30, 1891); cf. also remarks of David Davis, *ibid.,* 47th Cong., Special Session, p. 41 (March 23, 1881).

22. David Hill, "The Future of the Democratic Organization," *Forum,* 22: 654 (1896–1897).

23. David Turpie, *Sketches of My Own Time* (Indianapolis, 1903), pp. 343–347.

24. *Congressional Record,* 47th Cong., 2nd sess., p. 504 (December 21, 1882).

25. Cornelius Cole to Olive Cole, June 22, November 15, 1884, Cole Papers.

26. Speech delivered July 10, 1881, copy in Garfield Papers; *Congressional Record,* 47th Cong., Special Session, p. 220 (April 5, 1881).

27. Thomas Bayard to Manton Marble, August 27, 1875, Marble Papers, L.C.; Thomas Bayard to Samuel Barlow, November 24, 1878, Barlow Papers.

28. *Newton Booth of California,* ed. Lauren Crane (New York, 1894), p. 253.

29. Frank Hereford to J. M. Laidley, June 18, 1872, Hereford Papers, West Virginia Collection, W.V.U.L.

30. Francis Warren to Otto Gramm, January 28, 1897, Warren Papers; undated manuscript of Vance speech delivered sometime after 1890, Vance Papers.

31. Horace Chilton, *Notebooks and Diaries,* no. 1, p. 167 (1890–1894), Chilton Papers.

32. Turpie, *Sketches,* pp. 343–347. Cf. also Stephen White to John Irish, August 5, 1894, White Papers.

33. Evarts, *Arguments and Speeches,* III, 215–216; Horace Smith to George Hoar, July 4, 1895, Hoar Papers.

34. Horace Chilton, *Notebooks and Diaries,* no. 1, p. 126 (1891–1892), Chilton Papers. William Vilas to William Endicott, May 10, 1891, Cleveland Papers.

35. Richard Pettigrew to R. W. Wheelock, May 18, 1892, Pettigrew Papers.

36. A valuable survey of the works on government during these years is Ranney's, *The Doctrine of Responsible Party Government*. Henry Jones Ford, "The Cause of Political Corruption," *Scribner's Magazine*, 49:54–55 (1911); quoted in Ranney, *Responsible Party Government*, pp. 71–72. Frank J. Goodnow, *Politics and Administration* (New York, 1900), p. 1.

37. Ansom D. Morse, "What is a Party," *Political Science Quarterly*, 11:70 (1896); Bryce, *Commonwealth*, II, 5.

38. Morse, "What is a Party," p. 69.

39. Alexis de Tocqueville, *Democracy in America* (New York: Vintage Edition, 1954), I, 181–187. Quotations are from pages 181, 182.

40. Bryce, *Commonwealth*, II, 3–4.

41. Wilson, *Congressional Government*, pp. 93, 213–214.

42. Ranney, *Responsible Party Government*, pp. 53–54; Henry Jones Ford, *Rise and Growth of American Parties* (New York, 1900), p. 306. Cf. also Jesse Macy, *Political Parties in the United States* (New York, 1900), p. 7; and by the same author, *Party Organization and Machinery* (New York, 1904), p. 267.

43. Ford, *Rise and Growth*, pp. 127, 297.

44. *Ibid.*, pp. 310, 314, 316.

45. Morse, "What is a Party," p. 70.

46. Ranney, *Responsible Party Government*, pp. 59–61; Ford, *Rise and Growth*, pp. 322–323. For a clear statement of contemporary views, cf. "Toward a More Responsible Two Party System," *American Political Science Review* (Supplement), September 1950.

47. Geoffry T. Blodgett, "The Mind of the Boston Mugwump," *Mississippi Valley Historical Review*, 48:614–634 (1962). Morefield Storey, *Politics as a Duty and as a Career* (New York, 1889), pp. 7–10, quoted by Blodgett, pp. 631–632.

48. Charles F. Adams, "Individuality in Politics," lecture of April 21, 1880, quoted in Ostrogorski, *Democracy*, II, 449.

49. Marion Butler to the editor of the *Commercial Travellers' Home Magazine*, July 5, 1897, Butler Papers; cf. also J. P. Jones to the *Nevada State Journal*, November 3, 1894, Jones Papers, University of California Library, Los Angeles.

50. William Stewart to H. E. Taubeneck, December 16, 1895, Stewart Papers; speech delivered by Marion Butler, 1897, copy in the Butler Papers.

51. George Hoar to William Lovering, February 3, 1899, Hoar Papers.

52. Ostrogorski, *Democracy*, II, 656–657.

53. *Ibid.*, II, 658.

54. *Ibid.*, II, 441–451; Ostrogorski entitled this chapter on the Liberal Republicans and Mugwumps, "The Struggles for Emancipation." For similar conclusions see James S. Brown, *Partisan Politics, The Evil and*

The Remedy (Philadelphia, 1897), pp. 42–43, 47–51, 174–179. Cf. also the critique by Dorman Eaton, "Parties and Independence," *North American Review*, 144:550–564 (1887).

55. Cortissoz, *Reid*, I, 375–376.

56. Topeka *Commonwealth*, January 23, 1879; Omaha *Daily Herald*, January 3, 1887; Bismarck *Daily Tribune*, February 15, 1893. Examples could be easily multiplied; cf. Seattle *Post Intelligencer*, January 27, January 31, 1893.

57. E. C. Wall to William Vilas, December 24, 1891, Vilas Papers.

58. Ford, *Rise and Growth*, p. 303. Macy, *Political Parties*, p. 167; Morse, "What is a Party," pp. 69–70. *Congressional Record*, 47th Cong., Special Session, p. 203 (April 5, 1881).

CHAPTER IX: The People and Their Government

1. J. D. Meese to George Hoar, April 12, 1897, Hoar Papers.

2. William Everett, "The United States Senate," *Atlantic Monthly*, 97:157–166 (1906); "Notes," *American Law Review*, 28:274–278 (1894).

3. *Springfield Daily Republican*, February 3, 1892; *Seattle Post Intelligencer*, January 28, 1897. *Louisville Courier Journal*, March 4, 1897.

4. Stephen White to Charles Forman, April 17, 1896, and to E. H. Smith, May 7, 1897, White Papers.

5. George Hoar, "Has the Senate Degenerated?" *Forum*, (1897); C. W. Mott to John Spooner, May 6, 1898 Spooner Papers.

6. H. Van Holst, "Ought the United States Senate to Be Abolished?" *The Monist*, 5:1–22 (1894–1895); Boyd Winchester, "The House and the Election of Senators," *Arena*, 24:14–20 (1900); Alfred Russell, "Dissatisfactions with the Senate," *Michigan Law Journal*, 2:406–411 (1893).

7. Wallace W. Hall, "History and Effect of the Seventeenth Amendment," unpub. diss. University of California, Berkeley, 1936; Haynes, *Election of Senators*, pp. 100–115. The handbooks that appeared offer almost complete bibliographic guides to all the literature for and against direct election. See *Selected Articles on the Election of United States Senators*, (Minneapolis: Debaters Handbook Series, 1912); "List of References on the Popular Election of Senators," comp. A. P. C. Griffin, Library of Congress (Washington, 1904). "Election of Senators by Popular Vote," 61st Cong., 3rd sess., *Senate Report*, No. 961.

8. William Allison to George Hoar, April 17, 1899, Hoar Papers.

9. *The Federalist*, paper no. 62, (New York: Modern Library Edition, 1937), p. 403.

10. Donalson Caffery to a Louisiana Democratic Club, September 7, 1896, Caffery Papers, U.N.C.L. William Allison to Herbert Campbell, March 26, 1895, Allison Papers.

11. J. D. Meese to George Hoar, April 12, 1897, Hoar Papers.

12. Bryce, *Commonwealth*, I, 123.

13. *Congressional Record*, 53rd Cong., 2nd sess., p. 7775 (July 20, 1894).

14. Charles H. Fox, "Popular Election of United States Senators," *Arena*, 27:455–467 (1902). Haynes, *Election of Senators*, includes an excellent summary of both positions on this question.

15. *Congressional Record*, 49th Cong., 1st sess., p. 2749 (March 25, 1886).

16. Wilson, *Congressional Government*, p. 194; Bryce, *Commonwealth*, I, 121–122. Alfred Russell, "A Dissatisfaction with the Senate," Michigan Political Science Association, *Publications*, 1:46–48 (1893–1894); Condit Crane, "In the Seats of the Mighty," *Outlook*, 61:27–34 (1899).

17. *Nation*, 72:4–5 (1901). S. W. McCall, "Power of the Senate," *Atlantic Monthly*, 92:433–442 (1903). Everett, "Senate," pp. 157–166.

18. A. Maurice Low, "The Oligarchy of the Senate," *North American Review*, 174:231–244 (1902); William H. Moody, "Constitutional Power of the Senate—A Reply," *North American Review*, 174:386–394 (1902). Cf. also Dorman Eaton, "The President and the Senate," *North American Review*, 142:572–586 (1886), and Henry L. Nelson, "The Overshadowing Senate," *Century*, 43:514–515 (1902–1903).

19. Wendell Garrison, "The Reform of the Senate," *Atlantic Monthly*, 68:227–232 (1891). Cf. also, *New England Magazine*, 14:383–386 (1896) and 9:540–541 (1893).

20. Garrison, "Reform of Senate," pp. 227–232.

21. John Haynes, "Popular Election of United States Senators," *Johns Hopkins University Studies in History and Political Science*, 11–12:95–108 (1893).

22. Haynes, *Election of Senators*, pp. 167, 169.

23. John Spooner to D. N. Collan, April 4, 1899, and to D. B. Lovejoy, May 5, 1890, Spooner Papers.

24. Speech delivered by Orville Platt in 1900, quoted in Coolidge, *Platt*, p. 414. Henry West, "The Place of the Senate in Our Government," *Forum*, 31:431 (1901).

25. "Power of the Senate," *Nation*, 76:105 (1903) and 79:295 (1900). Garrison, "Reform of the Senate," pp. 227–232.

26. *Congressional Record*, 55th Cong., 1st sess., pp. 171–172 (March 23, 1897); cf. also remarks of Bryan, *ibid.*, 53rd Cong., 2nd sess., pp. 2775–2776 (July 20, 1894). John Haynes, "Popular Election," pp. 96–98; Haynes, *Election of Senators*, pp. 176–177, 187.

27. A. C. McLaughlin, discussion of remarks of T. E. Barkworth, "Should the United States Senators Be Elected by the People?" Michigan Political Science Association, *Publications*, 1:89 (1893–1894); *Florida Times Union*, May 5, 1891.

28. Haynes, *Election of Senators*, pp. 181, 185.

29. *Ibid.*, pp. 182–183, 189, 191. Cf. also Walter Clark, "The Election of the Senators and the President by Popular Vote," *Arena*, 58:453–461 (1894); John Haynes, "Popular Election," p. 99.

30. *Baltimore Sun*, January 8, 1892; Haynes, *Election of Senators*, p. 199. John H. Mitchell, "Election of Senators by Popular Vote," *Forum*, 21:385–397 (1896); E. P. Clark, "Electing Senators by Popular Vote," *Nation*, 74:222 (1902).

31. William Allison to Herbert Campbell, March 25, 1895, Allison Papers; James McMillan to G. S. Cassels, December 23, 1897, McMillan Papers.

32. Hoar's remarks on direct election were gathered in "Papers Relating to the Election of Senators by Direct Vote of the People," 60th Cong., 1st sess., *Senate Document*, No. 512. The speeches were delivered April 3, 6, 7, 1893.

33. B. A. Hinsdale, remarks in T. E. Barkworth, "Should Senators Be Elected by the People?" p. 94.

34. *Congressional Record*, 53rd Cong., 3rd sess., p. 74 (December 6, 1894). Ranney, *Responsible Party Government*, pp. 72–73, 85–86.

35. Haynes, *Election of Senators*, pp. 200–208, 223–225; *Cincinnati Commercial Gazette*, March 18, 1890.

36. Hoar, "Papers Relating to Senators," pp. 11–13.

37. William Allison to James Clarkson, April 25, 1893, Allison Papers.

38. Haynes, *Election of Senators*, p. 225. E. V. Robinson, remarks in T. E. Barkworth, "Should Senators Be Elected by the People?" p. 90; *Congressional Record*, 57th Cong., 1st sess., p. 2617 (March 11, 1902).

39. *Ibid.*, pp. 6595–6596 (June 11, 1902).

40. Hoar, "Papers Relating to Senators," pp. 15–16.

41. Haynes, *Election of Senators*, pp. 213–215, 228, 240–246. George Hoar, "Has the Senate Degenerated?" pp. 129–144.

42. Hoar, "Papers Relating to Senators," pp. 4–5.

43. George Edmunds, "Should Senators Be Elected by the People?" *Forum*, 18:270–278 (1894).

44. Ostrogorski, *Democracy*, II, 537.

45. Hofstadter, *Age of Reform*, chap. vi.

46. Russell, "Dissatisfaction with the Senate," pp. 46–48. Eulogy delivered at the funeral of Henry Dawes, 1903, Dawes Papers; newspaper clipping in the Richard Coke Scrapbooks, 1900, Coke Papers.

47. *Writings and Speeches of Grover Cleveland*, ed. G. F. Parker (New York, 1892), pp. 173–177. Haynes, *Election of Senators*, p. 181.

48. John McCurdy to John Sherman, January 19, 1891, Sherman Papers.

49. *Louisville Commercial*, April 8, 1897; George Parker to Charles Fairbanks, January 22, 1897, Fairbanks Papers. G. W. Griffith to George

Hoar, April 13, 1897, Hoar Papers. Edwin Maxey, "The Rule of the United States Senate," *American Law Review*, 38:61–67 (1904).

50. M. M. Trumbull, "The Decline of the Senate," *The Open Court*, 7:3895–3898 (1893); William Walton to John Reagan, February 25, 1896, Reagan Papers.

51. Ford, *Rise and Growth*, pp. 334–335; A. Lawrence Lowell, *Essays in Government* (Boston, 1889), pp. 21–22. Ranney, *Responsible Party Government*, pp. 63–65, 84–85.

52. Francis Warren to G. R. Palmer, March 14, 1892, Warren Papers.

53. Ostrogorski, *Democracy*, II, 557.

54. *Congressional Record*, 79th Cong., 1st sess., p. 123 (March 19, 1945).

INDEX

Adams, Charles Francis, 236
Adams, Henry. See *Democracy*
Addicks, John, 174, 186
Alcorn, James, 170
Aldrich, Nelson, 35, 101, 144–145, 167, 204, 210; as Senate leader, 44, 47–49, 52, 56, 58, 60–61, 66–67, 72, 136, 172, 182–183; early career and state politics, 47, 112, 159, 161; and Mills Tariff, 91; and McKinley Tariff, 92–93; and Gold Standard Bill, 106; and Appropriations Committee, 107; defends lobbying, 207. See *also* Caucus; Political party discipline; Political party leadership
Alger, Horatio, 258
Allison, William, 35, 152, 157, 187, 204; as Senate leader, 44, 47–50, 60–61, 66–67, 72, 108, 136, 172, 182–183, 189–190; early career and state politics, 46, 162, 177; awarding committee posts, 52, 56–58; Bland-Allison Act, 80; Mills Tariff, 91–92; Wilson-Gorman Tariff, 95; Dingley Tariff, 97; and Gold Standard Bill, 106; and Appropriations Committee, 107–108; business activity in Senate, 209–210; on direct election, 244, 252, 254; on the Senate's role, 245. See *also* Caucus; Political party discipline; Political party leadership
Amateurs in the Senate, 130–131, 158, 259. See *also* Political experience
Ambassadors: and protocol, 142; senators' view of, 157
American Commonwealth, 191, 232, 233–234, 245, 247
American Iron and Steel Association, 83, 91, 187, 206. See *also* Business interests; Swank, James
American Sugar Refining Company, 96, 183, 204. See *also* Business in-

terests; Havermeyer, Henry and Theodore; Lobbying; Lobbyists
American Wool Growers Association, 83. See *also* Business interests
Ames, Adelbert, 140, 170
Ames, Oliver, 193
Anthony, Henry, 47, 142, 180, 227; as caucus chairman, 16, 28–30
Anthony Rule, 39–40
Anti-Trust Act, 98
Appropriations bills, 86–87, 108
Appropriations Committee: assignments, 20–21, 49, 51, 52–53, 54, 58, 63, 107; powers of, 65–66
Arthur, Chester, 32, 76, 78, 88, 155, 163

Barbour, James, 171
Barlow, Samuel, 199, 211
Barnum, William, 209
Bayard, James, 13
Bayard, Thomas, 36, 38, 209, 213; and legislation, 78, 81, 84, 85; critique of lobbying, 208, 212; on party government, 230
Beck, James, 85; and conflict of interest, 212–213
Beveridge, Albert: and committee assignments, 55–57, 59, 60–61; concern for position, 144–145; on Senate life, 145, 151; counseled on politics, 149; Senate election, 162
Blackburn, Joseph, 63, 67, 68
Blaine, James, 155, 157, 179, 209; relations with Conkling, 31–33, 35
Blair Act, 86
Blanchard, Newton, 66, 94
Bland-Allison Act, 80
Booth, Newton, 230
Boston & Maine Railroad, 166–168. See *also* Business interests
Bourbon Democrats, 37–38, 67. See *also* Business interests
Brayton, Charles, 47, 161